# How to Do Media and Cultural Studies

# How to Do Media and Cultural Studies

## Second edition

### Jane Stokes

Los Angeles | London | New Delhi
Singapore | Washington DC

Los Angeles | London | New Delhi
Singapore | Washington DC

SAGE Publications Ltd
1 Oliver's Yard
55 City Road
London EC1Y 1SP

SAGE Publications Inc.
2455 Teller Road
Thousand Oaks, California 91320

SAGE Publications India Pvt Ltd
B 1/I 1 Mohan Cooperative Industrial Area
Mathura Road
New Delhi 110 044

SAGE Publications Asia-Pacific Pte Ltd
3 Church Street
#10-04 Samsung Hub
Singapore 049483

Editor: Mila Steele
Editorial assistant: James Piper
Production editor: Imogen Roome
Copyeditor: Kate Harrison
Marketing manager: Michael Ainsley
Typeset by: C&M Digitals (P) Ltd, Chennai, India
Printed by: MPG Books Group, Bodmin,
Cornwall

First published 2013
First edition published 2002

**Library of Congress Control Number: 2011945433**

**British Library Cataloguing in Publication data**

A catalogue record for this book is available from
the British Library

ISBN 978-1-84920-785-0
ISBN 978-1-84920-786-7 (pbk)

For Rose

# CONTENTS

# Contents

# LIST OF FIGURES AND TABLES

# PREFACE

Welcome to the second edition of *How to Do Media and Cultural Studies*. In the ten years since I first began writing this book there have been dramatic changes in the media landscape. The radical impetus of new technology has taken hold and the terrain of mediated culture has been transformed. Scholars of media and culture have risen to the challenge and new paradigms of research and investigation have grown up; new journals have been launched; new university courses have been designed and, in some instances, dropped. In view of all these changes, the desire to update the material in this book has become an absolute imperative. In conducting the research for this second edition, I have been humbled by the range and quality of research being published today. I am very grateful for the opportunity to update the first edition and to reflect on some of these advances. I am grateful, also, to the reviewers who have drawn my attention to errors and omissions in the first edition. No doubt many remain, but I am thankful of the opportunity to expunge some of the more embarrassing phrases and passages.

# INTRODUCTION

## WHAT IS THIS BOOK ABOUT?

How do you start to conduct your own research? Where do you go to get ideas? How do you design a good research project? How does it relate to the rest of your studies? What is the objective of doing research? This book aims to address some of these questions. When you start your first independent research project you are joining a research community with a long and diverse history. How can you know for sure that you are making a genuinely new contribution to the field? How do you know that you have something relevant to say? How can you be confident that your research will be credible? *How to Do Media and Cultural Studies* asks you to think about the philosophy behind the research as you engage in the practicalities of conducting research. It is aimed primarily at students of media and culture and explains some of the most common and useful methods of research that students can undertake, and describes the processes of designing, conducting and writing a successful student research project.

### Research methods in media and cultural studies

This book introduces students to a range of research methods which they can draw on in conducting their own investigations. It is designed to be used by students working independently or in the classroom to support modules in research methods or dissertation preparation. Research methods classes are relatively recent additions to the rostra of modules taught on media and cultural studies courses at undergraduate level with the consequence that the teaching of research methods can lag behind other teaching in media and cultural studies. However, an understanding of research methods is a crucial element underpinning what any researcher does, whether this is explicitly acknowledged or not. How we operationalize our ideas; how we interrogate our field; how we construct our questions – these are important questions which go to the heart of epistemology of the field. Without thinking about these issues we relegate ourselves and our field to unreflective, subjective description. In order to address these concerns directly, this new edition includes two new chapters in Part 1.

# PART 1: THINKING, THEORY AND PRACTICE

This second edition includes a new section, which presents some ideas for considering, firstly, *How we know anything about anything?* and secondly, *Why do we do Media and Cultural Studies?*

The first chapter of Part 1 investigates some of the principles which underpin research in most fields of study. Here we ask whether it is possible to know anything at all. How can we prove what we think we know? Chapter 1 investigates **epistemology** or the science of knowledge – what are the means by which we can prove or test our ideas and theories? What is it possible for us to say about the world? This chapter offers a general overview of the history of ideas and considers how important concepts such as epistemology, logic and argument inform our thinking. We discuss four different 'ways of knowing' which we label: 'orality', 'classical', 'modern' and 'postmodern'. Understanding these shifts in epistemology will help you to build a well-constructed argument and to understand some of the principles behind the research methods we discuss later.

The second chapter, 'Why Do We Do Media and Cultural Studies?', looks at the rationale and motivation underlying communication, media and cultural studies as fields of research. Here we consider how these fields came to be academic fields of study. The title of this book elides the difference between 'media' and 'cultural' studies and does not refer to the related field of 'mass communication' at all; this may cause some controversy among certain quarters as it may suggest a lack of recognition of the differences between these quite discrete academic areas. However, it is my contention that the fields have more in common than not, and this will continue to be so as the media blend into everyday life and all aspects of our cultural lives become increasingly 'mediated'. Scholars from every field may benefit from a consideration of what is happening in the neighbouring fields. For inter-disciplinarity to rise above the hollow buzzword it sometimes seems to be, it is necessary for us to look beyond the artificial boundaries which separate our fields, to consider what motivates us to research media and culture. In this chapter we briefly survey the history of research into media and culture and consider its location within academe. Chapter 2 explores the political motivation which is at the heart of our academic research, and touches on the institutional imperatives which shape it.

# PART 2: METHODS OF ANALYSIS

The second part of *How to Do Media and Cultural Studies* offers practical guidance to help you conduct your own research. We begin, in Chapter 3, with some ideas for getting started on your research project. Some suggestions are offered on how to originate your own ideas and how to design your research question; we also give advice on how to write a project proposal and how to design and conduct your project. The subsequent three chapters of Part 2 present you with more detailed support and advice, targeted to whether you are researching *industries*, *texts* or *audiences*.

We have learned the three-stage model of communication almost as a mantra: 'sender–message–receiver' or 'encoding/text/decoding' – it doesn't matter what you call it – we often conceptualize the communication process as constituting two distinct sets of people, *producers* and *audiences*, brought together through the *media*. As academics we could choose whether to study media *texts*, the readers or *audiences* who consumed those texts, or the *industries* which produced them. Yet today the reality of the media landscape is undergoing a revolution in the way media and culture are produced, distributed and consumed. The 'Arab Spring' of 2011, for example, taught us that many of our established ideas about mediated communications demand reconsideration. When people protesting in Tahrir Square used their mobile phones to generate, send and receive information via social network sites, we recognized that the traditional distinctions between media producers and consumers had been radically transformed.

In many regards we can see this as a revolution in media control. And at the same time this is an illusory revolution, as the economics of the media industry are still rooted in capitalist modes of production. The material reality is that the ownership of the means of producing messages rests in the hands of multinational corporations such as Microsoft and News International. The precise names may be different ones from those of ten years ago, and perhaps they will be different ones again by the time you read this sentence, but the location of power and wealth in the capitalist system we all inhabit remains unaltered. However much the look of it might change, the feel of it even, the fact remains that our media continue to be dominated by large corporations. At the same time, we realize that culture is increasingly media-dominated with people spending more time than ever using the media in cultural pursuits which are increasingly monetized. The factory system may be dead; we may well live in a 'post-Fordist' society; but it is far from being a post-capitalist one. There is a separation, fundamental to the operation of capital, between 'supplier' and 'consumer' which is echoed in the relationship between 'producer' and 'audience', 'writer' and 'reader'. This relationship is powerfully embedded in a culture dominated by the concept of exchange value. When studying the media (the means by which messages are exchanged), it is necessary to be mindful of the relationship between the party of production and the party of consumption; between the point of origination of the point of consumption, between those crucial functions of capitalist exchange – buying and selling. We would ignore the fundamental power base central to our media system if we did otherwise. It is for this reason that we follow the traditional divide to the study of media in the following chapters which are devoted to the study of *industry*, *texts* and *audiences* respectively.

Chapter 4 examines some of the ways we can research the media and cultural *industries*. The methods we focus on here are *archive research, discourse analysis, interview* and *ethnography*. The advantages and disadvantages of studying media and culture as the product of industries are discussed and the particular issues of access to media producers are considered. In Chapter 5, we think about the methods best suited to the research and analysis of the products of the media and cultural industries, the media *texts* themselves. The films, television programmes, music and performances which form the content of the media are more readily accessed and form the object of analysis for some of the most typical methods of media analysis for undergraduate researchers: *semiotics, content analysis* and *discourse analysis*. We also explore a set of methods I label '*typological*' – that is, those methods which consider texts as belonging to particular sets or types. In this section we look at *genre, auteur* and *star* study – all methods associated with film studies but applicable to any form of media and culture. The final of these large chapters, Chapter 6, looks at how to research the *audience* or the users or recipients of mediated messages. There are some special considerations to be taken into account when researching audiences. Here we concentrate on how you might use *surveys, focus groups, ethnography* and *oral history interviews*. Each of these methods are discussed and guidance given on how to conduct them.

An important characteristic of each of these main chapters is the presentation of 'case studies' to illustrate the various research methods covered. These 'case studies' are not proposed as canonical or typical; they are simply examples of the relevant research method and have been chosen to help students understand how that method is used and applied. Some are 'classics' of the field; others are relative newcomers. They are a rather subjective collection of books and articles which I hope will illustrate the methods discussed and inspire you to conduct your own research. I am sure that lecturers and students will find examples of their own to supplement those suggested here. Suggestions for further reading are given at the end of each chapter along with some ideas for activities to take your studies further. There are also weblinks to some relevant examples of research papers to support your learning.

## PART 3: PRESENTING YOUR WORK

In the final chapter, Chapter 7, matters of how to complete your dissertation are considered – how to write up the dissertation and how to present it. This edition also includes a new *glossary* of key words which are highlighted in the text in bold. I hope you will find *How to Do Media and Cultural Studies* a useful book; it is intended to be helpful and constructive. The proof of its worth is in your work. I wish you every success in your research project.

*Jane Stokes*

# PART 1

## THINKING, THEORY AND PRACTICE

*Part 1: Thinking, Theory and Practice*, provides some context for the subsequent discussion of research methods in Part 2. Media, communication and cultural studies are all fields of study which focus on a very broad topic: the cultural and mediated world. These are not disciplines in the sense of having a single focus of analysis. For example, psychology is about the study of the mind; history, the study of the past; or English literature, the study of texts. Our areas of study are topics which encompass the diversity of all of these and many other fields besides. One of the exciting consequences of the renowned inter-disciplinarity of media, communication and cultural studies is a promiscuous attitude towards research methods. During your studies you are likely to come across work which uses many methods of research such as focus groups, semiotics or economic case studies of businesses. This plurality of approaches may seem overwhelming when you come to write your dissertation and find that you can do anything from textual analysis to industry interviews. This book serves to help you identify which research method is right for you – from how to choose a topic and design a question, to how to conduct your own research and present your dissertation.

It is precisely because the range of methods we can use is so diverse that we need to spend some time thinking about the underlying rationale behind research of any kind. Chapter 1 asks the reader to consider *how we know anything about anything* and addresses some fundamental questions related to the philosophy of knowledge or *epistemology*. Here we explore the social, cultural and temporal specificity of knowledge and justification in general terms, thinking about ideas of argumentation, proof and validity from a philosophical perspective. The ideas we discuss here are relevant to many areas of study and provide a generalist theoretical perspective to aspects of the philosophy of knowledge.

The second chapter of Part 1 provides a historical overview of the different approaches that have been taken by scholars of communication, culture and media. It presents a survey of some of the main research themes and offers a brief historical perspective to the methods and approaches discussed in subsequent chapters. Here we also consider the material nature of research – how and why research is undertaken, to help us understand the motivations behind much media and cultural work. The two chapters which make up Part 1 are intended to provide the reader with some fresh perspectives on the ideology and practicalities of research and analysis which, it is hoped, will encourage readers to produce original, creative and reflective work when they come to write their own dissertations. The following material is offered with the intention of empowering a new generation of researchers to create new paradigms of research and ways of thinking by which we can investigate the exciting changes in our cultural world.

# HOW DO WE KNOW ANYTHING ABOUT ANYTHING?

## Aims and Objectives

- In the following, we explore the basis of epistemology, or the science of knowing, by considering how we know anything about anything.

- In order to investigate the relationship between technologies of knowing and epistemology we consider four broad 'ways of knowing':

  o the 'oral' tradition and pre-literate ways of knowing;

  o the classical, Aristotelian system of logic and rationality;

  o the way of knowing associated with conventional scientific knowledge or 'modernity'; and finally

  o post-modernism and discourse analysis.

- We offer some suggestions for further reading.

- Some follow-up activities are provided for you to take your studies further.

## INTRODUCTION

In this chapter we look at *how we know anything about anything*, exploring issues around *epistemology*, *logic* and *validity* to investigate changing ideas of knowledge and understanding. Looking at the philosophical bases underlying ideas of knowledge and research will help you to appreciate the different traditions of epistemology which operate within the study of media and culture. We consider some of the key questions from philosophy: What constitutes knowledge? What is the relationship between *knowledge* and *truth*? How do we make a *logical* argument? How do we know whether a statement is 'true' or 'false'? What is the relationship between reality and representation? How do we persuade other people that we are telling the truth? How does a researcher prove anything? These are questions about *epistemology* – the study of knowledge. They are the fundamental bases of how we know anything about anything.

The question of epistemology is crucial for students of media and culture as there is no prescribed method for us to use; no single way of knowing about media and culture. The research methods we use are borrowed from other disciplines, among them anthropology, economics, literary studies, psychology, political science and sociology. There are researchers studying the media in business schools, art departments, humanities and social science departments. The fact is that the way we know about media and cultural studies is not especially unique – many of the approaches we use could be applied to a host of other topics.

We could define research as the process of investigating the world to discover new things, and the goal of any research project is to add to our knowledge. Before we get down to the details of how to conduct your own research, this book begins by asking: *What is knowledge?*

## WHAT IS KNOWLEDGE?

This question goes to the heart of understanding any kind of research. Today we scarcely think about the processes by which we come to know anything – 'It all seems so obvious; you just know', I hear you say! However, one of the key ideas of communications, cultural and media studies is that it is precisely those things which seem most obvious – those things that we take for granted and that we don't question – these are the very things which we most urgently need to unpack. For it is precisely the ideas which seem 'obvious', 'natural' and 'normal' that exercise the greatest power over us; this is where the essential truths of our society rest – in the way we think about the world. Our world view is embedded in the *taken-for-granted* ideas which attach to the concepts of reality, truth and knowledge. An appreciation of the ontological construction of knowledge itself is a prerequisite to understanding the research processes in any field. In the areas of communications, media and cultural studies, where matters of epistemology and ontology are central to so much of our endeavour, this is so much more urgent. In a field of study where there seem to be so many paradigms for research, and so many apparently equally valuable modes of study, it is important that we spend some time thinking about what constitutes knowledge and the various paradigms of knowledge and epistemology.

## HOW DO YOU BUILD A TOASTER?

Knowledge comes in many forms. We all have 'common knowledge' – for example, that you need to connect the plug on your toaster to a power socket to make it work. But how many of us have the more 'specialist knowledge' that we would need if we were to build our own toaster? As societies have become larger and more complex, so the kinds of knowledge that each individual needs has changed. Work has become more specialized so that we each perform a relatively narrow range of tasks; the economic system in which we live allows us to pay someone else to make our toasters for us, while we earn money from performing other, perhaps equally specialized, tasks. We have acquired the necessary knowledge to be able to prepare our food using electronic technologies like toasters. However, we do all still 'know' that you can cook food using fire. Even though we may use a toaster every day, we do know that we could make toast under a grill or even over an open fire. The kinds of knowledge which we possess, about cooking and about many other things, differ through time. New technologies of food preparation, such as the grindstone or the blender, the microwave or the toaster, enable us to make different kinds of food, even rendering edible some things which were not so before, and changing how we think about food. Despite the fact that in the modern world we may use sophisticated technology and 'know-how' in conducting ordinary food preparation, we do still know that you can pick an apple off a tree and eat it when it is ripe. The old ways of knowing do not disappear: they linger still in our social memory or as the principles behind the new technology; they are there for us to draw on when needs must.

We can consider the different ways of knowing in general as somewhat analogous to technologies of food preparation. At different times, in different situations, particular kinds of knowledge are necessary and useful; it is great to be able to cook the perfect soufflé, but it is not going to help you prepare a meal on a camping trip.

## FOUR WAYS OF KNOWING

In terms of culture and communication, we might consider how different kinds of media used for the distribution and dissemination of knowledge constitute different 'technologies of knowledge'; thus, in the great evolutionary history of humankind, the technology which is deemed to separate humans from the beasts – language – is the single most important technology of all. The ability to verbally communicate is the foundation of every subsequent media technology. There are different ways of knowing which are in some regards successive, making older ways redundant: the keyboard may have replaced the pen for most writing tasks, but we will be teaching children to form the letters of the alphabet for a long time to come. We will see in the following discussion how different 'ways of knowing' are associated with successive media technologies and how they each play an important part in the processes by which we know anything about media and culture today.

In the following sections of this chapter we will look at four different 'ways of knowing'. First of all, we will consider the ways of knowing associated with the '*oral tradition*' – the epistemological foundations of the earliest civilizations before the introduction of writing (Ong, 1982). The second way of knowing, as writing was being introduced, is based on the know-how developed in the ancient Greek agora – a public space for decision-making by debate; we refer to this rhetorical method as '*classical*'. The birth of science and the spread of print technology are associated with our third period, the '*modern*', which laid the foundation of many of our contemporary modes of discourse. To describe a fourth way of knowing, following from the disillusion with the modern, we use the term '*post-modern*'. These four broad 'ways of knowing' are very general and open to challenge, but are posed as four schematic categories which provide a useful way of thinking about how different epistemological systems operate. Although presented successively, it will become clear that they are cumulative, so that, for example, the principles of story-telling that we can identify in the *Iliad* and the *Odyssey*, in *Beowulf* and *The Canterbury Tales,* are present in the highly complex media form of the Hollywood film and in the sophisticated oral culture of rap battles in Los Angeles street culture (see, for example, Alim, 2006). All four ways of knowing are used in media and cultural studies today; yet they are rarely expressly acknowledged. I contend that a lack of awareness of these different epistemological positions often blinds us to the insights of others working in our own field. Without an understanding of the specific ways of knowing that different scholars in our field employ, we are destined to be divided amongst ourselves at a time when the need to respect academic diversity seems to have never been more urgent.

## WAYS OF KNOWING IN ORAL CULTURES

Let us consider first the way of knowing associated with the '**oral tradition**' – a term used to refer to linguistic communication of the past before societies became 'literate', or to refer to societies which have yet to embrace writing. When we talk of 'oral societies' we are referring to societies in which history, science and belief are relayed exclusively through oral accounts and stories, passed down through generations. These are societies where the only repository of knowledge, culture and history is in the memory of its people. We can identify a strong oral tradition today when we tell a joke or recount a family story; it is present in our music – from classical *lieder* to contemporary rap. All human societies rely on language as a means of communication, and we do still learn a great deal about the world through oral forms.

Before we had computers, or books, or even writing, the main form of cultural transmission (of history, science or knowledge) was *spoken language;* there are some societies today where this is still the case. Walter Ong describes 'primary oral cultures' – those cultures 'untouched by writing' – and contrasts them with literate cultures (Ong, 1982: 31). An oral culture is bound by memory – human knowledge goes as far as one person can remember. The skill of remembering is highly valued in oral societies; the griots of Africa, for example, developed sophisticated mnemonic strategies for extending their memory and for being able to recall lengthy genealogies and stories (Ong, 1982).

There are still very high levels of illiteracy in some parts of the world; many millions of people can't read or write. Many millions, too, who grew up in an oral society, have had to adjust to the literate world. One such person is the Ugandan President, Yoweri K. Museveni, who describes his education growing up as a member of the nomadic Banyankole Bahima people of Southern Uganda during the 1940s and 1950s in his essay about 'The Power of Knowledge' (Museveni, 2005). The culture of the people, the skills, the morality and the history were all transmitted from one generation to the next via speech (Museveni, 2005). Museveni describes how each evening the elders would tell stories for the children and adults. These 'oftarama', he says, are evidence of the way in which memory is so important to oral societies. He says of these evenings:

> [They] were not only for the children to listen but for the adults to refresh and keep up the collective knowledge of the tribe, for example by scraping back together details remembered by different persons. (Museveni, 2005: 12)

Knowledge, among the Banyankole Bahima, as among other oral cultures, is verbally transmitted and is *collective*.

This point is also made by Bert Hamminga in his discussion of the differences between African epistemology and Western ideas of knowledge (Hamminga, 2005a). Hamminga argues that in Ugandan society knowledge is not something to be acquired by an individual, but is something shared by a community. People speak, not of what '*I* know', but of what '*we* know'. According to African epistemology, Hamminga tells us, 'the clan or the tribe is the knowing subject' (2005b: 59). There is a great respect for authority, but authority is something which is also shared by the whole community. He uses an analogy from nature to describe African attitudes to truth and power:

> All power, all truth comes up from the roots of the family tree, the dead ancestors, to the trunk, the elders, and passes up to the parents and children, the branches, leaves and flowers. (Ibid.: 61)

Power is not something external to us, nor is it associated with an individual; it is within the people as a collective. In pre-literate African society togetherness is a quality valued so highly that agreement is not just expected, it is required. Everyone has their own part to play and a group does not move without consensus – if someone veers from a point of view taken by the group, the rest of the group either wait until that person changes their mind or they all decide to follow; no action is taken until consensus is achieved. The idea that one would develop an argument to support a case is just foolishness: 'From the African point of view, arguments are a sign of weakness, of lack of power and vitality ... truth is not argued for but *felt*' (Ibid.: 61). And here Hamminga makes the point that the Bantu word for 'felt' is also 'heard' – knowledge is understood as something which you *hear*, which comes from a community acting with one *voice*.

Daniel Everett is a cultural anthropologist whose work provides an illustration of the distinctive quality of the epistemology of oral cultures. Everett first encountered the Pirahã people of Amazonian Brazil as a Christian missionary, intending to translate the Bible into the indigenous language. He spent several years studying the language and culture of the Pirahã, an experience he recounts in his book, *Don't Sleep, There are Snakes* (Everett, 2008). Living among the Pirahã he made many friends who helped him learn their language, but he made no converts and abandoned Christianity. Everett identifies several examples of the relationship between language and epistemology which challenged his literate, Western and Christian understanding of the world. When Everett wanted to know the words for 'right' and 'left' – he held out his hand and asked his Pirahã friend, Kóhoi:

'OK. This hand is the one that Americans call the "left hand". Brazilians call it *mão esquerda*. What do the Pirahãs call it?'

'Hand.'

'Yes, I know that it is a hand. But how do you say *left* hand?'

'Your hand.'

'No, look. Here is your left hand. Here is your right hand. Here is my left hand. Here is my right hand. How do you say *that?*'

'This is my hand. That is your hand. This is my other hand. That is your other hand.' (Everett, 2008: 215)

Everett could not discover how to translate 'left' and 'right' – a necessary pre-requisite to some fundamental ideas in Christianity, such as explaining the position of Jesus and the Holy Spirit in relation to God. When Kóhoi told Everett, 'The hand is up river', at first, this confused him even more. Later, when out hunting with a group of men, he noticed they gave directions to one another in terms of the river. Instead of saying '*go left*' or '*go right*' they would say '*go up river*' or '*go down river*'. It was then that he realized that the Pirahã oriented their world around the Amazon River which was such an important part of their lives.

In European and American culture, we orient ourselves relative to our own bodies – we believe ourselves to be at the centre and our sense of direction relies on us knowing our 'right' from our 'left'. This can be referred to as 'endocentric orientation' – when directions are understood in terms of one's own body. However, the Pirahã language is 'exocentric' in orientation, relying on a directional system external to their own bodies – *up river* and *down river*. The Pirahã example illustrates how the language and knowledge of an oral culture is embedded within geography and location. Nature and place play key roles in structuring a way of thinking that is in a synergetic relationship with one's sense of location and identity.

Knowledge and truth are historically contingent within oral cultures, changing as different economic and political situations demand. Ong gives an example of what has been called 'structural amnesia' taken from the research of Goody and Watt (1968) among the Gonja people of Ghana. At the turn of the century, British scholars working in Ghana recorded details of the etiological myth about the founder of the Gonja state, Ndewura Jakpa. They noted that Jakpa had seven sons and divided his kingdom into seven so that each son could rule a province. Sixty years later, the myth was again recorded by anthropologists, but by this time there were only *five* provinces in Gonja and the story had been altered to reflect this new political reality: in the more recent account Ndewura Jakpa had *five* sons and the destiny of the other two provinces was not mentioned; they had been lost from the history. Ong writes:

> … the part of the past with no immediately discernable relevance to the present had simply fallen away. The present imposed its own economy on past remembrances. (Ong, 1982: 48)

Language and demonstrations are the primary means by which knowledge is relayed in oral societies through forms which are still in use today: story-telling, singing and poetry. Much of our lives are still lived within this oral culture – much of our interpersonal communication with friends and family takes place verbally, despite the advances of 'social networking' and other means of mediated forms of personal communication. Think of the stories which circulate in your own family on holidays or ritual occasions – how many of these are told and re-told on every family get-together? These kinds of memory and recollection are recorded only in the verbal reports of family members, so that our sense of self, of family and kinship is still very much embedded in an oral culture in which recitation and repetition are important, if unacknowledged, parts of our cultural lives. In society more broadly, too, the mainstay of many media forms is the spoken word: one might think of radio, but also songs and poetry. A film or television programme without a script is a pretty rare thing. Language is the mainstay of human culture in oral and literate societies alike and remains the central means by which communication occurs.

The oral way of knowing prevailed in human society for more time than all the subsequent ones combined. The different manifestations of epistemology in pre-literate societies is doubtless vast, but we are unlikely to learn too much about them all mainly because, by definition, they were not recorded. The introduction of writing allowed the recording of human knowledge in a form more permanent than memory – and this in itself was revolutionary. The culture clash between literate and pre-literate societies has structured much of our global modern history. It is evident in places like Uganda where Hamminga did his research, and also among the poor, disenfranchised and dispossessed in every country of the world. High rates of illiteracy plague countries as rich as the USA, excluding people from participating in contemporary social, political and cultural life. The different uses to which working-class people put their newly acquired literacy in the early part of the twentieth century is the subject of a founding text of British cultural studies, *The Uses of Literacy* (Hoggart, 1957). The epistemological shift from oral to literate cultures is a cultural revolution with profound and continuing implications.

## THE IMPACT OF WRITING ON WAYS OF KNOWING

The advent of writing presented a challenge to orality. The earliest evidence we have of writing comes from Africa, where some 5,000 years ago the earliest marks were seen. Writing seems to have developed in Sumeria, in China and in Mesopotamia at around the same time. For most of its history, writing has been the preserve of the few. The idea of 'universal literacy' as a public policy is barely a century old, a tiny period of time in the history of human culture. The introduction of writing creates a different epistemic base; writing 'technologizes the word' according to Ong. Writing renders words and language abstract; it reduces the force, the power and the magic of the spoken word. Walter Ong contrasts 'orality' with 'literacy' to argue that the ways of knowing, of understanding the world, are significantly different in each kind of society. With the introduction of writing, knowledge shifts from being something that comes to you, to being something you can find out. Writing allows for records to be kept which cannot be 'contingent' or 'relative'; it makes for certainty and repeatability. Thus genealogies and etymological myths like those of the Gonja people can be recorded, and become harder to change in the light of subsequent real events. The word itself is a concrete thing when it is written; something which you can see on the page – its potency shifts. Literacy, it has often been observed, renders words less powerful, less awesome. It also ossifies language and makes truth an external to the human mind. The role of language and the spoken word is very important to our lives, and elements of oral culture prevail in our ceremonies and rituals – 'I pronounce you man and wife'; 'With this ring I thee wed'. For PhD students, we no longer have to recite the entire dissertation, but we are still obliged to have a 'viva' or a spoken 'defence' of our dissertation. In Islam, a man can be considered honourable only when he has learned, and recited, the whole of the Koran.

Oral ways of knowing have not been lost: they remain an important form of epistemology in the form of oral history and 'auto-ethnography' (Maréchal, 2010). Auto-ethnography is a research method which investigates the experience of the self using ethnographic methods and is most used in performance studies and english (Chang, 2008). The method relies on personal and subjective accounts of one's own experience, and values narration as a specific way of knowing. In our fields you are most likely to come across auto-ethnography within cultural studies, for example Ben Carrington's account of researching a cricket club (Carrington, 2008) or Alexander, Moreira and kumar's personal accounts of their experiences of fatherhood (2012).

Writing allows for the development of administrative systems, laws and so on. It permits a society to operate as a larger unit; allows for the greater reach of power across a society; and facilitates larger links and control over a bigger geographical area. Writing is central to the development of larger and more complex societies. The value of writing as opposed to orality was much contested by the ancient Greeks from whom derives our second way of knowing: classical epistemology.

## CLASSICAL EPISTEMOLOGY AND RHETORIC

The Greek city state or *polis* was organized around a central market place (*agora*) which served as a meeting place and was also the location of the debates which were both part of, and productive of, early democracy. This was a society which used slaves and subjugated women, but whose way of thinking and rules of rhetoric have been vitally important to the development of ideas of parliament and liberal democracy. The concepts of *logic* and *epistemology* developed during this time still resonate and are important constituents of all our work; these ideas go to the heart of how we construct an argument and make a reasoned case. Writing was a relatively new technology 2,000 years ago and was much debated. The threat was perceived to be that people would no longer be obliged to remember or use their mind to work things out, but would get lazy and rely on written texts. The ancient Greeks advanced their ideas through debate and developed a sophisticated system for thinking about rational argument. Many of our contemporary ideas about language and truth developed in the Greek city state.

*Rhetoric* is the term given to the art of debate as practised by the ancient Greeks. It comes from the Greek word, *rhetorike*, which dates from the fifth century when it was first used by Socrates in Plato's dialogue *Gorgias*.

Aristotle, Plato's student, wrote the first full exposition of rhetoric and proposed three different forms of argument – *ethos*, *pathos* and *logos*. These remain useful analytical categories which we can apply when developing our own arguments or when analysing those of others.

*Ethos* relates to the person speaking or giving you the information – are they reliable? Are they '*ethical*' and *honest*? Can you believe the speaker based on what you know about their character? For example, on the subject of climate change, someone says: 'I am the leading researcher of climate change; I have all the qualifications necessary therefore you should believe me.' Or: 'I am a farmer and I have noticed that the seasons are not changing in my 30 years of working on the land.' These are all appeals to ethos – to the honesty and integrity of the person speaking – and have no bearing on whether the argument itself is sound or reliable or has any basis in truth. Ethos relates to the credibility of the speaker and resonates with the more modern concept of *source credibility*. Thus, an oil company spokesperson is probably less credible and reliable when talking about climate change than an 'impartial' scientist.

The second form of argument, *pathos*, relates to how well the speaker draws on the listener's emotions – how are we moved by their words? A good speaker would be able to persuade the listener by playing on their sympathies. For example, the tabloid press often tell their stories in highly emotive terms, appealing to our *sentiment* and *feelings*. We may laugh or be moved to tears by some of the coverage, but either way we take notice and are moved. Using pathos appeals to our feelings or emotions, and we see this used in contemporary media of many genres; we are made sad by pictures of people in areas devastated by natural disasters such as earthquakes, or by the sight on the television news of a parent grieving the loss of their child in a war zone. These are rhetorical tropes designed to pull at our heartstrings. To return to our climate change example, we are moved by images of starving polar bears, which may well be losing their habitat owing to climate change but may equally be unaffected. Appeals to our love of animals and our sentimental side in making arguments about the damage done to wildlife and the wilderness (regardless of whether there is any evidence of any causality) can be very persuasive.

*Logos* is the logical basis of the argument. Does the argument make sense? Does each part follow logically from the previous one? In this case our rational self is being appealed to – we are taken through an argument, presented with evidence that the temperature is the highest since records began, so yes, there is global warming. If we are shown factual evidence of the changes in the climate and it can be proven that there is a relationship between $CO_2$ gasses and rising temperatures of the earth, then we are likely to believe it. Logos is that element of an argument which appeals to rationality and good sense. It is founded on a well-structured argument with credible evidence, and it has validity. Aristotle believed that the best way to make a case was through logos – through the appeal to rationality. This is certainly the rhetorical trope which has been most important in developing science and technology and which contributed most to the scientific revolution, which we will talk about later in the chapter. But before we do – let's consider some of the rules of argument that enhance our rhetorical skills.

## SO WHAT MAKES A GOOD ARGUMENT?

How can you demonstrate through the application of logic that something is true or false? For example, the idea that an argument should be built on sound premises is associated with the rhetorical trope of the *syllogism*. Syllogisms are sets of statements where a conclusion can logically be drawn from two preceding statements. If you can prove the first two statements, then the third is necessarily true. Thus, for example:

> All dogs are mammals.
>
> Rex is a dog.
>
> Therefore Rex is a mammal.

The conclusion – Rex is a mammal – is based on the two preceding premises. The first is a general statement relating to the definition of the category 'dog'; the second is a specific statement about a particular example, in this case, Rex. We can conclude logically that if 'All dogs are mammals' and that 'Rex is a dog' then Rex must be a mammal. However, the reverse is not necessarily true: if Trudi is a mammal, it does not follow that she is a dog. The logic of the syllogism is important to our understanding of how a well-structured argument can be made. Sometimes our work does involve categorizing objects, artifacts and events according to set criteria. For example, we can see how films and television programmes are designed and marketed according to genres which are a form of category order. We might phrase a syllogism thus:

> All musicals feature people singing.
>
> *Glee* features lots of people singing.
>
> Therefore *Glee* is a musical.

Does this follow? You can see that there is logic to this. If you can prove the first two statements to be true then the conclusion does indeed follow – it makes sense, it is logical: *Glee* is a musical. You can see from this example how careful you have to be about defining your categories, though, because

*Glee* is not a musical in the sense of 'a cinema genre in which music is heavily featured'. We have based our argument on *false premises* – *Glee* is not a musical because we dispute the assumed definition of 'musical' in the first premise. 'People singing' is necessary to musicals but is not the whole answer; it is not 'sufficient'. This is a useful structure to think about for an argument in a dissertation – in the first phase you establish a general statement as being true before going on to prove the second. An understanding of the basic rules of logic will help protect you from the danger of building your argument on unsound foundations. Classical philosophy teaches us to pay close attention to the logical structure of arguments; to build our case on sound premises and to establish the facts carefully. Constructing a good, well-reasoned dissertation requires you to be able to make a persuasive argument based on the tenets of Aristotelian rhetoric. The reader must be persuaded that you have the necessary *ethos* to be a credible speaker. The best way to demonstrate this is by showing you have read widely and have mastered your topic well. You can also prove that you are a credible speaker by discussing your personal experience. For example, if you are looking at the cultural lives of young people in your own neighbourhood, then the reader will be interested to know about your own background; it will add to your credibility as a speaker if you can say that your background has something in common with your subjects. Your use of language and figures of speech will enhance your essay through the judicious use of *pathos*, but the most important by far is that you design and develop a good research question which follows rules of logic and argumentation. We still adhere to the principle developed by Aristotle that, in academic writing at least, a logical, rational argument will be most convincing. When you read academic books and articles, you should consider how the arguments are built and developed. Some useful exercises to help you develop your skills in analysing and building arguments can be found in Stella Cottrell's book *Critical Thinking Skills* (2011).

## The allegory of the cave

The ancient Greeks railed against the impact of writing on the human mind even as they used writing to circulate their ideas. We can identify early studies of communication and culture in the writings of the ancients who concerned themselves with politics, philosophy, the arts and drama. In his *Republic* – written around 380BC – Plato creates a dialogue between Socrates and various interlocutors about the importance of the correct education for the 'philosopher-king' of the republic, a treatise on the training of the statesman (Plato, 2007). The importance of understanding dialogue and dialectics are crucial, and there is a strong emphasis on rhetoric and training in skills of public speaking and persuasion.

Plato is also concerned about ideas of 'truth' and 'reality', and 'representation' and 'verisimilitude' in art. The famous allegory of the cave is discussed in a dialogue between Socrates and his brother Glaucon. They consider the hypothetical case of a group of people who have lived in a cave their whole lives chained to a wall with only shadows of people outside cast on a wall to look at. Socrates asks whether the people in the cave: 'in every way … would believe that the shadows of the objects … were the whole truth?' (Plato, 2007: 241). He concludes that they would, and, since they would not know any different, they would not be troubled by their predicament. However, if a man was to break free and leave the cave, it would take him a while to become accustomed to daylight and to learn about the world beyond the cave. He would think back on his time in the cave and realize that the visions on the wall were not reality. If that man then returned to the cave, he would not be able to take part in the old world; he would know they were just images and he would be frustrated and angry. He would be an outsider, and would be vilified by the other people in the cave. The allegory of the cave shows that concern with images predates the modern era, for here Plato is considering how people apprehend *representation*. The 'cave' of this allegory has often been compared to the cinema or the television – if representations and images are all one sees, how then can one be educated to understand the truth? If one's world view is garnered only through the mass media, how can one have any understanding of the real world? This form of argument resonates with what Jean Baudrillard would later refer to as 'simulations' and themes within post-modernism relating to what is knowable in a mass-mediated society (Baudrillard, 1983).

## Beware the sophists

The *sophists* were philosophers and educators in fifth-century Greece (Duke, 2012). Gorgias of Leontini, the most famous of the sophists, argued that knowledge was ultimately unattainable, and so, why bother? C. Francis Higgins (2006) characterizes the sophism of Gorgias as a trilemma thus:

   i Nothing exists.

   ii Even if existence exists, it cannot be known.

   iii Even if it could be known, it cannot be communicated.

   *Source:* Higgins, 2006: n.p.

The sophists believed that since knowledge was unattainable and impossible to express anyway, one should train oneself to be successful in communication and to be able to construct a good argument in order to be a good leader, but not to be concerned about using language to understand 'reality'. Sophist philosophy was anathema to Socrates, who considered them to be a 'public menace' and was highly critical of their philosophy as they could speak very well, but what about? It is from this movement, and later writings about it, that we get our current word '*sophistry*' – the term has come to refer to an argument which may sound impressive but lacks substance and may be misleading. In terms of sophisticated rhetorical skill, there are many excellent sophists among the ranks of media and cultural studies scholars; certainly there is a great deal of work that is expressed through sophisticated arguments with varying degrees of reference to the real. Are they the 'public menaces' who Socrates vilified? In the next section of this chapter we are going to think about a third way of knowing – that associated with 'modernity'.

## THE MODERN WAY: SEEING IS BELIEVING AND THE SCIENTIFIC REVOLUTION

So far we have considered the shift in world view from an epistemology of 'hearing' or 'feeling' typical of Bantu and other oral societies, to one of 'rhetoric' and 'speaking well' in the classic period. We now come to consider the age of the Enlightenment and a shift away from what was called 'the Dark Ages' – when truth comes in the light, and observation and experiment become the means of knowing; when seeing is believing.

The Scientific Revolution was both the product of, and produced by, what we might call 'modern' ways of thinking (Henry, 2012). The project of the Enlightenment, so much associated with the rise of the modern, rests in the belief that human experience can be improved through science and technology and that we have a social obligation to ensure that improvements take place.

The mathematician René Descartes (1596–1650) wrote the principles of an epistemology which was to be the basis of much Western thinking in his 1637 *Discourse on the Method of Rightly Conducting One's Reason and Reaching the Truth in the Sciences* (Cottingham, 1999). The fundamental basis of Descartes' writing was that everything could be measured and that the world was accessible to scientific investigation by humans. All human knowledge was interrelated; Descartes used the metaphor of the *tree* to explain the relationship of the various areas of philosophy and science to one another:

> The roots are metaphysics, the trunk physics, and the branches are the various particular sciences, including mechanics, medicine and morals.
> (Descartes, quoted in Cottingham, 1999: 224)

The idea of 'natural philosophy' (what we would now call 'science') spread across Europe in the seventeenth and eighteenth centuries. It reached a high point in the French Revolution when the philosophy of *equality, liberty and fraternity*, presented a lethal challenge to that other triumvirate: *monarchy, the aristocracy* and *the church*. This is epitomized by the '*Encyclopedists*' who in 1747 published the first volume of what was known in English as the

*Encyclopedia, or a Descriptive Dictionary of the Sciences, Arts and Trades.* Denis Diderot and Jean Le Rond d'Alembert were the editors of the 17 volumes of essays, which were intended to collate all the existing human knowledge with the aim of understanding the world as a 'general system'. Today the assumption that one could collect all knowledge would be considered a vanity, but the *Encyclopedia* embodies a particular philosophy characteristic of the 'modern'. As Jean-Loup Seban says:

> As the most ambitious and expansive reference work of its time, the *Encyclopedia* crystallized the confidence of the eighteenth century bourgeoisie in the capacity of reason to dispel the shadows of ignorance and improve society. (Seban, 1999: 264)

In the 'modern' epistemology, everything is 'knowable' and progress is not only possible but is a historical inevitability. Scientists advance knowledge by proposing hypotheses which they then test against the available observable data before going on to make conclusions which add to the sum of human knowledge.

This was also the period of the rise of the nation state in its current form; and the quest for knowledge became associated with that of national identity (Anderson, 2006). The leaders of the nation states used a particular kind of scientific endeavour to promote the ideology of their supremacy, even competing with one another to employ the best scientists to work for them. Descartes himself was employed by the monarchs of Europe – it was as tutor to Queen Christiana of Sweden that he died, by some accounts after having caught a cold tutoring her in the early morning. The Royal Institute in London was set up by King George to ensure the British had an advantage in the battle for science.

The Scientific Revolution transformed ideas about epistemology – it created a shift in understanding the material world away from argument and logic (based on language) towards *observation* and *measurement*. Thus, while the early scientists called themselves 'natural philosophers', they were creating a philosophy based on an engagement, observation and understanding of the real ('natural') world. Scientists of the eighteenth and nineteenth centuries made machines and objects to enhance their skills of observation. The Science Museum in London is home to a collection of instruments which constituted state-of-the-art technology in the time of King George III (see the 'Science in the 18th Century' gallery, Science Museum, 2011).

The modern or scientific way of knowing then is based on observation and experiment. Knowledge is built up incrementally by a special class of people, *scientists*, who conduct experiments and test hypotheses. The assumption is that everything is knowable to humans through research in opposition to the ideas of the sophists.

We can think of research paradigms as being of two broad kinds: *inductive* or *deductive*. In media studies, questions of representation may come from observing a situation; for example the gay and lesbian activist group, Stonewall, hypothesized that gay people were under-represented in television for young people and set out to determine whether that was the case by a content analysis of these shows (Stonewall, 2010). They were able to reach conclusions based on their observations and confirm their original hypothesis. On the other hand, when Lisa Tripp wanted to investigate the use of computing by Latino school children, she was really not sure what she would find; her research was much more '*inductive*'. Although she started with a concern about how the lack of access might be influencing the performance of the youngsters at school, she found it was the social connections that they really missed and which the young people perceived as more of a concern (Tripp, 2010). Sometimes you have a theory or an idea and you want to 'test' it to see if it is true – this is the way scientific knowledge developed incrementally through the seventeenth and eighteenth centuries and is still the way most scientific (and social scientific) work is conducted. Sometimes you are just curious about a situation and you want to try to find out what is going on; you induce your conclusions from the situation. In either case you conduct research from a position of having a strong grounding in the theory and you are building knowledge from an established base.

The modern scientific method is based on the idea of universal truth. It assumes that knowledge is out there, waiting to be discovered. The idea that all human problems can be solved through the investigation of (social) scientists prevails in an epistemology dedicated to progress and improvement in the human condition. It is this concept of knowledge as positive and positivist that post-modern philosophers have challenged.

## THE REVOLUTION OF THE STRUCTURE OF SCIENTIFIC REVOLUTIONS

Within the scientific community there have been many debates about how we understand and interpret the world. Thomas Kuhn's 1962 book, *The Structure of Scientific Revolutions*, was a radical contribution to the theory of science. The traditional, modernist way of understanding knowledge (of epistemology) is that knowledge is always improving and evolving. The model of theory building and hypothesis testing central to modern epistemology is predicated on the gradual evolution of science. However, Kuhn argued that all the important breakthroughs in science had come as a result of something more like a *revolution* – a complete change in perspective. Kuhn argues that every so often in science there is a 'paradigm shift' – a leap away from one way of thinking and towards another. Once a paradigm becomes established, it becomes 'normal' and 'normal science' comes to dominate until the next revolutionary breakthrough (Kuhn, 1962).

Kuhn's work was just one assault of many against the belief in the unending scientific progress which characterized 'modern' epistemology. Was it after World War II when we saw how the technologies which promised so much in terms of human liberty could be used to slaughter so many millions of people? Theodor Adorno saw the Holocaust as the defining moment in the central struggle which he saw to be at the heart of civilization – the struggle between culture and barbarism (Adorno, 1967). Adorno's exhausted disillusion with the modern world is a theme which runs through much of the literature of the post-war period but disenchantment with modernity in the arts was expressed in many quarters.

In literature, the heyday of the 'realist' novel was marked by great works by Thomas Hardy in England, Tolstoy in Russia and Henry James in the US – authors who wrote works in which they created a whole world, integrated and integral. It was a world we looked in from above, as if we were looking down a microscope; an efficient world with a story-teller who spoke as if his characters were there for his delight – a world in which the narrator was 'the voice of god'. In the novels of James Joyce and Virginia Woolf, the so-called 'modernist' authors, we can see this world view disintegrating as the faith in the old order diminishes. In Woolf's *Mrs Dalloway*, for example, we see multiple perspectives on the world as Woolf (and her central protagonist, Mrs Dalloway) struggle to make sense of their world in a new way. The novelist gets to grips with the fractured identities and dislocated understandings of characters with partial views and different ways of knowing. James Joyce takes it further in *Ulysses* – the character named after the hero of Homer's poem – for here he builds a novel using every possible writing style. In a stream of consciousness – writing from the point of view of a particular character, a point of view liable to shifts and changes – it is contingent, subjective, flawed and partial. This challenges the model of the nineteenth-century realist novel, a novel in which the reader could rely on the absolute certainty that the author knew how it was all going to end. The literary high modernism marks a starting point for a post-modern sensibility which is also the beginning of media and cultural studies.

## POST-MODERN WAYS OF KNOWING

During the middle of the twentieth century, this 'modern' idea of scientific knowledge, sometimes referred to as 'positivism', began to look increasingly jaded. The spectre of fascism began to look like the historically inevitable outcome of the ideology of the machine age. A cynicism with the modern was one reason for the introduction of the term 'post-modernism'. The advances of science had not brought about the universal changes in the human condition which one might expect. In the wake of the war there was little to be proud of. A generation of scholars grew up to be cynical about the positive influences of science and technology. A way of knowing steeped in looking beneath the surface, in analysing the meaning of things, in dissecting discourse, in questioning appearances grew up. For the language we used no longer referred to the real world; to explain, decipher and understand 'natural philosophy'. Now we focused on understanding the social world, the realm of culture. Post-modernism began to dominate the epistemology of much of the humanities and social sciences in the middle of the twentieth century.

The post-modern shift can be seen in the work of Jean Baudrillard (1981); Baudrillard damned the reign of the sign in his work on *Simulations* (1983). Jean-François Lyotard wrote about the suspicion of grand narratives – the modern way of knowing relies on a big idea – that everything is knowable, that progress is inevitable, that good will overcome evil (Lyotard, 1984). These stories we tell ourselves are just that, stories. Lyotard examines how the 'narrative' way of knowing exists alongside the modern. Perhaps the most influential of the post-modern theorists is Michel Foucault (1991; 1998; 2002). Foucault uses psychoanalytical techniques and insights to investigate the social construction of criminality in his work *Discipline and Punish* (1991) and sexuality in *The History of Sexuality* (Foucault, 1998). In *Archaeology of Knowledge* (2002 [1972]), Foucault dissects the way we know, and provides an analysis of the relationship between knowledge and power. Foucault identifies the multiple processes by which discourse is used to shore up authoritarian control and maintain the status quo of even liberal societies. The impact of discourse analysis as a method used in media and culture has been profound, as it enables us to dissect the ideological position of the media and to recognize the location of power in language.

Gilles Deleuze and Félix Guattari (1994; 2004) further advance the move away from the scientific methods when they discuss the metaphor of the 'rhizoid' as a means of understanding knowledge. They eschew any idea of linear cause and effect; the importance of their work is that they highlight the complexities, the intricacies and the delicate nature of epistemology. In their idea of knowledge in relation to *immanence*, are they returning to an instinctive idea of knowledge more typical of the oral way of knowing? To something both pre- and post-modern – a knowledge which tries to cut out the whole of the Scientific Revolution?

One of the most infuriatingly interesting writers on the theme of post-modernism today is Slavoj Žižek. His book, *The Sublime Object of Ideology* (1989) unites Hegel and Lacan – philosophy and psychoanalysis – in order to discuss the operation of ideology within our culture. His television appearances, his blog and several books show an active demonstration of the idea that we need to engage with the media as we critique it. The work of media and cultural studies scholarship is to understand the world better through observing, yes, but also by acting and being part of it. The way of knowing by doing is evident in the current trend in media and cultural studies towards 'research by practice'.

A post-modern epistemology does exist; it is critical of epistemology itself. Post-modernism is self-reflexive – always considering that it speaks from a particular, specific, discursive position. We need to be aware of our own subject positions in relation to the discourses we have to work with. The post-modern scholar is *knowing* without assuming omniscience. The post-modern world in which we currently live recognizes the limits of knowledge, recognizes it as a discursive construct, and accepts and acknowledges that we always work within the constraints of the discursive limitations. The sensibility of the post-modern scholar is cynical and sceptical about the ways we discuss and consider the world. But we would fall into an ideological trap if we allowed ourselves to believe that the world itself is not real; or that our actions do not have consequences. The work that we do is devoted to ensuring a better world, and that may well be a myth of modernity, but it is a trick of post-modernism to accept it – we will return to sophistry and ignorance if we do not keep our work connected with the actually existing world.

## FOUR WAYS OF KNOWING COMPARED

In discussing the four ways of knowing outlined above we must be wary of creating a false teleology and assuming that each of these paradigmatic epistemologies brings us to greater enlightenment – this would be to reproduce the modernist myth of ever-advancing knowledge. When we look back on our necessarily cursory survey of the history of epistemology covered above we can see that they all still exist together in what Braudel called an 'ensemble of histories' (Braudel, 1975) – no way of knowing has superseded any other. The four ways of knowing which we have characterized as 'orality', 'classical', 'modern' and 'post-modern' are all still very much in evidence in the world in general and in the work of media and cultural scholars specifically. Contemporary post-modern epistemology re-values the located the situated and we find the narrative ways of knowing, typical of oral culture, in revival in areas like auto-ethnography. Indeed, narrative knowing has lived alongside successive ideologies of epistemology (Lyotard, 1984), and language remains the primary means by which we apprehend the physical world and one another.

Each epistemological model we have considered has a different relationship to technologies of communication. Language, the primary means of communication in oral societies, forms such as story-telling, singing and recitation being the dominant means of mediating culture. Location, geography, botany and animals provide significant reference points in cultures close to nature. Most communication takes place one-to-one and relies on co-presence; information is relayed physically through demonstration. The administration of the Greek city state required a special place to be developed for communication – the *agora*. This creates a separate, dedicated space for debate and decision-making in a society where specific classes are responsible for such activities. This technology, on which contemporary 'houses of parliament' (places of talking) are based, gives communication its own space. The Greeks developed sophisticated rules about the kind of talk which would take place in this special place – the rules of rhetoric, theories of statesmanship and ideas of philosophy emanate from this specific technology. The agora is a special place which, by including some people necessarily excludes others (notably women and slaves). The right to use this particular technology – a specific place to use language and a right and wrong way to speak – brings an ideology of language which is quite different from that of oral culture where decision-making is much more likely to be communal and inclusive. The greater social complexity creates a separate class who make decisions, and new technologies – specifically writing – grew up to ensure control over states. In the modern era we see the development of even more sophisticated nation states and more sophisticated technologies of communication to manage them, thus the spread of literacy in the Holy Roman Empire and the importance of the Bible for maintaining control over a global society managed from the Vatican. As societies became more complex, demands for inclusion from more people became more vociferous. Communication technologies including the book, the newspaper and scientific and other literature helped to create a more unified society as it grew and expanded and demanded complicity from more people (Thompson, 1995). The relationship between technologies of printing and the nation state have been documented by Benedict Anderson (2006). If the modern state is the nation state then the post-modern age is also the age of globalization – with the introduction of the trans-national media of broadcasting and later computing we have the possibility to transcend the limitations of the nation state so laboriously built up during the last three hundred years. Ideologies of 'globalization' and 'cosmopolitanism' are testament to a new kind of consciousness made possible in large part by the technologies of communication which enable discourse across time and space. We have a different epistemology to help us understand the world; the absolutism and universality of modernity have dissipated and become dispersed.

## DISCUSSION

We have considered how the idea of what constitutes 'knowledge' varies historically and is embedded within ideologies of nature, society, technology and language. We have looked at four different 'ways of knowing' and considered how they relate to media technology and social life. We can see how each epistemological framework is associated with a different mode of communication. We have also seen that the 'technologies of knowing' – of communication and media – relate in quite complex ways to the different 'ways of knowing'.

I hope this chapter has taught us that the very idea of knowing itself is controversial and contingent. We have to think about the ways of knowing implicit in our work and consider how these may be helping or hindering our research. We need to always be reflective, thoughtful scholars and avoid the 'taken for granted' and the 'obvious'. The way we think about the world, the tools we use to think and the language we use to express those ideas are all things we need to be open minded about. We have discussed some historical ideas about epistemology, trying to refute teleological motive. If we understand the various items in the epistemological toolbox of academic thinking, then we can be free to create and imagine new projects, new ways of thinking and understanding.

Within every academic discipline we can identify a prevailing *epistemology* or 'way of knowing' which will close off certain avenues of enquiry, and direct us to others, constraining our potential for investigation and understanding. If we can better understand the limits and possibilities provided by the way of knowing of our society and our discipline, I believe this will enable us to be more broadminded and to think 'outside the box' of prescribed research and analysis. The idea of this book is not to tell you the *correct* way to do media and cultural studies, or even to tell you the way I prefer to do it, but to help you to do media and cultural studies in your own way. Media and cultural studies have provided some of the means by which scholars have challenged the obvious, the necessary, the 'goes without saying'. Media and cultural studies have been at the forefront of adopting new philosophies to challenge our actually existing society. This is why we do it. This is why, in the words of Roger Silverstone, 'we *must* study the media' (Silverstone, 1999). In the next chapter we explore some of the specific imperatives motivating Media and Cultural Studies scholarship.

## FURTHER READING

Cottrell, Stella, 2011. *Critical Thinking Skills: Developing Effective Analysis and Argument.* 2nd edition. London: Palgrave Macmillan.
Providing examples of how to (and how not to) make an argument and helping develop your critical skills, this book is a terrific aid for anyone studying at undergraduate level.

Henry, John, 2012. *A Short History of Scientific Thought.* Basingstoke, Hampshire: Palgrave Macmillan.
This is a fascinating study chronicling some of the key historical shifts in the philosophy and practice of science.

Jensen, Klaus Bruhn (ed.), 2002. *A Handbook of Media and Communication Research: Qualitative and Quantitative Methodologies.* London: Routledge.
A rich theoretical discussion of some of the themes discussed here with close reference to the media and communication research. This edited volume

includes a number of contributions from leading scholars in communications research. Of special significance to the discussion above are the two chapters in Part 1: Klaus Bruhn Jensen's 'The Humanities in Media and Communication Research' and Graham Murdock's contribution 'Media, Culture and Modern Times: Social Science Investigations'.

Priest, Susanna Hornig, 1996. *Doing Media Research: An Introduction:* Thousand Oaks, CA/London: Sage.

This is a very engaging book. See especially Chapter 1: 'A Philosophy of Social "Science"', which gives a good, simple and straightforward guide to the basic binaries of qualitative/quantitative and inductive/deductive research.

# TAKING IT FURTHER ... ON YOUR OWN

*Thinking about media, culture, epistemology and everyday life*

Keep a diary of the sources of information you use during the course of the next week, whether it be to find out which movie to see or where your next class will be. Think about which medium you are using at each different hour during the day. Note what kinds of information or entertainment you garner from each different medium: computer, iPhone, book, newspaper, notebook. At the end of the week, compare the number and range of information media you have used. Do you use one more than another? Which medium are you likely to use for which kinds of information? Are some communication forms more suited to certain kinds of information than others? Think about the relationship between technology and knowledge – for example, what kinds of technology are suited to conveying 'interpersonal' communication and which for communicating with a large group?

*Rhetorical analysis of news reportage*

Select a current news story which is being reported across a range of different media. Choose one medium to focus on, for example, *newspapers, radio* or *the internet* and collect three news reports from different outlets on the same story. If you are looking at radio in London you might choose the BBC station Radio 4, a commercial news and talk station such as LBC, and the commercial music station Capital Radio. In class, analyse the reports to identify different kinds of argument being articulated. Identify how the various media forms use 'logos', 'pathos' or 'ethos'. Consider how the different kinds of argument are used by different media forms. Which is most persuasive and why?

## TAKING IT FURTHER ... BEYOND THE CLASSROOM

*Investigating past approaches to knowledge and epistemology*

Visit one of the great museums of science such as the Science Museum in London. If you can't visit in person, websites provide excellent resources for this exercise. Look at the collection of technology and identify three 'technologies of knowing' from different periods. Consider what epistemological framework encouraged the scientists of the time to believe that this would enhance their knowledge – and how. Think about the relationship between technology and epistemology in the modern age. What are the similarities and differences between our 'way of knowing' and that of people in the past? What are the technologies of understanding available to you? What are the dangers and opportunities of the internet as a means of knowing?

# 2

# WHY DO WE DO MEDIA AND CULTURAL STUDIES?

'We *must* study the media.' (Roger Silverstone, 1999: 12)

## Aims and Objectives

- In this chapter we provide a historical overview to some of the main movements in the study of media and culture.

- We consider some of the political motivations and the transformative agenda underlying the main trends in Communication, Media and Cultural Studies research and scholarship.

- Finally, the chapter offers some suggestions for further reading.

## INTRODUCTION

Why do we do media and cultural studies? There are many motivations for people to conduct research in media and cultural studies. For many of us, it is *new technology* which excites us – perhaps we are intrigued by the popularity of a new kind of phone or the CGI in the latest movie. We might be worried about the kind of 'surveillance society' being created when so much private information is available on databases kept by private and public organizations, on social networks or websites. It may be the enjoyment of playing games or watching television that makes us want to learn more about the *pleasure* derived from media; or it may be our appreciation of the artistry in a piece of work which drives us to learn more about the *aesthetics* of media or culture. Many of us are concerned that the media do not serve the *political* function that they should – the media are held responsible for keeping a check on our politicians and we want to ensure that they do this rigorously. Perhaps we feel horror at the media's coverage of war seems to normalize or even glamorize armed conflict. Each reader of this book will have their own answer to the question: 'Why study the media?' Later chapters of this book will give you some guidance and ideas about how you can conduct your own research. In this chapter we are going to consider *why* people have studied the media, looking at some of the main trends in the history of our field.

In Chapter 1 we talked about how we know anything at all and looked at some ideas and concepts which one might find across a number of different research traditions. Here I want to concentrate on the unique qualities of communication, media and cultural studies. How do researchers in these fields differ from those in any other? We can identify four main characteristics of media and culture research: the first is that the phenomena we research are the products of *human endeavour* – we are looking at cultural artifacts and these are, by definition, produced by people. There is nothing '*natural*' about the media and culture which surrounds us, and yet it often seems to us the most natural thing in the world. The first thing we have to learn about researching media and culture is that we can take nothing for granted. Indeed, it is those 'normal', 'natural' and 'taken-for-granted' elements of media and culture which are precisely the most ideologically loaded and which we must interrogate most closely. The second key characteristic is that, because we have to use *media to talk about the media*, it is self-referential. I am typing these words in my study now and you are reading them there and then – before these words can get to you I will have to send them to the publisher who will reorganize them and have them proof-read before sending them off to be printed and bound before being shipped back to the UK or Australia or wherever you are now, before you or the librarian buys the book, probably online, and my words become part of an information economy. It is a long journey, from my having these thoughts in my head to you apprehending them on the page. It is one which uses a range of methods of communication – reading, writing, word-processing, re-reading, emailing, editing, posting, printing, marketing, shipping, printing, shopping, reading – all mediated forms of communication. All media and cultural studies outputs contribute to the media and as researchers we are all, always, part of the phenomena we critique. This brings me to the third key defining characteristic of media and cultural studies: the escalating transformation of the mediated environment. The increasing mediatization of the cultural realm has been one of the prevailing themes in the history of Western culture for about the last 200 years. These changes have not gone unchronicled; people have been commenting on them, positively and negatively, since the beginning of what we have come to call 'Western civilization'. The process of the growth of media began apace during the Industrial Revolution in the mid–late-nineteenth century with the introduction of the steam press and cheap methods of printing, while advances in chemistry and physics brought us photography and the beginning of the cinema. The twentieth century witnessed the expansion of these as popular media, while radio, television and later computing were all added to the media landscape. Since the introduction of computer and microchip technology, the rate of change has been of a different order – the language of the gigabyte and hypertext protocols are now part of the everyday vocabulary of people who formerly worked with celluloid, magnetic tape, transmissions, negatives and so on – all media technologies which are dead or dying. The revolution being wrought, still, by computer technology is unrivalled in the history of human activity. The fourth feature is one that is shared with some other academic subjects – in our field, scholars are aware of the transformative power of media and, more importantly, of a media and cultural studies education. Many kinds of education are empowering to the individual; a media education enables one to see the world in a different way: to recognize mediated messages as *constructed* and *deliberate*. One of the liberating features of media studies is that it helps people to acquire a richer understanding of the roles of media and culture in their everyday lives. This can be a very transformational process in itself. Media and cultural studies, then, is the study of something which is: a) *cultural*, *not natural*; b) *reflexive*; c) in a state of almost *continuous flux*; and d) *transformative*. We must study the media because in doing so we can help monitor and direct it to bring about change for the better. In this chapter we review some of the main paradigms for researching media and culture.

## APPROACHES TO MEDIA AND CULTURE BEFORE MEDIA STUDIES

Media, culture and communication studies are relatively recent additions to the rostra of academic subjects taught within the formal education system. Many of the questions raised under the rubric of these apparently new subjects have antecedents which precede the establishment of these as areas for study. Questions about aesthetics, representation or the relationship between the people, the communication system and the state were all raised by the ancient Greeks and by successive philosophers throughout history.

The idea of what we can and cannot (should and should not) represent is one continuing theme in philosophy and theology as well as cultural history. Questions of representation go to the heart of all Abrahamic religions and they have often been contested. Consider the phenomenon of *iconoclasm*, or the destruction of icons. We saw examples of it when statues and images of Colonel Gadaffi of Libya were defiled and destroyed in the spring of 2011. The term *iconoclast* was first coined in reference to a Christian movement in Byzantium in about 730 when the Emperor Leo III ordered an image of Jesus Christ to be replaced with a cross at the entrance of the Great Palace of Constantinople (Gioia, 2005: 40). The first example of Muslim iconoclasm was in 630 with the destruction of idols at Mecca. In the history of Islam, Christianity and Judaism, there have also been several periods when symbols and icons have been destroyed. One of the most shocking examples of recent times was the destruction of the Buddhas in Bamiyan in Afghanistan in 2001 as part of a campaign to undermine Buddhist culture and tradition. The site has been made a world heritage site by UNESCO (2011). *The Times of India* reported on 6 February 2010 that Hindu icons were smashed in the temple at Sree Sree Rakshakali Temple at Ashrafdi village in the Narayanganj district in Bangladesh (*Times of India*, 2010). There are hundreds of other examples of the destruction of images by people of many faiths. The relationship between religion and representation can be of incendiary importance. Within Christianity, issues of representation go to the heart of the conflict between Protestantism and Catholicism which has shaped the history of modern Europe. As our world has become more globalized – as more interaction between peoples of different faiths and ideologies grows – so ideas about media and communication (what can and cannot be said, to whom, by whom) have the potential to result in conflict.

## THE INDUSTRIAL REVOLUTION, MODERNITY, MEDIA AND CULTURE

The biggest changes in the location of culture and its representation came in the period of the rise of the 'mass media', the time of the Industrial Revolution (about 1760–1880). Space does not permit us to do justice to the enormous impact this had for the role of media and culture in society during this period. John Thompson has written about the rise of modernity and its inexorable correlation with the rise of the mass media (Thompson, 1995). The rapid developments in transport and communication witnessed in Western society during the eighteenth and nineteenth centuries made people increasingly aware of social and cultural differences. In the nineteenth century, new towns and factories were growing rapidly; people were moving from the country to the city to find work and as they did so a new social class of people was forming: the 'working class'. The relationship we had to our livelihoods changed as we worked, not for ourselves, or as agricultural workers on the land, but for the manufacturer and the factory owner.

This changing relationship was observed, chronicled and reflected on by the writers of the day. The newspapers of that time were important media for discussion and debate of social change. One of the most important movements campaigning for social change in the nineteenth century was the Chartists who lobbied for an expansion of the right to vote. The Chartist newspaper, *The Northern Star*, launched in Leeds in 1837, rapidly reached sales figures of some 50,000, making it the biggest circulation of its time (Williams, 2010). There was a growing radical press in Britain in the eighteenth century, such as *The Poor Man's Guardian*, which grew up to serve and reflect the interests of the nascent proletariat (Curran and Seaton, 2010; Williams, 1998;

2010). The labour movement articulated its case through the expansion of the press and the rapid spread of ideas enabled by new technologies of printing and transport.

Karl Marx (1818–83) and Friedrich Engels (1820–95) are the two authors most readily associated with the growth of political movements arguing for a greater stake in the wealth of an expanding economy. Friedrich Engels was the son of an industrialist who was sent to England to manage his father's factory in 1842; he was horrified by the poverty he found. Engels undertook a study of the 'industrial proletariat' and their relationship to the labour movement in England in 1844–5 which resulted in his treatise *The Condition of the Working Class in England* (2011 [1845]). Here Engels describes the changes wrought by industrialization and the extent to which the working classes were being politicized in response. The relationship between capital and class are crucial determinants in the shaping of history. The central critique of capitalism can be summed up in relation to the exploitation of surplus value as follows:

> ... the cause of the miserable condition of the working class is to be sought ... in the Capitalistic System itself. The wage-worker sells to the capitalist his labour-force for a certain daily sum. After a few hours' work he has reproduced the value of that sum; but the substance of his contract is that he has to work another series of hours to complete his working day; and the value he produces during these additional hours of surplus labour is surplus value which costs the capitalist nothing but yet goes into his pocket. That is the basis of the system which tends more and more to split up civilized society into a few Vanderbilts, the owners of all the means of production and subsistence, on the one hand, and an immense number of wage-workers, the owners of nothing but their labour-force, on the other. (Engels, 1887)

The fact that the 'surplus value' of the working class can be taken for the enrichment of the owners of the means of production remains, over 150 years later, a fundamental law of the capitalist system and an abiding source of inequality and poverty. Engels and Marx were both revolutionaries, active in the struggles to improve the lot of working people in Germany and France – they were exiled from both countries for their revolutionary acts. Both knew the importance of the media for generating ideas and bringing about change. But the power of those in authority to control and shape the media, the means by which people are able to get information, could not be underestimated. In *The German Ideology* Karl Marx and Friedrich Engels wrote:

> The ideas of the ruling class are in every epoch the ruling ideas, i.e. the class which is the ruling material force of society, is at the same time its ruling intellectual force. (Marx and Engels, 1974 [1845])

Dominant culture is shaped by the ruling class and it is the task of those opposed to the control and domination exercised by the ruling class to stand up and object. Marx's work summed up the ideas and attitudes of many in the labour movement in the nineteenth century, and his three-volume analysis of capitalism, simply called *Capital* (Marx, 1990 [1867]; 1992 [1885]; 1992 [1894]), is seen by many to be the foundational work of communism. Marx and Engels, and many others in the labour movement at the time, saw their goal not just as commenting on the state of the working class in England or anywhere else, but in changing it. The writings of Marx and Engels are riddled with observations and comments which are of their time and which now read as sometimes embarrassing, sometimes infuriating. Nonetheless, their work is testament to an engagement with the economic and social world and a determination to help bring about social change through the use of the media in their books, pamphlets, articles and speeches. Perhaps the most important contribution of Marxism to our field of study is that it provides us with an understanding of the media and cultural world as having an economic, *material* base. We can never ignore that our society is founded on the capitalist mode of production, nor that the ruling economic class have a vested interest in shaping the thoughts and ideas of the rest of us. Marxist scholarship provides an important strand in media and cultural studies with a long tradition of work inspired by Marx including that of Antonio Gramsci (2011), György Lukács (2000 [1923]), Louis Althusser (Althusser, 1979; 1984), Jesus Martin-Barbero, 1993 and many others (Wayne, 2003).

Since the rise of the mass media, people have commented on it, noted it and reflected on its impact for good and bad. In the nineteenth century, societies were set up for the study of art; for example, the Arundel Society used the latest media technology of chromolithography to distribute prints of the finest art from the ancient world (Griffiths, 1980). The Romantics and the Arts and Crafts Movement were two schools of art which harked back to an earlier time but used modern technology, modern industry and commerce to spread their message. They were self-consciously creating a new kind of culture; reflecting on what culture was and what it could and should be. Thinking about how to reform the world through culture was a prevailing nineteenth-century interest. This is summed up in the words of one of the leading educators of the period, Matthew Arnold (1822–88), author of *Culture and Anarchy* (2009 [1869]), who famously wrote that culture is: 'the best which has been thought and said'. Culture was the means by which differences in social class could be eradicated. As an educator he was concerned to ensure that values of high culture prevailed. He was a key player in a continuing debate about the function of education as a means of giving people what Bourdieu would call many years later, 'cultural capital' (Bourdieu, 1984). The role of media and culture was subject to a great deal of debate in private and public life at the time of the Industrial Revolution. These ideas were central concerns to artists, academics, writers and politicians in the nineteenth century (Thompson, E.P., 2002; Thompson, J.B., 1995; Williams, 1961; 1963; 1975).

## THE TWENTIETH CENTURY

The nineteenth-century debates about the relationship between culture and society rang down into the early twentieth century. As the culture of working-class people came more to the attention of the upper classes, the debates about the role of culture in public life grew. The development of radio as a viable means of communication during World War I led to a series of debates about the cultural function of this new medium in the peacetime economy. In the US the technology was passed on to the Radio Corporation of America for them to commercialize more or less as they wished. Although there was a public service role for radio, and radio, was used as a community and an education broadcaster in many areas of the US, the main use was as a *commercial* system. In the UK, the public debate about radio was more circumspect; the British Broadcasting Corporation was given a monopoly over broadcasters, and any effective competition was rendered illegitimate after the BBC was made a corporation in 1926 (Curran and Seaton, 2010). Paddy Scannell and David Cardiff discuss the way the BBC gradually gained control over broadcasting in their study of early radio, which forms our case study on page 86 (Scannell and Cardiff, 1991). The role of broadcasting in raising the cultural standards of the nation was an integral part of the vision behind a national broadcasting service as envisioned by its founder, John Reith, the first Director-General of the BBC. The triple imperative to 'inform, educate and entertain' has come down to us from the progenitor of broadcasting in the UK. Reithian principles of broadcasting place a high value on culture as uplifting and edifying. The BBC was founded on such high cultural aspirations.

The discussion about the future of radio connected with debates about the role of culture in society which had been discussed by Matthew Arnold and was also the concern of a group of writers associated with the quarterly journal, *Scrutiny*, founded by F.R. Leavis in 1932. This journal, devoted mainly to literary criticism, was also putting the subject of English literature on the academic map. In so doing, it was recalibrating the relative status of the various arts in England. Most of the leading critics and writers of the day contributed, including T.S. Eliot, I.A. Richards and William Empson (Mulhern, 1979). Intellectuals of the day voiced their fears and anxieties about the rise of an increasingly 'mass' society. The most outspoken critic of the changes in cultural life was T.S. Eliot, the brilliant writer whose poem *The Wasteland* (1922) summed up everything that was cheap and tawdry and empty about the modern age. Eliot's *Notes Towards the Definition of Culture* (1948) reflected the ennui of an aristocratic class unsure of how to accommodate the social and political changes around them, certain only that change was inevitable and their way of life gone forever.

In the US, too, the early part of the twentieth century was a time of much reflection on the role of the nascent mass culture and its relationship to the social world. It was in response to concerns about the potential dangers of the *cinema* that the Payne Fund Studies were commissioned in 1929.

## THE PAYNE FUND STUDIES

In the US in the 1930s the role of culture, especially commercialized culture of the radio and cinema, caused much concern. The private Payne Foundation supported a series of studies to look at one aspect of this question: the impact of the cinema on young people (Jowett et al., 1996). The Payne Fund Studies comprised 13 different research projects conducted in the USA between 1928 and 1932 to provide a multi-disciplinary study of the relationship between young people and the cinema. A summary account by W.W. Charters was published in 1933 as *Motion Pictures and Youth: A Summary* (Charters, 1970 [1933]). As George Gerbner later wrote: 'The corruption of children and youth has … been the target of choice of all great cultural debates, from Socrates to media violence' (Gerbner, 1996: xi).

One of these studies, *The Emotional Responses of Children to the Motion Picture Situation* (Dysinger and Ruckmick, 1970 [1933]), used a 'physiological' approach to the study of young people's cinema-going. Dysinger and Ruckmick used monitors to measure the sweating and heartbeat of children and young people when viewing films. They found that the youngsters displayed physical responses while watching films, leading them to conclude that the movies did have an effect on young viewers. One of their findings was that adolescents of 16 years of age got more excited than children of nine during scenes involving themes of a romantic or sexual nature. They warned:

> When the pictures are finally shown in color … and when the stereo-scopic effect of tridimensional perception is added … an irresistible presentation of reality will be consummated. When, therefore, a psy-choneurotic adolescent, for example, is allowed frequently to attend scenes depicting amorous and sometimes questionably romantic episodes, the resultant effects on that individual's character and development can be nothing but baneful and deplorable. (Dysinger and Ruckmick, 1970 [1933]: 119)

The technology would create an 'arousal' in young people which could be dangerous, they warned in one of the most controversial of the reports. Another of the Payne Fund Studies looked at the influence of the cinema on the social attitudes of children. Ruth Peterson and Louis Leon Thurstone wanted to see how the attitudes of high-school children towards issues such as nationality, race and crime changed as a consequence of seeing films addressing these issues (Peterson and Thurstone, 1976 [1933]). They used a laboratory method of measuring attitudes 'before and after' exposure to films asking for children to fill in a survey about their attitudes to issues represented in the films. They found very little difference in children's attitudes as a result of seeing the films with the quite notable exception of D.W. Griffith's *The Birth of a Nation* (1915). This epic about the American Civil War shows very extreme anti-African-American sentiment. Peterson and Thurstone report:

> *The Birth of a Nation* had the effect of making children less favorable to the Negro. ... It was interesting to find that the change in attitude was so marked that, after an interval, the attitude of the group was definitely less favorable to the Negro than before the film was seen (Peterson and Thurstone, 1976: 38).

Other studies in the series showed less dramatic results, but it was the more extreme findings of the Payne Fund research which were exaggerated and sensationalized in the press. The publication of the Payne Fund Studies resulted in public outcry at the harm young people were subjected to by the cinema. The research findings were then used to support censorship of the cinema in the USA (Jowett, Jarvie and Fuller, 1996). We can see in this example the close relationship between media research and government policy. We might observe how one of the primary objectives of much contemporary research is to support the intervention of the state into media and cultural production. It has often been claimed that new media technologies have a deleterious impact on our young people. In contemporary debates these tend to focus on worries about young people's excessive use of social networks. Concern about the media having harmful 'effects' is a prevailing theme in media research, providing an important motivation for many media scholars to this day (for a good discussion of media-effects research see Barker and Petley, 2001).

## 'WHY WE FIGHT': PROPAGANDA AND WORLD WAR II

The kind of 'before and after' methods employed by Peterson and Thurstone, above, were frequently used in the study of the media in the mid-twentieth century. Sometimes this was with the goal of finding out how to better manipulate people, as is the case with propaganda and advertising – both instances of media being used to influence people's behaviour or attitudes. In the early phase of American involvement in World War II, the US government was faced with high desertion rates among the ranks which, it was believed, were a consequence of soldiers having little or no idea of the reasons for the war. Frank Capra was invited to make a series of films explaining '*Why We Fight*' to soldiers enlisted to fight a war for which they had little stomach. The US government believed that if people were informed of the issues they would be persuaded to fight with more enthusiasm. In Germany, Leni Riefenstahl had made *Triumph of the Will*, a beautiful film advocating the ugliest Nazi doctrines, and Capra had evidently seen this when he made his films in the US. There were seven *Why We Fight* films, each focusing on a different issue, for example, the British campaign. A number of 'before and after' surveys were taken to see how far people's attitudes had changed as a consequence of seeing the films. The series constituted state-sponsored propaganda to encourage American men and women to enlist in a war.

## THE FRANKFURT SCHOOL

The power of the media as a propaganda force was inescapable during World War II, but had been debated and discussed across Europe by intellectuals alarmed at the rise of the 'mass media' since the 1920s. Before the war, the mass political movements of fascism and communism relied on the mass media of the press, radio and cinema to create support for their philosophies of totalitarianism. In Germany in the 1930s the rise of the Third Reich and the persecution of Jews resulted in the wholesale emigration of Jewish German intellectuals to other parts of Europe or the US. A scholar who did not succeed in escape to the US, and who committed suicide at the border as he tried to escape Nazi-occupied France over the Alps to Spain, was Walter Benjamin. Benjamin's essay, 'The Work of Art in the Age of Mechanical Reproduction' was written in 1936 (Benjamin, 1968) and is one of the most evocative and provocative accounts of the relationship between aesthetics and technology. Its full impact on Media and Communication Studies was not felt until much later, when Hannah Arendt published a translation of it in 1968 (Scannell, 2003).

The culture shock for intellectuals from Germany coming to the US for the first time was colossal. Many were fleeing religious persecution and intolerance. Most were Jews who had been sacked from their jobs or otherwise exiled from Germany and from German intellectual life. The differences in their responses are sometimes seen to be epitomized in the experiences of Paul Lazarsfeld on the one hand and Theodor Adorno and Max Horkheimer on the other (Scannell, 2007). They had much in common: both parties had social justice at the forefront of their ambitions, both were radical thinkers. Lazarsfeld chose to work within the system, taking money from the radio corporations which dominated the media scene at the time, and conducting research for them in return. Lazarsfeld defined such work as 'administrative' – 'academic work in the service of external public or private agencies' (Scannell, 2007). He did, however, believe that the money made from these projects could, and should, be used to subsidize other work of a more critical nature, and was a supporter of Adorno and Horkheimer and their critiques of the television, radio and cinema industries. Perhaps the most renowned scholars of ideology in the media are Theodor Adorno and Max Horkheimer, whose essay on the 'culture industries' has been frequently republished (Adorno and Horkheimer, 1993). Adorno and Horkheimer argue that the American media convey a particular ideology in support of the status quo. For Adorno, industrially produced culture represses the potential for radical change by offering individual solutions to social problems (see, for example, Adorno, 1991). Adorno and Horkheimer's anti-capitalist ideology compels them to affirm that the media should be fulfilling a role more uplifting of the human spirit, which in turn would encourage people to rise up against the system. But, because of the industrial nature of artistic production under capitalism, it is not possible for the artifacts produced to have the liberating potential Adorno and Horkheimer believed they should. They believed that art should be uplifting and provide a transcendental experience, but the kind of work they found in their new home in the US was tawdry, cheap and pandering to the lowest common denominator. One can't help but feel that the clash is as much one between high- and low-brow culture as it is between a European and an American tradition.

Paul Lazarsfeld and Paul Merton are often credited with founding media studies in the United States, and their early work on radio is considered classic (Simonson, 2010). Peter Simonson and Gabriel Weimann (2003) provide an interesting evaluation of their work at Columbia University and particularly of their essay, 'Mass Communication, Popular Taste, and Organized Social Action' (Lazarsfeld and Merton, 1948). This essay, Simonson and Weimann argue, displays a critical edge to their work which subsequent accounts have ignored in summarizing their work as 'administrative'. The work of the Columbia school in the United States was politically engaged and committed to social justice. Merton and Lazarsfeld were critical of the way the mass media kept people entertained and disengaged from political life. Merton and Lazarsfeld were resolutely 'critical' in their approach; Simonson and Weimann argue that their work on mass communication integrates the role of the mass media in upholding the capitalist system (Simonson and Weimann, 2003).

Many of the research methods which were later to become standard in the social sciences were originated at Colombia. The 'panel study' for example which interviewed the same people at different times was used by Paul Lazarsfeld, Bernard Berelson and Hazel Gaudet in their study of changing voter intention in the Presidential election of 1940 (Lazarsfeld et al., 1968 [1944]). They wanted to see the extent to which people were influenced by mass media messages and concentrated especially on those voters who changed their intention during the campaign. From this research they observed that if there was any impact from the media, it was filtered through 'opinion leaders'. Paul Lazarsfeld explains it as follows:

> The mass media often reached their audiences in two phases. After opinion leaders had read newspapers or had listened to broadcasts, they would filter bits of ideas and information to the less active sectors of the population. (Lazarsfeld, 1967: vi)

It was the idea of the 'two-step flow' of communication which Elihu Katz and Paul Lazarsfeld were to investigate in more detail in their study of opinion formation in Decatur, Illinois (Katz and Lazarsfeld, 1955). The relationship between the media and public opinion has been an abiding theme in American communications and media studies subsequently. This early research proposed an object of analysis which is still at the heart of our subject – the relationship between the media and political behaviour.

American communications have another, less well known origin in rural sociology. In a country with such an expansive territory, it was difficult to reach remote rural communities. Communication to people across the whole country was difficult; the dissemination of information about the latest farming and agricultural techniques and technologies was stymied by the large distances information had to go to areas beyond the reach of early radio transmitters. An early example of a study which linked rural sociologists with communication theory is also a classic in the 'diffusion of innovations' literature: *Medical Innovation: A Diffusion Study* (Coleman et al., 1966). This paradigm was later popularized by Everett Rogers in his influential book, *Diffusion of Innovations* (Rogers, 2003 [1962]).

## TECHNOLOGICAL DETERMINISM AND THE SOCIAL SHAPING OF TECHNOLOGY

In Chapter 1 we discussed the importance of the technology of literacy for writing, and considered the work of Walter Ong, who discussed the relationship between writing and oral cultures (Ong, 1982). Ong is much indebted to the work of Harold Innis (1894–1952), the Canadian economic historian who studied the relationship between technology, economy and power in different societies. Innis proposed that, at different times different 'staples' dominate in an economy and that the group controlling these staples comes to dominate in other realms, often with unforeseeable consequences. Thus, for example, when timber supplanted fur as the main staple for trade in Canada, this created a shift in the balance of power; greater timber production led to the production of cheap paper which, in turn, was exported to the US and contributed to the expansion of the newspaper industry in the 1830s (Innis, 2008 [1951]). His work considers the relationship between different forms of communication and social class. In an essay published in 1945, Innis focuses on the English press in the post-war period. 'The English Press in the Nineteenth Century' describes the economic and regulatory environment in the English press and its influence on radical writing. This essay argues that the radical press was silenced by the actions of the state and the market. He concludes his essay with a prognosis for the future:

> And so we entered the open seas of democracy in the twentieth century with nothing to worship but the totalitarianism of the modern state. A century of peace gave way to a century of war. (Innis, 1945: 53)

For that is how the twentieth century looked in October 1945. The idea of progress and social progress as ever-advancing looked redundant. Innis writes:

> We have passed from the security and optimism which characterized the belief in progress in the nineteenth century to fear and pessimism and demands for security. (Innis, 1945: 37)

Innis's work in the area of the relationship between patterns of communication and the structures of power and authority is a (relatively) unrecognized contribution to our understanding of media and communications.

Many of the ideas which Innis proposed have come down to us through a figure more renowned in the field of media studies, his student Marshall McLuhan. When McLuhan wrote 'The medium is the message' in 1964 he set off a train of thought which ricocheted down the years (McLuhan, 1995 [1964]). McLuhan's theories about the relationship between media technology and society have been controversial, not least because of his often contradictory exegesis. In *The Gutenberg Galaxy* (1962) McLuhan proposed that the shape of a society in the age of print, dominated by Gutenberg's invention of the printing press, is significantly different from that in the current 'electronic age' characterized by television as the primary medium of communication. McLuhan's work is often over-simplified and misrepresented as claiming that communication technologies are determinative of social phenomena in a 'technological determinism'. The hypothesis that media technologies can influence social structure is an important theme in Elizabeth Eisenstein's work on the impact of the introduction of the printing press and moveable type in the development of secular society in modern Europe (Eisenstein, 1979). The relationship between mobile phone use and the 'Arab Spring' of 2011, for example, is often cited as evidence that new technologies can result in new forms of organization and patterns of communication which can challenge the status quo. The idea that technology can somehow *determine* or *shape* society is often quite nuanced in academic writing but can be over-stated in popular formulations. It has been countered by a number of authors arguing the counter case – that society shapes technology (see, for example, MacKenzie and Wajcman, 1999).

## THE FRENCH INFLUENCE
## AND *CAHIERS DU CINÉMA*

In France in the aftermath of World War II there was a renewed popular interest in American films after the pleasures of cinema-going had been denied to French audiences for so long during the Nazi occupation. When finally in the 1950s American films were shown once again in France, they attracted a great following. The idea that these were the output of 'mass production' and the propaganda machine of American corporations made in factory-like studios had engendered a dismissive attitude towards Hollywood movies. But in the early 1950s, the films of Howard Hawks, Orson Welles and John Ford, among other studio directors, were being recognized as great works of art by some writers in France. In the pages of the magazine *Cahiers du Cinéma* (launched in 1951) the writer André Bazin was one of those who argued that these directors were very much 'authors' of their texts, and they began to develop what has come to be called '*La politiques des auteurs*' (Hillier, 1985; 1992; Bazin, 2004; Bickerton, 2011). A central claim was that these films were the work of a single organizing intelligence, despite being mass-produced in the highly industrialized Hollywood studio system. Intellectuals up to this point had often dismissed Hollywood film as made for the market and therefore not worthy of serious academic consideration. However, there was a political intent in shifting critical attention away from the work of recognized 'geniuses' of literature and fine art towards the unsung heroes of mass-produced movies. André Bazin and other authors could see a commonality in films by Howard Hawks or Douglas Sirk which enabled their work to rise above the constraints of genre or studio. To advance the idea that an American mass-produced popular form like the Hollywood movie could be considered 'art' was shocking and revolutionary, especially in France, where official orthodoxy valued national culture above any other. It was the expression of a trend in French culture to appreciate rather than deprecate the American influence on popular culture which extended also to art and jazz. Among the writers who contributed to *Cahiers du Cinéma* were Jean-Luc Godard, François Truffaut and Eric Rohmer – some of the most important directors of the 'new wave' of French film-making in the 1960s. The writings published in *Cahiers du Cinéma* were highly influential in film studies and the idea of the 'auteur' was taken up by other movements in cinema; it resonated with the Art Cinema movement in the UK which had celebrated the work of revolutionary Russian directors, such as Sergei Eisenstein and Dziga Vertov, the surrealist movement and the Italian futurists. *La politiques des auteurs* had a powerful impact on British and American intellectual life as it served to recalibrate the relationship between high and low culture, mass production and the romantic charismatic myth of the artist. This approach has a contradictory place in the history of media and cultural studies; the idea of an 'auteur' runs counter to many of the ideas of cultural studies because it

seems to re-inscribe the myth of the 'charismatic artist' at the heart of industrial culture, suggesting an elitism which runs counter to the celebration of
mass culture at the heart of cultural studies. Yet the idea of the *auteur* resonates with popular ideology and has had a powerful influence on the work of
subsequent generations of media and cultural studies scholarship.

## MASS CULTURE DEBATES IN THE 1950s

In 1950s America there were heated debates about the role of 'mass culture'
in society, and US intellectuals had very complex relationships to the dominant media forms of radio, cinema and publishing. C. Wright Mills' *The Power
Elite* (1956), Rosenberg and White's collection *Mass Culture: The Popular
Arts in America* (1957) and Norman Jacobs' *Culture for the Millions* (1961)
are important contributions to the debate about the role of mass media in
a culture increasingly dominated by large corporations. C.Wright Mills discusses the relationship of various groups to the social and political elites who
wield the most power. He considers that a vital public is essential to the operation of a democratic society and believes that the media have an important
role in informing people about political life. Mills fears that the principles
of democracy and equality on which the USA was founded are under threat
from the abuse of power which occurs when there is no critical and informed
public. In order to maintain a balance of power, again a founding principle of
the United States' constitution, it is necessary to have a plurality of 'publics'
able to articulate their position and to operate as a check on the dominant
class. However, in a society dominated by 'mass culture' this process is stymied. Mills argues that the mass media became markets, and public opinion
subject to control and manipulation, even intimidation, by those media markets (Mills, 1956). Mills has shifted the focus of debate away from the examination of voter behaviour studied by Katz et al., towards the behaviour of the
media in controlling and manipulating public life.

   The work of Dwight MacDonald offered a powerful critique of mass culture which is summed up in his essay in Rosenberg and White's collection
(MacDonald, 1957). For MacDonald:

> Mass culture is imposed from above. It is fabricated by technicians hired
> by businessmen; its audience are passive consumers, their participation
> limited to the choice between buying and not buying. The Lords of
> *Kitsch*, in short, exploit the cultural need of the masses in order to
> make a profit and/or to maintain their class rule. (MacDonald, 1957: 55)

MacDonald's critique of mass culture was part of a bigger discussion about
the role of mass culture in society which was occurring in the US during the
1950s and 1960s. The collection of essays by Rosenberg and White highlights
the concern among scholars of various fields about the shifting power bases

in the US and about the force of industrialized, commercialized culture on American culture (Czitrom, 1997; Peters, 2004; Simonson, 2010). This debate has continued as a thread in public debate about the media. An interesting exegesis on, and addition to, this discussion can be found in Herbert Gans' work, *Popular Culture and High Culture* (Gans, 1974). Gans identified the putative conflict between 'popular' and 'high' culture and argues that there is much which they share, but he maintains that different groups in society necessarily have different 'tastes'. The idea of 'taste publics' is something which we find in the later work of Pierre Bourdieu (1984) – an important theorist of the relationship between 'class' and 'culture'.

## THE FOUNDING OF BRITISH CULTURAL STUDIES

Three British writers are recognized as spearheading the paradigm shift which was to lead to the development of what subsequently came to be known as British cultural studies. Richard Hoggart, Raymond Williams and E.P. Thompson all wrote key books in the late 1950s and early 1960s which were to change the prevailing way of thinking about culture and its relationship to the mass media (Hoggart, 1957; Thompson, 2002 [1963]; Williams, 1961; 1963 [1958]). Each put the working class central to the story of English public life (Inglis, 1993; Turner, 1996). World War II had wreaked havoc on the economy and had thrown open to public scrutiny the horrors not only of war, but also of the British class system. The economic divide between rich and poor had long been understood and chronicled, but these authors were delineating the extent of cultural differences between sectors of society. In the 1950s, Raymond Williams was a lecturer in adult education and was building on Marxist history in Britain when he wrote *Culture and Society* (1963 [1958]) (Storey, 2009a). Raymond Williams' contribution to what was later to become cultural studies was profound (see, for example, Williams, 1983; 1989a; 1989b). Richard Hoggart explored the culture of the working class in his book *The Uses of Literacy* (1957). He discusses the particular artifacts and pleasures that working-class people enjoy. This was a foundational text in what later became known as British cultural studies, a field of study Hoggart was instrumental in founding. E.P. Thompson's *The Making of the English Working Class* (2002 [1963]) enlightens us as to the history of working-class radicalism and the fight for democracy. These three writers helped to sum up a new attitude towards class and culture. Their work both promulgated and reflected a greater social consciousness of the specificity of working-class life. They helped bring 'culture' down from the elevated heights of 'the best that has been thought and said' (Arnold, 2009 [1869]) to something we could all study – culture as a 'way of life' (Williams, 1963 [1958]).

The revolutionary changes of the 1960s were expressed in the civil rights movement, in black power struggles, in the growth of the women's liberation movement and increasing calls for gay rights. These changes were necessarily evident in the cultural realm. You could find evidence of changing social mores in the radical theatre and drama of the day, such as Joan Littlewood's Theatre Workshop and the 'kitchen sink drama' of which John Osborne's *Look Back in Anger* gave us the archetypal 'angry young man'. Shelagh Delaney's play *A Taste of Honey* (1961) was one of several made into films (dir. Tony Richardson) and contributed to a renaissance of British social realism expressed in films like *Saturday Night and Sunday Morning* (dir. Karel Reisz, 1960); *The Loneliness of the Long Distance Runner* (dir. Tony Richardson, 1962) and *Up the Junction* (dir. Peter Collinson, 1968). The celebration of working-class mores and values filtered through to television, too, after the introduction of commercial (also known as independent) television after 1955. For example, the soap opera *Coronation Street*, which is still running, was launched by Granada television as a counter to the cosiness of the BBC family drama *The Lloyds*. Some radical, innovative television was aired, for example, ITV's *Armchair Theatre* (1956–68) and the BBC's *Play for Today* (1970–84) and *The Wednesday Play* (1964–70). One of the most famous of these, directed by Ken Loach, was Jeremy Sandford's *Cathy Come Home* (1966) which had a direct impact on social attitudes towards homelessness. The late 1950s and the 1960s were revolutionary times in a number of ways. Social ideas and attitudes towards issues of class and culture were changing radically. It is from such ferment that cultural studies was founded in Britain.

# THE 1960s AND CULTURAL STUDIES IN ACADEMIA

The institution of 'cultural studies' as a separate discipline to be taught in universities was first proposed by Richard Hoggart when he founded the Birmingham Centre for Contemporary Cultural Studies. He used money donated by Penguin books to establish the Centre in 1964. Apparently the publishers had given Hoggart the money in appreciation of his help at the trial of the novel *Lady Chatterley's Lover* by D.H. Lawrence (MacCabe, 1999) – both the novel and the censorship trial faced by Lawrence and the publishers are in themselves manifestations of British class conflict. The institutional establishment of something called 'cultural studies' within the academy was, as Colin MacCabe argues, 'a fundamental political task' (MacCabe, 1999: v). MacCabe compares the introduction of cultural studies with the introduction, a generation earlier, of English into the curriculum. The Centre for Contemporary Cultural Studies at the University of Birmingham became home to a radical centre for the research of popular culture.

American antecedents to contemporary cultural studies are typically traced back to the Columbia school and to the mass culture debates of the 1950s. There is another antecedent, however, in the study of America's indigenous people, whose culture was investigated and researched by early scholars of anthropology; the study of *popular culture* in the US has an important origin in research into *folk culture*. One key figure in the popular culture movement in the US was Ray Browne (1922–2009) who established the first degree in popular culture anywhere in the world, at the Department of Popular Culture, Bowling Green State University, Ohio, in 1967. Browne was also a founder of two important journals, the *Journal of Popular Culture* and the *Journal of American Culture*, both of which continue to publish leading-edge scholarship. The relationship of Ray Browne's department to the rest of the American academy is quite complex and the department he set up at Bowling Green State was often controversial, by Browne's own account (Browne, 2006). Bowling Green State remains a centre for the study of popular culture and offers teaching at all levels there. The location of popular culture studies in the US, with its close links to folk studies and anthropology, was quite different to the more radical historical and literary antecedents of cultural studies which were being developed at the Birmingham Centre for Contemporary Culture.

In the 1960s the focus of interest in 'mass culture' was shifting towards an understanding of working-class culture as worthy of serious study. In no small measure this was because of the influence of popular music and pop art. During the 1960s artists high and low were turning their attention to the culture of the people. Thus, when Andy Warhol said 'pop is liking things', his droll statement summed up a massive social and cultural shift in American life. Debates about mass culture which had dominated public discourse in the work of Dwight MacDonald and others were rendered old-fashioned and out-dated, while in the UK the shift from 'mass' to 'popular' culture signalled a great shift in political attitudes towards media and culture.

## THE 1970s' MEDIA EDUCATION MOVEMENT

One consequence of the rise of popular culture as a serious object of study in the 1960s was an increasing desire to translate this into education and consciousness raising. The counter-cultural movement was growing against the mainstream media during the 1970s. The power of the television networks in the US and the 'cosy duopoly' of the BBC and ITV in the UK were under siege. Media systems faced criticism from women, people of colour, trades unionists and disabled people among others campaigning for greater diversity on television. David Morley worked in such a context when he wrote *The 'Nationwide' Audience*, a study of how politicized trade-union members interpreted the early evening news magazine programme in a different light to some other groups (Morley, 1980).

Throughout the 1970s academic interest in the media grew, partly in response to government debates about how access to the airwaves should be extended. In 1975 the first media studies degree was launched at the Regent Street Polytechnic, London, as Paddy Scannell recounts (Scannell, 2007: 198). Four years later, *Media, Culture and Society*, now one of the leading academic journals in media studies, was launched by a group of academics at the Polytechnic (now the University of Westminster). James Curran makes clear the political motivation behind the study of the media in his introduction to the first issue of *Media, Culture and Society* (Curran, 1979). In this statement of intent for the new journal, he makes it clear that the very idea of media studies is to challenge hegemony. He argues that the neglect of media and cultural industries as an area of study within the university system can be accounted for by 'the snobberies of the upper reaches of the educational industry' (Curran, 1979: 1). The journal was established to challenge the hegemony of both the media industry and the educational establishment.

## THE TURN TO THE READER

In the 1970s, semiotics and structuralism were trends in academia which focused on the text as the location of meaning and textual analysis provided the basis for much media studies research. The importance of Marxism and debates about ideology which sprang from the work of Louis Althusser (1979; 1984) led to a focus on the modes of production, the ideological content of texts and, to a lesser extent, the processes of production. During the 1980s, some key studies shifted the attention of media scholars away from the analysis of texts and towards the investigation of the text in the mind's eye of the reader. The idea that the meaning of texts was created in the reading began to gain currency with the impact of feminism and other civil rights issues on cultural studies: the idea that the personal was political led to work which focused on the way audiences read texts. The age of the reader emerged out of a political engagement with popular culture which was committed to empowering the users of texts. Issues of textual reception began to replace those of hermeneutics or production. The history of the changes in the way audiences have been researched has been discussed by Ien Ang (1991), David Morley (1992), Sonia Livingstone (1998) and others (see also, for example, Kitzinger, 1999).

David Morley and Ien Ang are both authors of key texts in the history of audience research. David Morley's work on how different audiences understood the news programme *Nationwide* (Morley, 1980) is a key study. Morley watched episodes of *Nationwide* with several different groups of people – evening-class students, school students, trades unionists – and noted how the meanings of the same text differed according to who was watching. His later research on how families watch television pays more attention to the location of reception by interviewing families in their own homes (Morley, 1986). The idea of focusing on the audience and the meanings and uses they put to the media may have been anticipated in the 'uses and gratifications' research of communication research, but here it became empowering, most especially for feminist researchers who took up the idea of empowerment of the audience through counter-hegemonic interpretations.

# FEMINIST INTERVENTIONS

The 1960s was a time of social unrest – the civil rights movement and the women's liberation movement were both manifestations of a cultural revolution in which wholesale discrimination against people on the grounds of race, colour or sexuality simply would not stand. There were several influential books addressing the role and representation of women in society, including Simone de Beauvoir's *The Second Sex* (1961) and Betty Friedan's *The Feminine Mystique* (1963). Naomi Wolf's searing attack on the representation of women in the media, and particularly the way the magazine industry conspires to sell us 'the beauty myth', was a best-seller (Wolf, 1990). It is a terrifically well-researched book with a sophisticated argument but a simple message that we could all understand – the contemporary idea of 'beauty' is actually enslaving to women. In 1976 the first issue of the journal *Signs: Journal of Women in Culture and Society* was published, and feminists turned their attention to the role of media in reinforcing gender stereotypes and divisions (van Zoonen, 1994).

The question of the use of media by women was given more serious academic attention in the 1980s. Tania Modleski's book *Loving with a Vengeance* (1982) was a key text in proposing the study of 'Harlequin Romances' novels for women. Modleski set out to explore the narrative structure and the production processes of these novels, so long derided as mass-produced escapism. Feminist research into *readership* has a powerful progenitor in Janice Radway's *Reading the Romance* (1984) which, like Modleski's research, explores the counter-hegemonic readings of women's romances.

In the UK, Annette Kuhn's *Women's Pictures* (1994 [1984]) was influential in generating the realization that film, media and cultural studies, all of which came out of established academic disciplines, still carried with them the baggage of a kind of careless misogyny – during the 1980s a number of works challenged the hegemony of a masculine-dominated discourse. bell hooks is perhaps the most celebrated of many black feminists who directly address popular culture in her work (1987).

The 1980s were a time of radical change in the media landscape – the hegemony of the networks was being challenged in the US by the expansion of cable and satellite television. In the UK and Australia, new channels to cater to audiences not served by the majority of services grew. Independent television production companies were being supported in a new commissioning strategy at Channel 4, especially aimed at bringing a wider range of people to work in television. At the time, Jane Root worked for Cinema for Women, a feminist film-making collective, and wrote a popular book about television: *Open the Box: About Television* (Root, 1986) which sets out, for a popular audience, some of the key ideas of media studies. The history of feminist media studies is considered by Angela McRobbie (2008) and also by Liesbet van Zoonen (1994).

# SEXUALITY, THE BODY AND QUEER THEORY

Michel Foucault's *History of Sexuality* (1998 [1976]) has had an important impact on media and cultural studies by virtue of both its content and its method. Foucault analyses the social construction of one of those elements of human culture which seems most innate – sexuality. Foucault's method, which has come to be labelled 'discourse analysis', deconstructs the exercise of social power and control at the heart of our social practice and language. The idea that sexuality, of any kind, may be a construct, is quite radical. The idea that we daily reinforce our own repression through the language we use is even more so. These are the areas of debate that Foucault's work has stimulated.

The impact of feminism on our area is quite well recorded, but during the 1980s there were several voices considering ideas of masculinity. Questions about the media and male sexuality began to be heard in the 1980s (see, for example, Metcalf and Humphries (eds), 1985). Issues of sexuality and the body were brought to the fore by the devastating impact of AIDS/HIV on a whole generation of young people. The 1980s saw the loss of so many young creative intellectuals as thousands of people died before their time.

The idea of gender as performance – something which we daily enact – is central to the writings of Judith Butler, whose book *Gender Trouble* (1990) has been enormously influential on subsequent writings. It was Teresa de Lauretis, however, who first coined the term 'queer theory' to describe a resistance to the constraints of gender (de Lauretis, 1991) – the term 'queer' being re-appropriated in the same way African Americans took the word 'black' and transformed it into a word signaling power and resistance rather than repression and prejudice. The study of gender and sexuality continues to be an important and abiding theme in the work of media and cultural studies.

# POST-COLONIALISM, IDENTITY, RACE AND DIFFERENCE

Stuart Hall has been one of the most influential scholars in helping us to address issues of identity and race in the media. One of the first works to come out of the Birmingham Centre under his leadership was the study *Policing the Crisis: Mugging, the State and Law and Order* (Hall et al., 1978). This multifaceted study explored the relationship between young people and the police and looked at representations of 'muggers' – people who commit street crime. The study revealed racist attitudes on the part of the police and the press which served to control and denigrate young people of colour. The question of representation, specifically of the representation of race and ethnicity, has continued to be a key theme in Hall's own work (see, for example, Hall, 1997) and in media and cultural studies more generally. It is a theme to which we will frequently return in the course of this book.

## NEW MEDIA, NEW PARADIGMS?

Throughout the history of the media, the impact of new technology has engendered new ways of thinking about the media in relation to the social, and that is no less the case today with the introduction of computing and social networking. New paradigms for investigating media production have developed with on-line ethnography and other innovations. The reconfiguration of the audience, from passive 'receivers' of media messages to active 'fans' engaging with the media products, has been a key theme in recent research. This approach has been linked with the work of Henry Jenkins (1992) who investigated the way media fans appropriate and 'poach' identities and themes from the media in new ways of conceptualizing the idea of 'fan culture'. The phenomenon of the 'fan' is one of the most recent ways of thinking about the construction of the audience (Gray, Sandvoss and Harrington, 2007; Hills, 2002; Sandvoss, 2005).

Media and cultural studies scholars are quick to respond to new trends in media content. For example, the advent of the ordinary person as 'celebrity' in television programming post-*Big Brother* has spawned a significant amount of research (Rojek, 2001; Turner, 2004). The idea of the 'celebrity' has opened up a whole new way to study television content and audiences. New media forms spawn new configurations of research paradigms. Space does not allow for a full consideration of the diversity of themes currently being addressed by scholars in our fields. Suffice to say that the transformative agenda of communications, media and cultural studies has been, and continues to be, a key organizing principle for our work.

## CONCLUSION

This chapter has highlighted some of the reasons *why we do media and cultural studies*; the main impetus is what MacCabe calls: 'An emancipatory social project' (1999: *v*).

In the beginning of this chapter we considered what was unique about media and cultural studies. We noted that it is about the study of *cultural* (as opposed to natural) phenomena; that it is *reflexive* – we need to use the media to discuss the media; and that it is subject to enormous and rapid *change*. But having discussed the motivations of research in this chapter, it is clear that a fourth reason is the overriding one: we do media and cultural studies to make a difference – to make a difference to the world; to make a difference to the way we understand and think about the world; to bring about positive change. Media and cultural studies are *transformational* subjects – they are political, social and humanist subjects. We can learn from astrologers about the movement of the heavenly bodies, but if we want to learn why people ever wanted to build a telescope in the first place, then that's a question for cultural studies. We do it because not only do we want to look at the stars, we want to know why we ever dream of reaching for them.

It is up to you to now consider how to use the information you have about scholarship of the past. You need to think about what themes or topics interest you – do not be swayed by fashion or fads or what you think your supervisor would like. In the next part of the book we present some approaches and methods that you could use to conduct your own research and we look at how you can get started on your research project. The best research project you can do is one based on your interests: What do you care about? How do you want to make a difference?

## FURTHER READING

Katz, Elihu, John Durham Peters, Tamar Liebes and Avril Orloff (eds) 2003. *Canonic Texts in Media Research: Are There Any? Should There Be? How About These?* Cambridge: Polity.

An interesting collection of essays proposing 13 'canonic' pieces of media research, including texts from the American communication tradition, such as Kurt and Gladys Lang (Katz and Dayan, 2003), and Europeans including Walter Benjamin, Raymond Williams, Stuart Hall and Laura Mulvey.

Murdock, Graham, 2002. Media, culture and modern times: Social scientific investigations. In Klaus Bruhn Jensen (ed.), *A Handbook of Media and Communication Research: Qualitative and Quantitative Methodologies*. London: Routledge, pp. 40–57.

Jensen, Klaus Bruhn, 2002. The social origins and uses of media and communication research. Chapter 16 in Klaus Bruhn Jensen (ed.), *A Handbook of Media and Communication Research: Qualitative and Quantitative Methodologies*. London: Routledge, pp. 273–93.

These two chapters in Klaus Bruhn Jensen's useful edited collection provide some interesting insights into the topics discussed in this chapter.

Scannell, Paddy, 2007. *Media and Communication*. London/Thousand Oaks, CA: Sage.

With nine chapters, each focusing on a key moment in the history of media and communication studies, this book neatly spans the British and American traditions of study and provides fascinating historical context to a range of research paradigms.

Storey, John, 2009a. *Cultural Theory and Popular Culture: An Introduction*. Harlow, Essex: Pearson Education.

And the companion reader:

Storey, John. *Cultural Theory and Popular Culture: A Reader*. Harlow, Essex: Pearson Education.

Together these two books provide an excellent history of cultural theory and the main traditions of research into popular culture in the British cultural studies tradition. There is also a companion website at www.pearsoned.co.uk/storey.

# PART 2
## METHODS OF ANALYSIS

# 3 GETTING STARTED

## Aims and Objectives

- This chapter will help to get you started on your own dissertation.

- We consider first of all how to identify your *topic* or general *subject of interest*.

- In the first stage of developing your topic into a workable research question you are asked to consider whether your main focus is to be on the *industry, texts* or *audiences*.

- The chapter then helps you to design your research question by asking you to consider three core elements of your research: your *object of analysis*, your *research method* and your *theoretical approach*.

- We discuss the importance of good design to your *project proposal*.

- The chapter then suggests some further reading.

- The last section proposes some activities for you to do to 'take it further' on your own, in class or beyond.

## INTRODUCTION

In the first chapter of this book we looked at some *ways of knowing* and considered how ideas of epistemology influence the kinds of questions we can ask about media, culture and society. Chapter 2 provided a historical survey of the rationale behind the study of media and culture, looking at selected moments in the history of our field. Now we turn to thinking about how you can conduct your own research. In your university work to date you have probably *read* several examples of research in books and journals and now it is time for you to *produce* your own work. If you have previously been given the title of the essay and the longest piece you have written is

3,000 words, to be asked to design and write an 8,000- or even 10,000-word dissertation on something original can be daunting. This chapter, indeed this book, is designed to help you make the leap from being a *reader* of research, to being a *producer* of your own work.

## GETTING STARTED

In the following sections we are going to discuss how to design your research question, taking you through the process from 'coming up with an idea' to 'writing your project proposal'. We consider how to design a research question and the importance of identifying your *object of analysis*, *research method* and *theoretical paradigm*. Subsequent chapters (4–6) will guide you in more detail through some of the main methods of research we can adopt, and the final chapter (7) will give some advice on how to finish and write up your dissertation.

## Coming up with an idea

The first task is to decide what subject you are going to study; the areas covered by communications, media, film and cultural studies are so diverse that the task of deciding *what* to research can seem overwhelming. The best dissertations reflect the interests, beliefs and ideas of the persons writing them. I cannot tell you what topic to choose, I can only give you some things to think about to help you identify what it is about your subject that most fires you up. What do you feel passionate about in the world of media and culture? Think about your own beliefs and values – can you conduct a project which allows you to find out more about the things that are really important to you?

For example, from her experience working with Latino children in Los Angeles, Lisa Tripp was concerned that some children were under-performing at school because of their lack of access to the internet at home. Tripp hypothesized that parents' attitudes to the computer might be contributing to their children's under-achievement in school, and she set out to find out more by interviewing families about their attitudes. She published her findings in '"The Computer is Not for You to be Looking Around, It is for Schoolwork": Challenges for Digital Inclusion as Latino Immigrant Families Negotiate Children's Access to the Internet' (Tripp, 2010). Tripp's essay is discussed further as a case study in Chapter 6. Sometimes, like Lisa Tripp, we are driven to investigate what we perceive to be an inequality. At other times, it may be that we recognize a disparity between official policies, publicly espoused, and private attitudes in relation to media and culture. For example, it seemed that the general consensus in the Netherlands in the 1980s was that the American television soap opera *Dallas* was an example of US cultural imperialism which no-one in their right minds should watch. And yet *Dallas* had high ratings indicating that it was being watched, and presumably enjoyed, by millions of Dutch people. Ien Ang set out to find out what people liked about *Dallas* and she wrote about her findings in her very influential book, *Watching 'Dallas'* (Ang, 1985). Marcia Morgado found hip-hop fashion fun and exciting and was intrigued as to why it seemed to elicit more feelings of disgust and disdain from other people she knew (Morgado, 2007). Morgado went on to research the *semiotics* of hip-hop dress to find out why it elicited such extreme reactions in her essay which is discussed as a case study in Chapter 5. If there are things which are important, or strange, or intriguing to you about our contemporary media and cultural world, then these are the kinds of things you should consider studying for your dissertation, as these are likely to keep you interested and engaged across the period you have to study. Researching a topic because you read about it in a book or because your supervisor suggested it will not necessarily motivate you to stick with it; the topic has to come from the heart and be something you really believe in and care about.

Below is a questionnaire for generating ideas for the project for you to administer to yourself! Read through these questions and give them some careful consideration. This might be an activity you want to do in class or with a peer.

**FIGURE 3.1**   Questionnaire for generating project ideas

Think about your own uses of media and culture:
1. What genres of media do you **use** the most?
2. What genres of media do you most **enjoy** using? Are they the same as above?
3. Are you part of a media or cultural **community** which you could research, such as a dance group or campaign network?

Think about your own beliefs and values:
4. Do you think there is a group which is **unfairly depicted** or **misrepresented** in the media?
5. Is there something which occurs in media or culture which particularly **supports your own values** and/or point of view?
6. Is there something you **would like to change** about the media, culture or communication?

Consider your subject area:
7. What interesting changes are taking place in the areas of: a) **new technology**, b) **regulation** and c) **social or cultural phenomena**?
8. Is there an **event**, contemporary or historical, which you think has had an important influence on the media and which you would like to investigate?
9. What **access** do you have to media content, institutions or audiences which you could study in your project?

Think about your studies so far:
10. Is there any **area of your studies** so far which you would like to look at in more depth?
11. Is there a **researcher** whose work you particularly admire? What do you like about her/his work?
12. Did a **specific module, lecture or seminar** particularly inspire you to research a topic?

## Think about your own uses of media and culture

A good way to start thinking about the topic for your research is to reflect on your personal interest in the field. Ask yourself what areas of culture or media interest you the most. Think about how you interact with culture and the media in your own daily life. Do you spend more time on social networks, watching television, listening to music or playing games? Keep a diary of your media use and make a note of how you use different media – is it for relaxation, socializing or entertainment? What kinds of enjoyment do you get from using media and culture? Which is your favourite medium and why? Would you describe yourself as a fan or a connoisseur of any particular medium or genre? Many excellent projects are written by students about programmes, films or music that they admire. If you are part of a subculture or scene, perhaps you could research the attitudes and behaviour of fellow members of your group. If you are a member of an online community, such as a *Facebook* group, your co-members can make an excellent resource: after all, they share your passion and are probably keen to talk about their interest. Perhaps you have experience of working in the media, or access to people who work in the media and who would be amenable to being interviewed. Your own knowledge, experience, .contacts and interests are invaluable resources in conducting original research.

## Think about your own beliefs and values

Consider how your personal beliefs and values are addressed or ignored by the media and cultural world. Is there something about the media which you find clashes with your own value system? Is there something you would like to change about the media? Think about the disparity between how things *should* be and how they actually are. For example, it is held that the press should work as a check on the power of the state, performing the function of a 'Fourth Estate', yet it can be taken to task for not doing this. You may build your dissertation around taking an instance where you think the press should conform to this role and discovering whether it does so. Is there a section of society, a social class or group who you think are poorly represented? For example, the Roma people and Travellers are persecuted across Europe. In October 2011 a group of Roma families at Dale Farm in Essex, England, were evicted from their established sites with no provision of a location for them to go to (Walker, 2011). This community had taken their case to the High Court in the UK and had been in a long-standing confrontation with the local authorities. A good research question might be to look at the media's contribution to the tensions which grew up between the Traveller and the settled community around Dale Farm. How are socially marginalized groups, like the Travellers in the UK, represented in the media?

## Consider your subject area

Your research should be original, but should also engage with your field of study; one of the best ways of ensuring that you do both is to find out about the latest developments in the field. To find out about what is happening in your subject area, look at the relevant academic journals. Look through the latest issue of *Media, Culture and Society* (http://mcs.sagepub.com/), *Cultural Studies* (http://www.tandf.co.uk/journals/routledge/09502386.html) or *Screen* (http://www.gla.ac.uk/services/screen/) – you may find them available electronically via your university website or you can go to the periodicals section of the library and browse the physical artifacts. What themes are dominant? Are there any articles which use interesting methods you could emulate? Search on the electronic databases such as SwetsWise, using some of the keywords that have come out of answering the questionnaire for generating project ideas (Figure 3.1). Read a recent article on your topic and find out how that topic is being addressed – how would/could you do something similar, but unique to you? Visit the website of the leading publishers in the field such as Routledge (www.routledge.com), Palgrave Macmillan (www.palgrave.com), Pearson Longman (www.pearsoned.uk), Wiley-Blackwell (www.wiley.com) and Sage Publications (www.sagepub.com). The online catalogues of these publishers will provide information about the latest books in media and cultural studies and other useful supporting material. Identify which topics are of current concern to academics – consider how you could research similar themes. You will need to start building a bibliography now, so make sure you keep a record of the full details of all the books and articles you find – you may need to refer to them later.

Keep up to date with the news in your topic area. Log on to relevant websites with news about your area of interest, follow the Twitter feeds of key people in the industry and read their blogs. Find out what the current areas are for debate and discussion in the media and cultural pages of the national papers. Listen to radio programmes such as BBC's *The Media Show* which is available online or via podcast. Get in the habit of reading a national newspaper that includes good media and cultural coverage such as the *Guardian* in the UK (www.guardianmedia.co.uk) or the *New York Times* (www.nytimes.com) in the United States. Magazines such as *Empire* or *Sight and Sound* are great for news and interviews about the latest developments in the cinema. Trade papers such as *Variety*, *Broadcast* or *MediaWeek* are invaluable sources of information about what's happening in the media and cultural industries.

The media world is changing rapidly and it is sometimes hard to keep up. This is where you come in – as a media scholar you can help explain and interpret current developments in the media and cultural world. What recent changes do you find most fascinating? Think about what is going on in the real world of technology, government and regulation, social change and economics:

- *Technological* – look at the implications of the latest media technology; how are they influencing industry and audiences?

- *Regulatory* – consider how recent governmental legislation or decisions (for example, the Leveson Inquiry in the UK or EU legislation on music copyright) may influence the media system.

- *Social* – examine how new media and cultural phenomena are being used.

- *Economic* – who owns which institutions? Are new companies entering the market? Are some folding? Why? How do shifts in patterns of ownership influence 'control' of the media?

Each of the above is constantly changing, and scholars of media and culture are at the forefront of examining the impacts of such changes. Use a wide variety of sources to find out about current developments in the academic community and the wider media and cultural spheres to get inspiration for your work.

## Think about your studies so far

The dissertation is intended to be the culmination of all your work on the degree to date. By now you will probably have taken several modules or courses in the field. The project is a good opportunity for you to pursue in more detail areas of interest which you studied during your course. Spend some time with your course and module guides to remind yourself of what you have been studying. Go through your notes, reflecting on classes or lectures you found especially interesting. Think about the topics you have covered on your course so far. Can you identify a theme or topic which you would like to investigate further?

One excellent starting point is to ask yourself what has interested you the most about the research you have read. Most research is generated by testing theories of previous scholars in new situations: is there any work that you have read which you can build on in your own research? For example, David Morley's book *Family Television* studies how the structure of the family is reflected in the way people watch television (Morley, 1986). One of his main conclusions is that patriarchal power structures are reflected in television-viewing habits, but Morley acknowledges the limitations of his study, which is based on a narrow demographic range of mainly white, middle-class families. You might be inspired by this study to ask whether members of other demographic groups use television in distinctive ways. For example, your own family background may differ from those Morley researched. A study of the decision-making processes around television viewing in extended or single-parent families, for example, would make an interesting comparison with Morley's research. Alternatively, you could ask: 'Who controls television viewing in households which are not based around family relations, as in student accommodation or when groups of friends live together?' Is it the owner of the television? Are decisions about television viewing made by the person who is most similar to the patriarch in the group – the person who earns the most perhaps; or the person who pays the subscription charge? Or does everyone watch television on their laptop these days? Has Morley's idea of *'family television'* been displaced by new technology and the proliferation of viewing platforms in the home? You could use the same methods as Morley, but by applying his ideas to a different situation you could come up with some new ways of thinking about how we watch television a generation later. Another way to build on Morley's research would be to interview groups of people about their collective media habits, as Morley does, but apply that method to something other than domestic television. For example, you might interview a group of friends who regularly use social networks to make social arrangements about the decision-making processes involved in making plans together. How do social networks operate when this group makes plans for how to use their leisure time? Or you could look at the family unit, as Morley did, but investigate how families decide which channels they are going to receive on their television subscription service. Morley's focus on the dynamics of group decision-making around the media is very productive of new ideas. There are numerous ways in which you could apply a method of research that has been used by previous researchers to new situations or media. Start by re-reading research which you found particularly interesting, paying close attention to the methods used. Think about how the researcher's approach may be adapted to new situations or environments.

## If in doubt, brainstorm!

Brainstorming is a great way of generating ideas and a useful technique for helping you to think about what you really want to do. When you have thought about the questions raised in the *Questionnaire for Generating Project Ideas* (Figure 3.1), allow yourself the time to indulge in a brainstorming session. You can do this alone, in a study group or in class. First get a very large piece of paper and some marker pens. Give yourself a set period of time to cover it with writing – 10–15 minutes, depending on how many of you there are. Write down each and every topic that you could, would or might like to study. Don't edit your ideas – be spontaneous and write everything down, almost like automatic writing. Make sure you keep writing, as quickly as you can, for the whole time. When the time is up, go and have a cup of tea or take a walk. Come back to the sheet of paper after about ten minutes and read it. Now, think about what connections you can make between the ideas you have written down. Take a different coloured pen and draw lines between similar or linked ideas. Create categories for your ideas. Can you identify common themes? Is there one idea which seems to dominate everything else or do you have several distinct ideas? Write a list of any ideas which could provide you with potential research topics. Next, think about how you could put these ideas in order of what interests you the most. Is there one topic which seems more appealing than the others? You may have several different ideas at this stage or you may still be stuck; but don't worry – talk through your concerns with other students in your class or with your tutor. By the end of your brainstorming session, you should have at least a couple of ideas which are worth pursuing further and you will have thought more about what interests you and why (see 'Taking it Further … On Your Own' at the end of this chapter).

## Use your supervisor

You should talk to your tutor or supervisor at an early stage in the design process to get guidance on how to approach your chosen subject area. Each university will have its own expectations and criteria: your tutor will be able to advise you on these. Your tutor will also know whether there are any special resources available to you locally relating to your topic. Early discussions can save you from going down false paths, so make an appointment to see your tutor as soon as you have an idea. Make regular appointments to meet your supervisor and stick to them. At some universities it is a requirement that students meet regularly, on specified days; take advantage of these meetings. Students who discuss their project regularly with their supervisor do much better in the final assessment than those who don't. Supervisors constitute a valuable resource provided for you: make the most of them!

## Use your peers

Peer reviews and buddy schemes are two of the ways in which students are encouraged to share their work with their fellow students. Your classmates are going through the same problems and issues as you and it is often helpful to talk to them about how things are going. Some universities formalize this by having a 'peer review' element of the dissertation. This usually involves students looking at one another's work and offering constructive criticism in the form of a review or evaluation. This can be very helpful, especially if you think of it as someone to offer support and encouragement. If your university does not have such a scheme, why not get together with someone in your class whom you trust, with whom you can meet up or chat online and discuss your progress? The dissertation is something you have to write and research on your own, but that does not mean it has to be a solitary activity – if you can share it with someone going through the same thing then that can really help to keep you on track.

## Read around your subject area

When you have settled on your subject area, you should begin to read as much as you can about it. Identify the key literature, but also read around your subject area; investigate related areas or similar topics for ideas on theoretical approaches and methods of analysis. The research project is an opportunity for you to add to the knowledge which already exists, but you can't do this until you are aware of what is already known and written about your subject. If you find that there are hundreds of books and articles on your object of analysis, you have probably not narrowed it sufficiently. Read the most frequently cited and/or recent books and articles on the topic and find out which are the main areas of contention. Could you find out something about these? Is there an area which the literature seems to have missed? Or a new phenomenon which the research hasn't caught up with yet? If, however, you find nothing has been written, you are probably not looking in the right place or are being much too specific. Redefine your search terms and try again. As you read, take careful notes on what research has been done in your area of interest and by whom; you will need this information when you come to write your literature review (see Chapter 7). Once you have decided on a subject area, read some books and articles about your subject, and discuss it with your peers and your tutor. You then need to work on developing your research question. The research question is what will guide your project, so it is crucial that you define it very carefully. In the next section we give some guidance on how to conceptualize your research question.

## The range of topics for student projects

If you follow all the stages discussed in the chapter so far you should have come up with quite a few different ideas for topics you could research. If you have not already done so, write them down now. The box below lists some of the topics that students could study.

---

### Examples of subject areas for research projects

African-American masculinity in *The Wire*

*Al Jazeera* Television

*American Girl* dolls marketing

Apps advertising

*Big Brother* as a global brand

British films about Anglo-Asian families

Celebrity culture in the tabloid press

*(Continued)*

---

*(Continued)*

Disabled people in the media

The e-book

The economics of *Facebook*

The films of Quentin Tarantino

Football coverage on the internet

*Glee*

Iranian cinema

Internet shopping

The iPhone and youth culture

Jedward

The Kindle

Local newspapers

Magazines and websites for teenage girls

The military in computer games

*Million Pound Drop*

Newspaper coverage of the war in Afghanistan

Perfume advertising

*Priscilla, Queen of the Desert*

*Shameless* in America

Student protest and the media

Viral advertising

*Vogue* magazine

As you can see, this is a wide range of subjects, and I am sure that your own list of ideas does not look out of place among these. Note that these are *not* questions but topics or subject areas. In the next section of this chapter we will discuss strategies for honing in your **object of analysis** and considering the design of your **research question**.

## DESIGNING YOUR RESEARCH QUESTION: INDUSTRY, TEXT OR AUDIENCE?

In constructing your research question it is important to remember that we ask different questions, in different ways, depending on which part of the communication chain we are investigating. One way of thinking about this is to consider how any medium has three elements: a) something which generates the message, b) the message itself and c) the receiver of the message. Stuart Hall (1981) considers how this process of 'encoding' and 'decoding' is not a direct chain – rather, it is contaminated with feedback and noise as Claude Shannon had described it some years previously (Shannon, 1949). The direct process might be figured thus: *encoding → message → decoding*. Yet, the 'encoded' message is rarely formed exactly as intended and seldom received as intended. It is useful, for analytic purposes, to break the communications chain into these three separate phases: *producer/text/audience*. In an age when the differences between 'producers' and 'audiences' are breaking down, and when the idea of the 'text' itself is problematic, these categories become harder to sustain. However, for the purposes of conceptualizing your research question, they remain useful analytical tools. Consider whether your primary interest is the people who **produce** the media or cultural artifact you are interested in; the **text** or event itself; or the **audiences** who use and consume it. Look at the list of examples of subject areas for research projects above – each of these topics can be narrowed down further to focus on either the *industry*, the *product* or the *user*. Your research question will take on a different focus depending on which you choose. Let's take a closer look at three of the items from that list: the e-book reader, the Kindle; the television programme *Glee*; and newspaper coverage of the war in Afghanistan – all of which are feasible research topics. Figure 3.2, focusing on the industry, text or audience of your subject area, gives examples of how you might further narrow these *general subject areas* into potential *objects of*

**FIGURE 3.2**   Focusing on the industry, text or audience of your subject area

| Subject area | Industry | Text | Audience |
|---|---|---|---|
| The Kindle | When, where and why did Amazon launch the Kindle? What is the response of the book publishing industry to the Kindle? | Do books look different on the Kindle? What is the aesthetic appeal of the Kindle and e-reader technology? | What do people like about the Kindle? When and where do people use the Kindle? |
| *Glee* | What genre was *Glee* intended to be at its launch? What precedents are there for a television musical? Are there any successful ones? Why/not? | Do the characters reinforce or challenge stereotypes? To what extent is *Glee* a post-modern text? | Given that *Glee* was designed as an inter-generational show, do people watch together as a family? How far do fans of *Glee* identify with the characters? |
| Newspaper coverage of the war in Afghanistan | What is the attitude of news producers to war coverage? How much control do the military have over access to news and information? | What are the main ways in which the news from Afghanistan is framed? How do newspapers use images to tell a story about war? | What are people's attitudes towards news coverage of the war in Afghanistan? How do people understand the issues of the war from the news they read? |

*analysis* depending on which aspect of the communication process you wish to concentrate on.

Let's take the example of the US television series *Glee*. You might want to find out more about how such an unusual show as *Glee* was produced in the first place. Researching the history of the production process would make an excellent case study of the television *industry*. If you think a particular executive or the determination of the writers resulted in a particular attitude towards the representation of young people, then you should consider an archival trawl of the trade journals to research the personnel involved in the production of *Glee*. The theme of how young people come to terms with social attitudes towards them is a constant theme in *Glee* which includes story-lines around homosexuality, disability and teen pregnancy. If you want to study the representation of gay characters in *Glee*, your method would be a *textual analysis* based on the analysis of the representations of the gay characters, especially Kurt Hummell (played by Chris Colfer). Kurt is a young man whose working-class father is accepting of his son's homosexuality and many of the story-lines centre around the problems other people have with Kurt's sexuality. You might consider how Kurt's character compares with other representations of gay young men coming out. For example the two main gay characters in the British television programme *Shameless* – one from each of the main families figured: Ian Gallagher and Mikey Maguire. What do these tell us about working-class gay people? Jane Lynch is a lesbian actor who plays straight woman Sue Sylvester in *Glee* – a lonely, frustrated, angry cheer leader coach who taunts and antagonizes our hapless hero, Will Schuster. Lynch brings a powerful off-screen persona as a happily married lesbian woman to the text through various interviews and her autobiography (Lynch, 2012). The actor's off-screen persona, renowned for her lesbianism, brings a delightful subtext to the narratives. Studying the star of this, or other texts, as the creator of meaning as discussed in Chapter 5, can be a very productive means of studying texts in relation to the extra-textual discourse.

Matters of how frequently something is represented are best understood through *content analysis*, while questions of what those representations mean would be more directly answered by *semiotic analysis*. If you are interested in gay people's attitudes towards, and opinions about, the representation of gay people in *Glee*, your concern is not with the texts themselves, but with the *audience* – you would probably choose the *focus group* or the *interview* if you wanted to take this approach.

To sum, then, we can say that research into communications, media and culture can be divided into three broad areas, each with its own preferred paradigms of research: *industries*, *texts* and *audiences*. In Chapters 4–6 we consider how you can conduct research in each of these areas respectively. Within each of these areas, it is theoretically possible to employ any method used in the humanities or social sciences, but, in practice and by convention, each has a different set of methods associated with it, as we will see when we come to discuss these in the next section of the book. Before continuing with your question design, think again about your general topic or subject area. Create a table like the one in Figure 3.2. Write down all the things that interest you about your subject area and list them according to these three stages of industry, text and audience in the communication process. Now, is there one which seems to be more important? Is there a theme which is more evident than the others? Do most of your questions seem to relate to how and why something is *produced*? In this case the industry should be the real focus of your enquiry. Is it the *aesthetics* of the films or television programmes themselves which mostly concern you? If you are interested in analysing how the narrative works or the construction of a particular social theme, then you are going to be focusing on the analysis of texts. Alternatively, perhaps it is the influence texts or products have on their audiences or on people's opinions and attitudes – which you wish to investigate, then the chapter on audiences is most useful to you.

## THE KEY ELEMENTS OF A RESEARCH QUESTION

When asking questions about media and culture you need to think about three key elements of your research question. The three parts of any research project are: a) the *object of analysis*, b) the *research method* and c) the *theoretical paradigm*. These should be logically interconnected and should justify one another such that they all coalesce within the research question. We might think of them as three intersecting circles as in Figure 3.3.

**FIGURE 3.3** The key elements of a research question

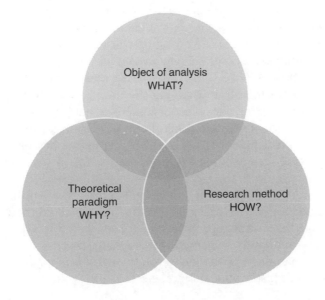

You may begin from any one of these, but in the early stages of your research project you need to think about the three elements as requiring equal focus and attention. Your attention might focus on one or the other at a given moment, but you should remember that all three demand equal consideration in your planning.

## The object of analysis

Let's focus first of all on your *object of analysis*, the 'what': the aspect of the subject which you are going to study in detail. Narrow your focus to a single aspect of the subject, or to one key character, theme or feature. Your object of analysis should be manageable – sufficient to keep you busy but not too much to handle. If you are interested in newspaper coverage of the war in Afghanistan, for example, your object of analysis will comprise a list of exactly which newspapers, online or hard copy, on which days. You may further focus on the coverage of a specific event, on a specific day; perhaps comparing coverage in two or three newspapers or websites. One can more readily expand the parameters of research – for example, by adding another news source, or comparing domestic and overseas coverage – than narrow your focus once you have started. So find the smallest unit you want to examine and define it as carefully as possible. By narrowing your subject area to a workable object of analysis, you will be able to concentrate on exactly what interests you about it.

## The theoretical paradigm

Theories are tools to help us think. In doing original research at undergraduate level, you are unlikely to be developing new theoretical models or having dramatically profound theoretical insights. Our use of theory, then, is purely pragmatic: we need to find a theoretical paradigm which will be useful and help us to investigate our chosen *object of analysis*. In Chapter 1 we looked at some of the different ways of knowing which underpin the theoretical positions taken by scholars. Take some time to consider what kind of theoretical paradigms you want to use. In defining the theory, you are thinking about *why* you are interested in your object of analysis. What is it about your chosen subject that you find interesting? What theoretical approaches can you bring to bear on your investigation? This might be glaringly obvious or incredibly difficult to unpack – depending on the exact nature of your question. But spending some time reflecting on *why* you are interested in this topic will bring to the fore the crux of your study. You need to draw on the existing literature, so think about how previous scholars have justified their research in this area. What theoretical approaches have been taken to your topic? How have previous researchers explained why they are interested in the subject? The theoretical paradigm is what gives you the *rationale* for your research. It should help you to justify your subject selection and your method of analysis.

The theoretical paradigm will help to explain why you are undertaking your project. Your university or college may have expectations that you write your dissertation using strict scientific methods or they may have the expectation that yours is a discursive essay – take some time to talk to your supervisor about these fundamental questions. Be sure of which epistemological tradition you are working in; this will help you to connect your theoretical paradigm with your research method.

## The research method

We have discussed the *what* and the *why* of your research project. You also need to be planning *how* you are going to conduct your research. You will improve the overall quality of your work if you spend as much time thinking about how you are going to approach your subject as you did settling on the subject itself. The research method you are going to adopt will depend largely on how you define your *object of analysis* and theoretical approach. You may have decided on the research method before you select your theory or object of analysis. It may be that you are fascinated with semiotics or inspired to do discourse analysis because of your previous learning. That is terrific and in such an instance the choice of method will suggest particular theoretical approaches and objects of analysis. The question of the *how*, *what* and *why* of your project should be developed in relation to one another, and as you research each separately you will find that the three relate to one another and grow together in a way unique to you, and you will work towards designing a research question organically.

## WRITING YOUR RESEARCH QUESTION

The research question sums up what you are going to address or answer in your dissertation. It will provide a narrative motivation for your work, structuring your argument and shaping your discussion of methods and analysis. So, in summary, the wording of your research question should ensure that you can answer the following three questions:

1 *What* are you going to research? (Can you clearly define your *object of analysis*?)

2 *Why* is this topic of interest? (Does it relate to a specific *theoretical paradigm*? What are the broader implications of your topic?)

3 *How* are you going to conduct your research? (What approach will you take or which *method* will you employ?)

The research question may or may not be the title of the project. If it is not the title, the research question should be clearly stated within the first paragraph in one concise sentence. Your research question should be on a topic which will sustain your interest for the duration of the study. The thinking phase may be time-consuming, but it is cheap and it doesn't hurt anyone! When you have limited time and resources, as most people reading this book do, it is better to spend your time constructing a well-designed study and ensuring that you avoid pitfalls of poor design.

## Identifying sources and resources

What you decide to examine for your project will invariably be influenced by what you can access: it is impossible to research media texts, audiences or institutions if you can't get hold of appropriate materials. If you are interested in doing a textual analysis of some obscure films, for example, make sure you can get hold of copies of them that you can view before you commit yourself to that subject. You will probably write a better project if you use films readily available on DVD or to download, if only because you won't spend so much time trying to get hold of them. There is a wealth of physical and virtual archives you could use, as discussed in Chapter 4 (see pages 83–89). You may decide to design a study based on one to which you do have access, for example in the special collections of your university library.

If you are interested in researching audiences, why not use your friends, neighbours or family as resources? University students make good subjects (they are easy to get hold of and can be readily bribed!). Your friends are probably interested in your work, and might well be flattered if you ask them to help out. Most social science operates within the paradigm of 'objective' scientific research typical of the 'modern' perspective as discussed in Chapter 1, and many of the methods are based on sample sizes which reflect such a perspective. This paradigm places a high value on 'impartiality' and 'objectivity' which is not possible if subjects are personally known to researchers. However, one must always balance scientific integrity with pragmatism. As a student, you may have reservations about asking complete strangers to be respondents in your studies, and you should not be pressured into doing this if you don't want to. However, if you need lots of questionnaire responses, your fellow students are usually suitable to approach, even if you don't know them personally. Students in the canteen or bar may be willing to spend five or ten minutes answering your questionnaire. You may want to send a questionnaire via SurveyMonkey or a similar online survey tool. People who share your interests and lifestyle are often willing to help out, so think about asking neighbours or members of your church or fellow music fans if they are interested. People with the same enthusiasms and interests are usually more than happy to talk about their obsession. If you have worked in a study group successfully during the rest of your academic career, encourage the others in the group to keep meeting during the project: you will all benefit from discussing your ideas and progress with one another and it will help prevent you from feeling isolated. Perhaps you could set up an online chat group of fellow students to help you study.

## REVIEWING THE LITERATURE

Your research question should be informed by previous research so make sure you read as much as you can about your subject. You can begin with the documents you have already used on your course: if you took a course on the subject area you are researching, begin by looking at the reading list and the articles you may have downloaded in your studies. Next, do a search of the library catalogue of your university to find out what books and journal articles have been written on the subject. Think about whether you want to get involved in this debate. Use the bibliographies of books and articles you have read to find more titles which may be relevant to you. You need to read widely and to think a lot about what you are reading, but it is rarely necessary to read everything. Acquire the habit of making decisions quickly as to whether a book or article is going to be of relevance to you. In the first instance, spend between three and five minutes looking at the title, chapter and section headings to decide whether it has any relevance to your topic. If it does, spend a further ten minutes scanning the contents of the relevant chapters or sections: look at the headings and the first sentence of each paragraph only. Make a note of the title, author and other details, and then put the book aside and write down the main topics covered and a couple of sentences about how it relates to your research question. Then move on to the next book or article. Aim to skim through several books and articles in this way, drawing up a list of around five to ten of the most useful texts. When you have made a list of the books, articles and websites which you have identified as being relevant, assess the importance of each one to you – you should not read the entire piece until and unless you have ascertained, by skimming and speed reading, that it is directly relevant to your subject. If you find four to ten books or articles that you will read and use in detail, you are doing very well. Most of the material you read will be relevant only as background reading, and you don't need to do more than scan it. Stella Cottrell provides an excellent guide to various reading strategies in her book *Critical Thinking Skills: Developing Effective Analysis and Argument* (Cottrell, 2011).

The literature review is an important part of most dissertations. It comprises a survey of the existing literature in the area and discusses how your work relates to that literature. Ideally this should include literature relevant to the three main elements of the research question we have discussed in this chapter – your object of analysis, research method and theoretical paradigm. You need to consider how previous scholars have addressed each of these three elements and show how you are interpreting this literature in your own study design. Guidance on how to write a literature review is discussed more fully in Chapter 7 (see especially pages 209–210).

# WRITING YOUR PROJECT PROPOSAL

By now you should have come up with a topic for your research project, identified whether your main interest is in the production, text or the audience for the topic, and considered your research method, object of analysis and theoretical approach. In this section, we are going to look at how to conduct the first main piece of writing involved in the project: the proposal or outline.

Whether it is a requirement for completion of your project or not, it is highly recommended that you write a proposal or outline. You need to get down on paper exactly what you are planning to do, and you need to show it to your tutors and listen to what they say about it! Getting feedback on your proposal before you begin is essential. All universities will have different requirements for writing a proposal, so you should make sure you know what the rules are where you are studying. The following is suggested as an indicative list of contents.

## Indicative list of contents for a dissertation proposal

Your dissertation proposal should include the following:

1 A statement of your **research question** including a rationale for why you have chosen this topic.

2 A description of the **aims and objectives** of the study – Why do you want to do this? What do you hope to find?

3 A description of your **object of analysis**.

4 A summary and a justification of your **research method(s)**.

5 A statement of the **theoretical paradigm** you will be working within including how this relates to your object of analysis and your research methods.

6 A **literature review** of relevant reading.

7 A **timetable** of when work will be undertaken.

8 An indicative **bibliography**.

The list above shows the main components of a proposal. Your proposal should include your research question as a title: this should be as self-explanatory as possible, and suggest the three key elements of the research project. The aims and objectives of the study should be stated clearly – the reader needs to know what you are expecting to discover. You must carefully define your *object of analysis* and be as specific as possible; for example, if you are going to discuss a particular advertising campaign, state when and where (in what medium) it can be found. Indicate how you are going to access it; for example, are you going to access online discussions, download newspaper articles via a database such as Nexus UK, or use DVDs in your university's library collection? Define your research methods and justify them in relation to your object of analysis. You should provide a discussion of how you decided to use this approach rather than any other. The fifth point in the list refers to the *theoretical paradigms* – here you need to say what theoretical work you have drawn on in deciding on your project.

You should reflect on the epistemological basis of your design. When we looked at four of the main 'ways of knowing', in Chapter 1, we considered how our research relates to particular epistemological positions. You may be working in the oral tradition – perhaps using autoethnography to tell a story about your own experiences. Alternatively, yours might be a textual analysis working within the rhetorical or hermeneutic tradition derived from Aristotelian philosophy. Often you will be using methods such as questionnaires which assume an epistemic base in the scientific positivist mode; if you are using discourse analysis then your theoretical paradigm is more likely to be in the tradition of post-modern research.

In your *literature review* you should demonstrate that you have read the relevant literature, including that related to your epistemological base, as discussed above. Your proposal should include a schedule with sensible estimates of how long things should take. Draw up a detailed timetable of when you need to get things done by, starting with the submission date and working backwards. Plan your work carefully and realistically, allowing yourself plenty of time to write up your findings. I advise you to allow at least one-third of the available time just for writing, so if you have one 12-week semester in which to conduct the entire project, make sure you leave the last four weeks to write the final draft and make revisions. Get going with any arrangements which involve other people as soon as possible – you don't want to rely on being able to interview people in March, only to find out that they take their annual vacation then. Make sure you can get access to any libraries or special collections, and book appointments as early as possible in your timetable.

Getting started is one of the most difficult parts of writing your research project, as you have some very important decisions to make. You need to spend time thinking about the issues and deciding what is really interesting and relevant to you. You should settle on something which will sustain your interest through the duration of the assignment. Have a look at the questions in the checklist for your project design below. Can you answer every question honestly and fully? Don't go on with the project until you are able to address all the points raised.

## Checklist for your project design

1 Does your research question make sense? (Is it logical? Does it flow?)

2 Is the project feasible? (Can you do it in the time available?)

3 Do you have access to the object(s) of analysis?

4 Can you locate sufficient appropriate academic literature?

5 Is your question unique to you?

6 Does your question build on previous research?

7 Have you discussed your idea with your supervisor?

## Time management and the project

Time management is one of the main problems students have to face in completing their dissertation. You may be combining your studies with working, or have family responsibilities which may place big demands on your time. Writing the project can be more difficult than other assignments because of time management; you have to exercise very strong self-discipline in undertaking the research project. Often the only deadline your university will give you is the final one – when that is several months away, it is sometimes tempting to get on with other things and put the project on the back burner. This is asking for trouble! When you are working on the project, you have to organize your own time. Get your diary now and think about when you can spend time on your project. Ideally, you should try to do a little every day – set aside at least an hour each day to focus on the project.

It is helpful, too, if you can work with a friend or 'study buddy'. Having someone who is in the same situation to talk over problems and issues can really help. If your university has a 'buddy' scheme, take advantage of this. Many universities organize such schemes using the university internet teaching system – if you don't have one at your university perhaps you could ask for one to be set up? Whether or not the formal structure exists, I suggest you pair up with someone in your class who you can meet regularly to talk about how your work is progressing.

You might also try to think about how to integrate studying for the project into your everyday routine. For example, every time you go to the library, find some references for the project; every time you see a friend whom you like to talk to about ideas, have a chat about how your work is going; every time you pick up a book for another class, have a look and see if there is any information relevant to your project. Try to write something every day, and give yourself regular time slots during the week when you can work on the project.

A little bit regularly will get the job done more efficiently than leaving yourself a block of time at the end when there may well be other pressures which you are not able to foresee. The extent to which you are left alone to conduct your project will differ according to which institution you are at and, sometimes, according to the personality of your supervisor. I would advise you to arrange several meetings with your supervisor and to make sure that you keep to them. Regular meetings to talk over how things are progressing (even if they are not going particularly well) are very important in helping to keep the project at the top of your agenda.

The following three chapters look in greater detail at how to study *industries*, *texts* and *audiences* respectively. They will guide you through some of the main themes and approaches that you could use to conduct your own work.

The project is one of the few opportunities you get to do your own research, and think about things which are of interest to you. Make the most of it. Enjoy!

# FURTHER READING

Cottrell, Stella, 2011. *Critical Thinking Skills: Developing Effective Analysis and Argument.* 2nd edition. London: Palgrave Macmillan.
When it comes to evaluating material and developing your critical-thinking skills, I can recommend Stella Cottrell's book, which also includes lots of useful classroom activities and exercises.

Bell, Judith, 2010. *Doing your Research Project: A Guide for First-time Researchers in Education and Social Science.* 5th edition. Buckingham: Open University Press.
Swetnam, Derek and Ruth Swetnam, 2009. *Writing your Dissertation: The Best-selling Guide to Planning, Preparing and Presenting First class Work.* 3rd edition. Oxford: How To Books Ltd.
Two excellent guides on how to write a dissertation.

Deacon, David, Michael Pickering, Peter Golding and Graham Murdock, 2007. *Researching Communications. A Practical Guide to Methods in Media and Cultural Analysis.* 2nd edition. London: Bloomsbury Academic.
A particularly recommended book about researching media and culture.

Jensen, Klaus Bruhn (ed.), 2002. *A Handbook of Media and Communication Research: Qualitative and Quantitative Methodologies.* London: Routledge.
This provides an excellent survey of various approaches to media and cultural research with several thorough examples.

Pickering, Michael and Gabriele Griffin (eds), 2008. *Research Methods for Cultural Studies.* Edinburgh: Edinburgh University Press.
This edited volume has some interesting articles by leading researchers in media and communication. The first two chapters are relevant to our discussion above, and several other chapters offer more detailed guidance.

# TAKING IT FURTHER ... ON YOUR OWN

*Focusing on your object of analysis*

If you have a general idea but you can't quite think how to narrow it down, this exercise should help you focus on what really interests you. Do a brainstorming session – write down on a piece of paper as many questions as you can about the topic; give yourself ten minutes and aim to completely cover the paper with ideas. Then look again at Figure 3.2 'Focusing on the industry, text or audience of your subject area'. Draw a table with three columns headed: 'industry', 'text' and 'audience'. Write down how you might use these categories in relation to your chosen topic. Let's take the example of games: anything to do with how and why they are made and marketed would fit under 'industry'; all issues about gaming content such as characterization and design should be listed under 'text'; and the theme of how games are received, what people get out of playing, and so on, relates to 'audiences'. Refer back to your 'brainstorming' sheet and decide whether the contents of your brainstorming session can be listed under these three categories. When you have copied your ideas to the three columns, ask yourself which aspect of your topic is of most interest. Could you write a research question focusing on the contents of one of your three columns?

# TAKING IT FURTHER ... IN CLASS

*Defining objects of analysis*

This activity is designed to help students understand the importance of the object of analysis. You will need two sets of cards, one with examples of 'topics' and another with examples of 'research methods' on each card. Some examples are given below:

Examples of 'topics':

- The TV show *Glee*
- *The New York Times*
- The stage show *Jesus Christ Superstar*
- *Al Jazeera* news website
- *Twitter*

Examples of 'research methods':

- Content analysis
- Semiotics
- Interviews
- Ethnography
- Focus groups

Working with a partner, randomly select one card from each set so that you have one card with a 'topic' on and one with a 'research method'. You will need to decide whether it is appropriate to look at 'audiences', 'producers' or 'texts', or some combination. Next, identify an appropriate 'object of analysis' for applying that method to that topic. You should then design a research question incorporating the 'object of analysis', the 'topic' and the 'method' before reporting back to the whole class on your findings. How would a different 'object of analysis' necessitate a different research method? How far does your topic limit your research method and vice versa?

# TAKING IT FURTHER ... BEYOND THE CLASSROOM

Take a look at the home pages of a key journal in your area. Look at the themes covered in these journals and select a recent article which interests you. How could you extend that study or pick up on a theme that relates to your own life experience or interest in the field? Here is a list of some journals that may be useful:

*Communication, Culture and Critique (http://wileyonlinelibrary.com/journal/cccr)*

*Cultural Studies* (http://www.tandf.co.uk/journals/routledge/09502386.html)

*Feminist Media Studies*

*Historical Journal of Film, Radio and Television* (http:

*Media, Culture and Society* (http://mcs.sagepub.com/)

*Screen* (http://www.gla.ac.uk/services/screen/)

*Television and New Media*

# 4 RESEARCHING INDUSTRIES: STUDYING THE INSTITUTIONS AND PRODUCERS OF MEDIA AND CULTURE

---

## Aims and Objectives

- The main aim of this chapter is to show how production industries have been researched in media and cultural studies.

- We offer some guidance on conducting your own research into the media and cultural industries.

- The chapter discusses the opportunities and challenges provided by selected approaches to research, and offers some case study examples. In this chapter we focus on four research methods:

  1 archive research

  2 discourse analysis

  3 interviews (including oral history interviews)

  4 ethnography.

- Some suggestions for further reading are offered.

- We finish the chapter with some suggestions for follow-up exercises, and activities for private study and for teachers to use in class.

---

## WHAT ARE THE MEDIA AND CULTURE INDUSTRIES?

In this chapter we are considering media and culture as the product of an **industry**, and also considering the different ways we can research cultural production. Both the terms 'media' and 'culture' are very complex words with contested histories and diverse, though frequently intersecting, etymologies. We may think of the culture industries as including the press, publishing, drama, music, cinema, broadcasting (television and radio), computer games, the internet and mobile telephony. However, within academia some areas have been more thoroughly studied than others. Researchers of the media have often had quite a narrow range of interest, concentrating largely on *broadcasting* and *the press*. The area of *cinema* is left almost exclusively to film-studies scholars while many industries, such as *publishing* and *print-making*, receive scant regard. Within the field of cultural studies, as opposed to media studies, the focus is more likely to be on culture from the point of view of *communities of users* and less commonly on culture as the product of an industry. Academics follow trends which also restrict the kinds of things we research. Thus, during the 1970s and 1980s media research was dominated by paradigms derived from *semiotics* and *structuralism* with a concomitant focus on media *texts*. These were later displaced by a focus on *audiences* in the 1980s and 1990s, as *reception theory* became more fashionable. The vast terrain of the media and cultural landscape has been well-trodden in relatively few places. The paths worn by previous academic study are there for you to learn from and consider, but you should feel free to make your own way; there are no rules about where you may roam. After all, many of our key media forms today, such as social networking or viral messaging, are relatively recent phenomena and new modes of investigation have arisen to investigate them.

The idea of a *culture* as an *industry* has highly political (and politicized) origins, as we saw in Chapter 2. Theodor Adorno and Max Horkheimer are often credited with first coining the expression in their essay, 'The Culture Industry: Enlightenment as Mass Deception', which was first published in 1944 (Adorno and Horkheimer, 1993). As political Marxists and cultural conservatives, the idea of industrializing culture was something quite abhorrent to them and to many other scholars in the 1940s and 1950s. The romantic myth of the charismatic artist creating '*art for art's sake*' retains a powerful potency. The aspiration for culture to be transcendent or 'sublime' and to be uplifting remains, although often overshadowed by the imperative for culture to have an *economic* significance. In many countries around the world, the *culture industries* are promoted not only as a public good, but also as a means of wealth production. The communications, media and culture industries contribute a large amount to the economies of modern Western societies. In Great Britain, the contribution of those industries to the economy is estimated to be about 5.6% of GVA (gross value added), employing 2.3 million people directly and indirectly and constituting about 8% of all businesses (Department for Culture, Media and Sport, 2010). The culture industries, including film, music and other media, have an important role materially as well as culturally. How do we reconcile the spiritual, enlightening qualities of culture with the economic imperatives of contemporary realpolitik?

As researchers of the media and culture, we spend a lot of our time thinking about a range of ideas relating to the role of the various industries in society. We sometimes forget that the vast majority of people who work in the business of making cultural artifacts do so in order to make money, and, as in any other industry, the profit motive is a strong determinant of why particular decisions are made. When studying the media and culture it is important to bear in mind that market forces and economics are the most significant forces determining what is done. The culture industries are involved in the production of artifacts which need to compete in the market place. Even the most charitable arts organization needs money to survive, and acquiring funding is a major part of the activities of private companies and non-profit-making organizations alike. The economics of the market place applies to everybody, and there are no culture industries which operate entirely outside these forces. The drive to survive is what spurs on most organizations, whether they be profit-making or charitable concerns, and in the real world that means making money. Whatever culture industry you are going to study, you must make sure that you understand the economics of the industry and how organizations make their bread and butter.

Most of the research into media industries is *instrumental*, conducted by and for particular companies with the purpose of advancing their own aims and objectives. There are several research organizations which collect reliable information about specific parts of the media industries. For example, information on television-viewing is collected by the Broadcasters' Audience Research Board (BARB) and is used widely by the television industry to monitor programmes and to develop programming strategy. In addition, companies conduct research into their own market position and that of their competitors. There is a wealth of administrative research which is produced solely for business purposes, and can also have value to academics; public companies are obliged by law to publish their accounts, and most companies issue an annual report which contains information on their activities for the year. Administrative data can be used by academics as a secondary source in their research, especially where it can provide facts and figures which would otherwise be too expensive to collect. Most research into the culture industries, then, unlike academic research, does not have the growth of knowledge as its goal, and the information is not gathered to advance a theory of any kind. The vast majority of research into the media and culture industries is *administrative* and *functional*, having practical uses and applications for the relevant industries.

Some of the research which is conducted in the private and public sectors is not available to the general public because it is considered proprietary; that is to say, it is the property of the company which commissioned it. Often research costs a lot of money to support, and the funders do not want to share the knowledge they have acquired because they have obtained it in order to improve their status in the market place.

In most countries in the West, including the UK and the USA, governments take an active interest in the media and culture industries. Broadcasting is one of the most heavily legislated media industries in Britain, with each successive broadcasting institution established by an Act of Parliament. The BBC, for example, funded by licence fee, was established in the UK during the 1920s at a time when many other industries were nationalized or being brought under state control. The director-general of the BBC is appointed by the board of governors, who are in turn selected by the government of the day. Successive governments have left their mark on the development of the BBC and the media system in the UK. During the Thatcher period, the philosophy of laissez-faire which instructed Conservative economic policy fed into media and cultural policy (Goodwin, 1999). Whether or not state funding exists for a particular culture industry is clearly dependent on prevailing governmental attitudes. At various times, support for media and culture industries has been justified on the grounds that cultural products can help to forge national identities or push political agendas. At other times, they have been supported on the same grounds as other industries: to provide employment and economic opportunities.

National governments clearly have the strongest influence on the shape of media industries in their own countries, but the European Union has increasing powers to influence the shape of the media in its member states (Collins, 1999). The significance of legislation and the regulatory environment on the culture industries provides an interesting research area. The impact of changes in regulation on particular industries and their operation could provide an interesting focus for your work. Whatever your topic, it will help you to understand the way the culture industries work if you find out about current legislation and follow the debates about pending changes in regulation. The relationship between politics and the media is particularly valuable for anyone interested in the power of the media (Wheeler, 1997). The idea that one should 'look to the money' to understand the workings of the media underlies the project of material analysis which is at the heart of the work of much media scholarship.

## STUDYING THE MEDIA AND CULTURE INDUSTRIES

In the history of our field, the workings of the media and cultural industries have been much less studied than the texts they produce or the audiences who consume them. It seems that scholars in the humanities and social sciences are all too willing to study media texts, such as films, games and television programmes, but are reticent to study the media industries. Michele Hilmes goes as far as to note that: 'to propose the serious study of media industries is a bold and iconoclastic task' (Hilmes, 2009: 30). Partly, as Hilmes explains, this is because of a long-standing tradition of a separation between the business world and that of universities. Partly, it is that the social sciences and humanities within academia are too ready to dismiss 'business' as outside of their sphere of engagement. Moreover, within media studies education there has always been an uneasy relationship between 'theory' and 'practice'. At stake in this dichotomy is the way that theorists and practitioners interact, which in turn relates to the relationship between the 'academy' and the 'industry'. In the past, scholars of the media and culture have neglected to engage with the industry while the media industries, in turn, have refused access to scholars. This is now shifting, with the publication of some important books on the culture industries including David Hesmondhalgh's *The Culture Industries* (Hesmondhalgh, 2007) and Jennifer Holt and Alisa Perrin's *Media Industries: History, Theory and Method* (Holt and Perren, 2009). Since 2000 we have seen a greater engagement by scholars with industry.

The most significant imperative behind the re-invigorated interest in the media and culture industries has been the changes in the processes of production themselves. Perhaps we are living in the *Network Society* (Castells, 1996; 1997; 1998) or the *Digital Age* (Negroponte, 2000) – call it what you will, there can be no doubt that, in the Western world at least, computer technology is engendering one of the epochal revolutions of our social and cultural lives. There will inevitably be a new form of social consciousness as a consequence, a revolution as important as that which occurred in the shift to print culture (Balvanes, Donald and Shoesmith, 2009). The changes wrought by the silicon chip and its related technologies overshadow in scale those of the steam engine and all the machines of the Industrial Revolution. The technological transformation of the media industries in the last 20 years has been unprecedented, revolutionizing the means by which media and culture products are made, distributed and consumed. Where the media were once considered 'mass media', produced on a *factory* scale for *mass* consumption, there is now greater potential for domestic-scale production. Where, until about 30 years ago, a printing press was something which you might find only in the city – now a printer can probably be found in most of the private homes of any street in any city in the developed world. The film stock alone to make a film used to cost more than the average monthly salary; today you can save a film on a data stick costing the price of a lunch (probably a cup of coffee by the time this book is published!). Media production is no longer the sole preserve of big business: the revolution in media technology means that the old barriers to entry no longer exist. Whether they have been permanently eliminated or are simply being rebuilt elsewhere, time alone will tell.

The introduction of new technology has caused a revolution in the processes of production in the media and cultural industries. In the UK, as in many other countries, the media industries were among the most centralized and highly unionized. The era of conservatism in the late 1970s and 1980s, with the twin figureheads of Ronald Reagan in the US and Margaret Thatcher in the UK, brought devastating assaults to working conditions of people in the traditional industrial sectors. The media and cultural industries were the targets of a right-wing backlash which saw public funding for the arts dramatically reduced and a commercialization of the sector. The impact of the introductions of new 'labour saving' technologies allied with a Keynesian economics policy resulted in a massive transformation of the media industries. When News International moved their entire printing press and editorial office to Wapping in 1986, it created one of the biggest confrontations between unions and employers to be seen in Britain. The breaking of the unions at News International and their diminution in power has been well documented elsewhere (Gopsill and Neale, 2007). The ability of the media to act as an effective check on the state, to comprise a powerful 'public sphere' or 'Fourth Estate', was seriously hampered by the close relationship between media conglomerates such as News International and the policy of the state. For them to be working hand-in-hand created serious damage to the democratic function a free press should perform. At a time when the press are subject to a continuing examination by Parliament in the UK at the hands of the Leveson Inquiry we may well ask – are the press fulfilling their role as executors of the public sphere?

The digital revolution may have changed the means and processes of production; it may have altered the kinds of companies which dominate the list of media corporations – but not so greatly as to influence the basic relations of capital. The capitalist system has proved remarkably resilient. Bill Gates, the CEO of Microsoft, may be the presentable face of computer capitalism, but his empire remains a dominant capitalist force in the media landscape. Steve Jobs, head of Apple, died a multi-millionaire, having built up a massive media empire. The new media forms are produced by surprisingly old-fashioned means, often using outsourced labour and exploitation of labour on a massive scale. In the culture industries a creative working environment does not always exist at every stage of production.

It is our task as media and cultural researchers to address these issues head on. We can recognize that the industry is in a state of almost permanent revolution; but at such times scholarly reflection can offer valuable interpretation. Think about how the social revolution of the post-war period in Britain produced the foundations for the later development of cultural studies in the work of Raymond Williams, Richard Hoggart and E.P. Thompson, founders of our field (see Chapter 2 pages 41–42). The challenges they faced in understanding the enormous social and cultural changes of their time were desperate. Ours, although far different, are every bit as dramatic. We, too, are in a phase of phenomenal technological revolution, great social change and enormous economic transformation. Much of this change is taking place at the interface between media and society. We have the privilege of being able to research these dynamics; the study of the media and culture industries just gets more and more interesting. Here are some examples of the kinds of areas of enquiry that you might investigate in researching the media and cultural industries.

1   The response of a particular organization or industry to new technology.

2   The impact of new legislation, changes in the regulatory environment, or public investigations such as the Leveson Inquiry, on an organization or industry.

3   The reasons for the introduction of a particular media phenomenon such as cable television or mobile telephony.

4   The industrial rationale for an expansion of a genre, for example the birth of 'scripted' reality shows like *The Only Way is Essex*, spawned as the progeny of the internationally franchised brand *Big Brother*.

5   The impact of a change of personnel or management on a company or industry, such as in the case of a take-over or the appointment of a new director or CEO.

6   An exploration of how different genres of cultural products are related to different patterns of work and professional practice.

7   The impact of the ideology or belief systems of people who work in the media and cultural industries.

8   A comparative study of working practices either in two different workplaces or at two different points in time.

# FOUR METHODS OF RESEARCHING THE MEDIA AND CULTURAL INDUSTRIES

There is a wealth of research into the media and cultural industries by economists and business researchers who consider them just as they would any other industry. Organizational communication, media economics and political economy are all areas of scholarship with long and distinguished histories. The industries themselves, and various agents of the state, also undertake research of an 'administrative' nature. What are the methods student researchers can utilize to investigate the media and cultural industries? In this chapter we concentrate on four of the main methods the student researcher can use to investigate the processes of production. Figure 4.1 shows the methods we will be discussing in this chapter, including the possible object of analysis for each method and listing the specific case studies we will discuss in the following pages.

**FIGURE 4.1** Four methods of researching the media and culture industries

| Method | Object of Analysis | Case Studies |
|---|---|---|
| **Archive Research** | Documents (e.g. institutional records in letters, memos and publications); journals and books (contemporary and historical); recorded interviews and digital archives and databases. | Paddy Scannell and David Cardiff, 1991. *A Social History of Broadcasting. Volume 1: 1922–1939. Serving the Nation.* Oxford: Basil Blackwell.<br><br>Sue Arthur, 2009. Blackpool goes all-talkie: cinema and society at the seaside in thirties Britain. *Historical Journal of Film, Radio and Television,* 29(1): 27–39. |
| **Discourse Analysis** | The talk and conversation of media workers; literature produced by media industries for internal purposes; trade literature and advertisements; published and unpublished comments and observations of industry insiders; cultural products addressing media and culture, for example, television programmes about television such as *Curb Your Enthusiasm.* | John T. Caldwell, 2008. *Production Culture: Industrial Reflexivity and Critical Practice in Film and Television.* Durham, NC/London: Duke University Press.<br><br>Chrys Ingraham, 2008. *White Weddings: Romancing Heterosexuality in Popular Culture.* New York/London: Routledge. |
| **Interview** | Opinions and attitudes of industry workers; people's ideas and perceptions about the industry; Reflections and recollections about the past (oral history interviews). | Jeremy Tunstall, 1993. *Television Producers.* London: Routledge.<br><br>Stefan Haefliger, Peter Jäger and Georg von Krogh, 2010. Under the radar: industry entry by user entrepreneurs. *Research Policy,* 39: 1198–213.<br><br>Stuart L. Goosman, 2005. *Group Harmony: The Black Urban Roots of Rhythm and Blues.* Philadelphia: University of Pennsylvania Press. |
| **Ethnography and Participant Observation** | Working practices of an industry, company or organization; the behaviour of people at work; the social interaction and relationships between people at work. | Hortense Powdermaker, 1951. *Hollywood, the Dream Factory: An Anthropologist Looks at the Movie-Makers.* Boston: Little, Brown and Company.<br><br>Anthony Cawley, 2008. News production in an Irish online newsroom: practice, process and culture. In Chris Paterson and David Domingo (eds), *Making Online News: The Ethnography of New Media Production.* New York: Peter Lang, pp. 45–60. |

*Archive research* is the most commonly used research method in any kind of project; it involves exploring published and unpublished sources collected in archives, libraries or databases. These may be physical, such as books, magazines or memos; or virtual, for example electronic or internet-based resources such as digital archives. In our discussion we focus on two case studies that use archives to research media history: Paddy Scannell and David Cardiff's *A Social History of Broadcasting* (1991) and Sue Arthur's 2009 essay, 'Blackpool Goes All-Talkie: Cinema and Society at the Seaside in Thirties Britain'. We discuss the differences between 'library', 'archive' and 'desk' research and consider how these constitute vital components of any research project. Archives comprise just one part of the *discourse* about media and culture and we consider here how we can analyse the discursive practices which surround the industries. John T. Caldwell investigates the discourses of professional practice among 'below the line' film and television workers in Los Angeles (Caldwell, 2008). Chrys Ingraham's research looks at a much less frequently studied cultural industry, that of the *wedding industry*. In *White Weddings* the author takes a *feminist materialist* approach to the study of the white wedding industry to unravel discourses of *heteronormativity* across a range of cultural products related to weddings (Ingraham, 2008). Asking questions of people who work in the industry can provide an excellent way of collecting original, first-hand data for your research project. Jeremy Tunstall has been a prolific investigator of the media industries and uses *interviews* as his primary method in his classic study from 1993, *Television Producers* (Tunstall, 1993). *Interviews* and *ethnography* are combined to research the phenomenon of *machinima* and its *'user entrepreneurs'* in a more recent study by Stefan Haefliger, Peter Jäger and Georg von Krogh (2010). Under this category we also consider the *oral history interview* as a means of researching industry workers about the past and take as a case study Stuart Goosman's study of *'doo-wop'* groups of the 1940s (Goosman, 2005). Our fourth method is *ethnography*, which is the method preferred if you want to investigate people's *behaviours* and *social interaction* in the workplace environment. One of the first people to apply ethnographic methods to the study of contemporary Western media was Hortense Powdermaker whose study of the Hollywood film industry during the aftermath of World War II provides a 'classic' case study (Powdermaker, 1951). Ethnographers since have often taken news production as their object of analysis, and our second case study by Anthony Cawley looks at the newsroom of the online edition of *The Irish Times* (Cawley, 2008). The following sections of this chapter will guide you through each of these four methods in turn, highlighting the possibilities for student researchers.

# ARCHIVE RESEARCH

One of the most frequently used of all methods of research is *archive research*. This is not to be confused with 'library' (sometimes referred to as 'desk') research. In most of your university assignments you will have been required to do some kind of *library research*, for example, going to the library to find books and articles, searching online databases to find relevant journal articles or using online newspapers to find out some background information. In writing your dissertation you need to use all these archive resources and more. As discussed in Chapter 3, it will be necessary for you to identify and investigate the three key elements of your research questions: the *object of analysis*, *research method* and *theoretical paradigm*. In the process of this preliminary work you will inevitably be required to undertake library research. We use the term archive research to refer to any project in which the contents of an archive constitute your *primary* source or your object of analysis. Thus, for example, if you wanted to research the history of *Vogue,* an important part of your research would involve identifying an archive where you could find copies of the magazine which would comprise your primary object of analysis. Examples of the kinds of material you could investigate using archive research include contemporary newspapers, television documentaries, art work, websites, blogs, books and journal articles.

Electronic archives are growing at a rate which will make this section of the book outdated as soon as it is written. There are some wonderful online archives available as libraries and museums around the world see the publication of material on the internet as fulfilling an important part of their mission to disseminate knowledge of their collections. Thus the great art galleries of the world, the *Louvre* (www.louvre.fr/llv/commun/home), the Victoria and Albert Museum (www.vam.org.uk), the *National Gallery* in London (www.nationalgallery.org.uk) and the *Guggenheim* in New York (www.guggenheim.org) all have terrific online archives and collections. The *British Library, Bodleian Library* (http://libguides.bodleian.ox.ac.uk), *Library of Congress, New York Public Library* and *Boston Public Library* – all of these have great printing-history archives and collections. The *British Universities Film and Video Council* (BUFVC) provides film and television programmes to schools and colleges. Its website is also home to a 'federated search engine' which enables you to access nine different search engines of relevance to researchers in film and television studies (http://beta.bufvc.ac.uk/).

When researching the culture industries we find huge variability in the amount and kinds of material held by different archives and collectors. If we take the example of British television, we find a wealth of information about the BBC at the *BBC Written Archives Centre* in Caversham, England.

This extensive archive includes letters, memoranda and BBC publications dating back to the founding of the BBC. The Written Archives Centre has provided the basis for one of the biggest histories of the BBC, initiated by media historian Asa Briggs (1961; 1965; 1970; 1979; 1995) which draws extensively on the archives. Other scholars have used the archives for smaller, more focused studies. For example, James Chapman researched the BBC's relationship with the anti-war film, *The War Game*, commissioned by the BBC and never shown. Previous studies on the controversy surrounding the film had focused on reports in the press, and the director Peter Watkins' own account of what happened. Chapman is able to reach a different interpretation by examining the correspondence found in the BBC archive about the programme, in his book, *The BBC and the Censorship of 'The War Game'* (Chapman, 2006).

The *Paley Center for Media* (formerly the Museum of Television and Radio) house their physical collections in New York and Los Angeles. They include extensive libraries of material related to the media industries with a special emphasis on broadcasting. If you can't get to New York or Los Angeles you can access their large and expanding online collection at www.paleycenter.org with a good range of interviews, presentations and seminars by media professionals. The section 'She Made It', for example, is about women in the television industry and includes interviews and debates with female television workers(The Paley Center for Media, 2008). In 2011 The Paley Center for Media hosted a conference on the 'Next Big Thing' which focused on digital media and the direction of new media – many of these presentations are available online (The Paley Center for Media, 2011).

Online archives and interviews can also be found on more generalist sites such as *YouTube*, *Wikipedia* and the *Internet Movie Database*. These sites should be approached with caution because of the more subjective nature of the way they are collected, but they can provide excellent sources for your project and provide a lot of rare material, especially in relation to the television industry. Alan McKee has compared the strengths and weaknesses of *YouTube* versus Australia's *National Film and Sound Archive* (NFSA) (McKee, 2011). He compares the two sources for their suitability to his research into Australian television history in an article published in the journal *Television and New Media*. In terms of access, McKee finds *YouTube* preferable and more 'user-friendly', but the information about the items lacks the kind of production details necessary for serious research such as personnel records and transmission dates. When considering the ranges of the collections, he finds that the NFSA is stronger on news and current affairs while *YouTube* better reflects the popular history of Australian broadcasting. The internet, through open access services like *YouTube*, enables everyone to contribute to an archive and this necessarily reflects a broader range of interests. Official archives like the NFSA (one might include here the BFI in Britain or the American Film Institute) have institutional biases which come through in their collections. The bias of these archives towards news and documentary and away from popular output has often been noted and has left the national collections of many countries with massive lacunae. There are an abundance of specialist sites online which provide archives of varying degrees of inclusivity and usability.

According to Brendan Duffy, there are broadly two different kinds of approach when it comes to archive research – *source-oriented* and *problem-oriented* (Duffy, 1999). *Source-oriented* document research is undertaken when the investigation of the source material motivates the research. In this kind of research, one would begin from the position of having access to an interesting archive or set of resources which one wishes to investigate. For example, a student at the University of California Los Angeles might have access to the extensive film library held there; alternatively, students at the University of Kent can access the archive of the British Centre for the Study of Cartoon and Caricature. In the course of your initial investigation, you may find that there is a physical archive or collection local to where you work or study on which you could base your research. The research question you developed would depend on your own interests, but the archive itself will have given you the initial impetus to conduct the research.

The *problem-oriented* approach to document research takes as its starting point a problem which one has developed out of reading other accounts or secondary sources. Here the documents may provide the object of analysis, but the research question has been generated independently of the documents themselves. The problem-oriented approach 'involves formulating questions by reading secondary sources, reading what has already been discovered about the subject and establishing the focus of the study before going to the relevant primary sources' (Duffy, 1999: 107). One might thus develop a question about the formation of a particular media company or of a piece of media legislation from reading around the subject. The archives of that company or relevant trade journals may then form the primary source. Rebekah Lynn Burchfield wrote her PhD based on the archive of nearly one million items held at Bowling Green State University's Music Library and Sound Recordings Archives (Burchfield, 2010). The University of East London is home to several archives, including the Refugee Council Archive and the East London Theatre Archive (ELTA) (http://www.elta-project.org/home.html). Find out whether your university has an archive which you could access.

Our first case study, by Paddy Scannell and David Cardiff (1991), looks at the social impact of broadcasting in its early days. Scannell and Cardiff draw on archive material from a wide range of sources to tell the complex and fascinating story of the beginning of radio from a social perspective

## Case Study

**Paddy Scannell and David Cardiff, 1991. *A Social History of Broadcasting. Volume 1: 1922–1939. Serving the Nation.* Oxford: Basil Blackwell.**

Scannell and Cardiff's *A Social History of Broadcasting* (1991) is an exploration of the social significance of British broadcasting focusing on the years 1922–39. During this period, broadcasting in the UK became coterminous with the British Broadcasting Corporation (BBC). The primary sources for Scannell and Cardiff's research were the archives of the BBC Written Archives Centre (WAC) at Caversham. At the WAC, the authors were able to consult minutes of BBC management boards and departmental meetings, policy files, production records, transcripts of broadcasts, press cuttings and other documents to piece together an account of the routine work of broadcasting. They also researched various BBC documents and publications, including the *Radio Times* and the *Listener*. The BBC archives did not provide their only source: the legislative context was gained through researching official government sources, including the reports of various government committees and *Hansard* (the official report of proceedings in Parliament). An awareness of the social impacts of broadcasting was garnered through analysis of periodicals of the day, including *Radio Pictorial* and *Radio Magazine*, and the music press, including *Melody Maker* and *Musical Times*.

Although the BBC is a central player in the narrative Scannell and Cardiff create, they insist that their book is not a history of the corporation. Instead, they make a larger claim for their project, arguing that it 'attempts to account, historically, for the impact and effect of broadcasting on modern life in Britain' (p. x). This is planned as the first volume in a series and concentrates on the early days of broadcasting in the pre-World War II period. This is when broadcasting became 'a state-regulated national service in the public interest' (p. x).

Key to the social history of British broadcasting is the idea of *public service broadcasting*, which is explored in the introductory chapter. In Part 1 Scannell and Cardiff focus on: the relationship between broadcasting and politics, looking at how controversial subjects were dealt with by the BBC; at the management of news and political debate; and at broadcasting and two key issues of the 'between the wars' period in Britain – unemployment and foreign affairs. Part 2 looks at the production of information in the BBC departments responsible for news, features and talks. Part 3 looks at music and variety, with chapters on various aspects of music policy, taste, entertainment and variety. The final part looks at how broadcasting relates to its audiences and how the BBC negotiated relationships between the 'national' and 'regional' services. Scannell and Cardiff's book is a large-scale study of nearly two decades of broadcasting history. It is an example of how historical accounts draw on a wide range of archive material.

Scannell and Cardiff's social history provides a model for how we could approach the study of any cultural industry. Radio had an important effect on the lives of British people in the 1930s. This study highlights various factors which shaped those developments. Scannell and Cardiff's work is wide-ranging and comprehensive, drawing on multiple sources and based on many years of study, reflection and research. Readers of this book may not be able to emulate this study in terms of scale and depth. However, in an example of how small-scale, locally-based studies can produce great research, we can consider the article by Sue Arthur from the *Historical Journal of Film, Radio and Television*. Arthur's essay about the cinema economy in Blackpool in the 1920s and 1930s draws on local newspaper archives to study the cinema industry in the important transitional period from 'silent' to 'talkies'. It provides a terrific example of how interesting, thoughtful research can be conducted using relatively humble resources such as the local history library held at any town hall or municipal library around the world (Arthur, 2009).

## Case Study

**Sue Arthur, 2009. Blackpool goes all-talkie: cinema and society at the seaside in thirties Britain. *Historical Journal of Film, Radio and Television*, 29(1): 27–39.**

In the late 1920s, Blackpool, in North-West England, had a lively entertainment industry with state of the art amusements and music hall theatres catering to the growing numbers of working-class people who could afford to take a day-trip or a week's holiday to the seaside. The theatre owners of Blackpool produced shows featuring performers of national and international acclaim and exhibited the latest American films.

In 1927 the 'talkies' were introduced to British cinema audiences when Al Jolson sang to his 'Mammie' in *The Jazz Singer*. This was the first time sound was synchronized with image in a feature-length film. The UK was the first country in Europe to adopt the new technology but the equipment was expensive and there was no guarantee of a long-term return. How did the exhibitors in Blackpool respond to the introduction of sound? Did they risk losing their established audience by introducing an expensive new technology which many thought was just a passing fad?

To answer the question of how Blackpool cinemas responded, Sue Arthur takes as her *object of analysis* advertisements and editorial copy in two local newspapers, the *Blackpool Times* and the *Evening Gazette*. By researching articles and advertisements for the cinema in the period 1929–30, Arthur is able to chronicle the introduction of sound and to follow some of the surrounding debates.

*(Continued)*

*(Continued)*

The first cinema to convert to sound was the *Hippodrome*, cashing in on the early Easter holiday by showing Al Jolson in *The Singing Fool* in March, 1929. Gradually other cinemas followed suit until, by July 1930, Blackpool was 'all-talkie' – and the film listings in the local papers showed every cinema exhibiting a sound picture. Arthur argues that this study has implications for our knowledge of the cinema industry more broadly. She says:

> The Blackpool example adds to our understanding of film-going in the 1930s by showing that where people had a real choice of entertainments and the spending power to choose, talking pictures very quickly constituted a real competitive attraction. (p. 37)

This study shows how a relatively small research project based on local history libraries and archives can generate valuable insight into the history of the media and cultural industries.

Whether you are using physical or virtual archives, you will need to prepare your research carefully. You will need to manage the amount of material held in the archive; if you are doing what Duffy calls 'problem-oriented' archive research, make sure that the archive in question houses the material you need. Your problem or research question needs to be well-defined – make sure you have discussed it with your supervisor. The main problems you need to avoid are: too much information and too little. Contact the archive well in advance of your visit to ensure that you can get access to the collection and that the material you want to look at is available. You will almost certainly need to visit more than once, so ensure that you allow sufficient time for this at the planning stage. Draw up a list of questions that you want to have answered by your analysis. Think about your overall research question – how can the material you are going to see help to address your thesis?

Researching an archive collection, whether it is of films, ephemera or written material, can be immensely rewarding. If you are researching a collection which has not been previously studied, it is exciting to uncover something which no one has looked at from a scholarly perspective before. Using an archive of original material allows you to generate data first-hand from primary sources. However, what you find in the archive is not always what you expect, so be prepared to be flexible and ready to shift your focus in the light of the discoveries you make.

# DISCOURSE ANALYSIS

Discourse analysis (also discussed in Chapter 5) is a method which requires you to undertake close analysis of texts, visual and verbal. Discourse analysis of the media and cultural *industries* requires you to analyse the texts which are not those produced for the media market, but the 'extra-textual' messages which are part of any industry. This might include internal information, promotional matter, corporate websites or annual reports. The media and culture industries don't only produce media texts for distribution in the media and cultural economy. They also produce material which is for industry consumption only. The 'discourses' they produce about themselves, for example in trade cards, industry-oriented marketing and press releases, contribute to a discourse about the industry which we can usefully analyse. These form the basis of John Caldwell's research which provides our next case study, looking at the industrial culture of film and television workers using discourse analysis as a major research method.

---

## Case Study

**John T. Caldwell, 2008. *Production Culture: Industrial Reflexivity and Critical Practice in Film and Television*. Durham, NC/London: Duke University Press.**

John T. Caldwell (2008; 2009) considers the language and images industry insiders use to communicate with one another as objects of analysis in his research into the Los Angeles film and television industries. Caldwell's work focuses on publicly available 'discourse' and on participant observation among those who work in the industry. He integrates several methods, including textual analysis, interviews, fieldwork and historical and archive research to investigate the cultural practices and belief systems of 'below-the-line' workers in Hollywood. Caldwell undertook his fieldwork in 1995–2005 when new working practices were being introduced in Hollywood including the increasing use of short-term contracts and the casualization of labour. In the chapter, 'Trade Stories and Career Capital' he explores the discourses of work found in conversations between people who work in the industry. Caldwell studies the stories insiders tell one another, applying the kind of narrative analysis usually applied to the films themselves to the stories producers tell one another. He considers 'trade story-telling' an important element of this discourse and he shows how ideas and attitudes of entertainment workers help engender a set of cultural values which runs through the industry.

---

Caldwell discusses how difficult it is to get access to workers in Hollywood and refers to the work of Hortense Powdermaker, an anthropologist who had researched Hollywood in 1951 (Powdermaker, 1951) (discussed later in this chapter – see pages 103–107). The access that Powdermaker acquired some 50 years before Caldwell did his research allowed her first-hand access to some of the most powerful decision-makers in Hollywood. By the time Caldwell conducted his fieldwork, access to such people was highly limited, ruling out much ethnographic research of the powerbrokers. But finding ways to get access to workers lower down the hierarchy, for example at trade fairs and conventions, was much easier. These people and their 'discourses' provide a vital resource.

We can all recognize the film and television industry as part of the 'culture industry', but what about weddings? Chrys Ingraham's research makes us realize how important 'white weddings' are to maintaining an ideology of *heteronormativity*. This research also helps us to understand the significance of weddings as part of the culture industries. Events management generally is a relatively recent area of research, and reading this study convinces me that it is one which we should consider researching more often.

## Case Study

**Chrys Ingraham, 2008. *White Weddings: Romancing Heterosexuality in Popular Culture*. 2nd edition. New York/London: Routledge.**

Weddings may not usually be considered among the culture industries, but Chrys Ingraham shows how the white wedding industry is very much a part of the ideological construction of what is 'normal' in Western society. Ingraham shows how the discourses of 'heteronormativity' assumed in the wedding industry have become a dominant ideological position. The exclusion of homosexuality, bisexuality or transsexuality from cultural representations makes everyone feel not only under an obligation to be straight, but to consider that everyone else should be, too. This 'normative' imperative, Ingraham argues, creates an environment in which anyone who does not conform to the norm is treated prejudicially.

This study explores the operation of the 'ideological complex' of weddings – including both the economic phenomenon of the wedding industry itself and the films and television programmes which daily support the ideology of heteronormativity. The white wedding industry is analysed for both its economic and ideological power. Chapter 2 of the book explores the 'wedding–industrial complex' in order to 'make visible the historical and material foundation upon which the operation of the heterosexual imaginary depends' (p. 39). Ingraham notes that, despite the decline in the number of people getting married in the US, the amount of money spent on the wedding industry is increasing. Globalization and travel is one key factor in the expansion – more Americans are getting married overseas, inflating costs. People are being encouraged to spend more and more money on their weddings as a cycle of increasing consumption is stimulated by the prevalence of weddings in the media and popular culture. This industry is big business – and growing.

Ingraham shows how, despite the apparent advances in feminism, the content of popular culture, especially films and television programmes, serve to support the idea of the wedding as the most important day in a woman's life.

By providing compelling images, popular film, television and the internet commodify weddings and create the market, the desire, and the demand for the white wedding. (p. 172).

This creates an anti-intellectualism which reinforces traditional ideas of femininity and the 'heterogendered division of labor' (p. 205).

When Ingraham's book was first published in 1999 there was little research into white weddings as a cultural and media phenomenon. In the years since then it has been studied more widely, but Ingraham's work is a model for critically analysing the relationship between media content and the operations of a particular culture industry – weddings themselves.

This book is supported by a website hosted by the publishers, Routledge, Taylor and Francis Group, which also provides some useful slides and weblinks (Routledge, 2011).

Discourse analysis, then, can be applied to a range of media and cultural phenomena. The television industry discourses of Caldwell and the wedding industry discourses of Ingraham are subject to careful analysis of the subject positions of the speakers. Within any discourse analysis, the *interlocutors* (speakers) need to be identified and their subject positions specified. It is necessary as a first step to identify *who* is speaking. With what authority (ethos) do they speak? How are the discourses framing the subject? Whether it be weddings or television production – what is the attitude towards the subject? What *frames* are being invoked? It is necessary to consider the different kinds of 'voices' and how these are set within broader 'frames'. Furthermore, who is the assumed audience? Who is being addressed and what is the assumed nature of the relationship (e.g. friend, colleague, boss)? What is said and what is unsaid? What is the tone of the discourse? What are the functions of the discourse (explicit and implicit)? You may wish to refer to the Aristotelian devices of rhetoric – *ethos, pathos* and *logos* discussed in Chapter 1 (see pages 11–13); for discourse analysis goes to the heart of understanding how speakers are positioned and the kinds of truth claims being made.

Discourse analysis is often associated with Michel Foucault and his work on the role of discourse in securing inequalities of power. See, for example, Foucault's work on *The History of Sexuality* (1998 [1976]), on prisons and criminality in *Discipline and Punish* (1991 [1975]), and on *The Archaeology of Knowledge* (2002 [1972]). You need to consider what kinds of power are at stake in the discourse you are studying and how the discourse contributes to the articulation of power. The analysis of power relations in discourse helps to identify the ideological position from which media products are made.

Industry discourse can be found in advertisements and i-dents, in trade journals and corporate and industry level websites. The internet has opened up whole new areas ripe for discourse analysis as media corporations like the BBC or the *New York Times* adopt a web presence to serve their brand. The work of the players in the media and cultural industries in self-promotion or peer-to-peer communication provides us with terrific resources for our research as Caldwell and Ingraham both show. The more typical application of discourse analysis is to texts made by the media and cultural industries, as we discuss in the next chapter. However, these texts are what Roland Barthes (1984) might have called 'motivated' in that they are carefully controlled and produced. Subjecting trade discourses to analysis as Caldwell does, or identifying an ideologically loaded economic exchange in an everyday cultural practice, as Ingraham does, provides us with a very rich analysis of ideology at work in the media and cultural industries. The next method we are going to examine explores how we can use media workers themselves as subjects, by asking them about their work.

## INTERVIEWS

The interview as a method in media and cultural research enables us to find out about people's ideas, opinions and attitudes. Interviews are a useful way of researching the media and cultural industries, not least because the method is familiar to industry workers. In this chapter we will consider how to interview people in the workplace while in Chapter 6 we consider interviews of audiences (see pages 176–187). Interviewing workers in the culture industries enables us to study attitudes towards cultural industries as workplaces, the rationale behind the production process, and the relationship of workers to their audiences. One of the pioneers of using interview research to investigate the culture industries is Dorothy Hobson. Hobson's 1982 investigation of the early evening British soap opera *Crossroads* used both producers and audiences as subjects. Her investigation of the audience for *Crossroads* was one of the first pieces of major research in Britain to look at the way the viewers of such a devalued television programme enjoyed, appreciated and used the television text. *Crossroads: The Drama of a Soap Opera* (Hobson, 1982) was instrumental in bringing greater emphasis to the audience's role in interpreting the text. It was especially timely in raising the level of debate about women's genres and is now a classic of feminist television studies (See Chapter 2, page 45 for further discussion). But this ignores the large part of the book that is devoted to the analysis of the attitudes and opinions of the people who made *Crossroads*. Hobson investigated the processes of production of *Crossroads* and interviewed the producers, editors, writers and performers of the programme. She found that, despite the fact that the show was perceived as depressing and downbeat by many critics, the producers felt they were making an uplifting programme in which characters overcame adversity with a spirit of hope and optimism. It is interesting that Hobson also interviewed the performers and found that in several cases their real-life character bore a resemblance to their on-screen personae – an observation which, for Hobson, explains the high level of 'realism' of the performances.

Interviews have often been used to study British soap operas. The research of Lesley Henderson (1999), for example, elicits some interesting insights into how and why soap operas address serious social issues such as breast cancer or domestic violence. Henderson interviewed personnel who worked on the leading television soaps in Britain, including *Coronation Street*, *Brookside* and *EastEnders*. People at various levels of the production process were interviewed, including writers, producers and script editors. One scholar whose work has tended to use a large sample of employees in the media industries is Jeremy Tunstall (1977; 1983; 1993; 1996; 2007) whose work on the British television industry provides our next case study.

## Case Study

**Jeremy Tunstall, 1993. *Television Producers*. London: Routledge.**

In writing *Television Producers* (1993), Jeremy Tunstall and his research assistants, Mark Dunford and David Wood, interviewed 254 producers working in British television. Tunstall focused on the role of 'series producer' or 'series editor', as this post was considered 'the highest level of person who is in regular daily editorial or "hands-on" control of the content of a series or programme' (p. 5). The management role of the producer is given careful consideration and Tunstall raises the question of whether the producer can be seen as an 'auteur'.

The role of television producer was in a state of flux at the time of the interviews. Between 1955 and 1982, there had been only two large

*(Continued)*

*(Continued)*

organizations, the BBC and ITV, running television and there was a very stable pattern of employment and career paths for producers. The era of the mature duopoly, in which the BBC and the ITV networks pretty well controlled British television history, was coming to a close by the early 1990s. Moreover, the full impact of the launch of Channel 4 and the Thatcher revolution was taking effect on the British television industry, so there were many factors to create uncertainty for all television workers.

Subjects for the study were identified by looking through trade publications and at credits listed in the *Radio Times* or at the end of broadcast television programmes. Tunstall insists that no particular attempt was made to make the interviewees representative of the industry as a whole, beyond the fact that they were selected from across the main programme genres, including documentary, sport and comedy. Letters were written requesting interviews and were followed up by telephone calls. Interviews were arranged to take place in the offices of the subjects during the period March 1990 to July 1992, and the standard length of an interview was about 70 minutes. The interviewers followed a prepared list of questions, administering the same open-ended questions to each producer, although these did change slightly as the study progressed. The interviewees were given assurances of anonymity at the time of the interviews, and although some gave permission for their names to be used, most of the subjects are quoted anonymously.

Subjects were interviewed about their careers and the changes in the role of producer during their time working in television. Tunstall found that the producers were aware of their employment becoming more casualized. Jobs which had once been seen as secure for life were now more typically offered as short-term contracts. At the same time, the research found that producers were becoming more autonomous and had greater freedom in their work. Tunstall concludes that, although producers are key players in television, they cannot be said to operate as *auteurs*. Instead, he finds that the *genres* according to which television programmes are made are the most important determinants of professional mores and values. In British television, it seems that departments operate along fairly fixed generic conventions which shape the working patterns within the industry.

This wide-ranging interview method is typical of Tunstall's work. Tunstall has explored the changing culture of the workplace of culture industries in the increasingly global media economy. For example, Tunstall interviewed over 200 people working in the British newspaper industry in the 1990s, comparing their contemporary experience with that of the 1960s in his book about *Newspaper Power* (1996). He identifies dramatic changes in the constitution of the newspaper and increasing power of the editor. Tunstall examines the relationship between media systems around the world. He has charted the period from the rise of American control and domination of the media in *The Media are American* (Tunstall, 1977) to the increasing globalization of media control in his more recent book, *The Media were American* (Tunstall, 2007). Changes in the processes of production have been multivalent since Tunstall's study as he himself is the first to observe (Tunstall, 2007).

One of the key relationships Tunstall was keen to explore in the case study above was that of the relationship between the 'creative' and 'non-creative' workers in the television industry. The prevalence of 'creative' workers is often viewed as one of the key characteristics of the culture industries and has thus attracted a great deal of academic interest (Hesmondhalgh, 2007; Holt and Perren, 2009). Relatively little work has focused on our understanding of the 'non-creative' staff in the media and cultural industries. One recent study which uses interviews to investigate the relationship between 'creative' and 'non-creative' people in the television industry is by James Paul Roberts (Roberts, 2010). Roberts interviewed 45 people working in British television, mainly within drama departments during 2007–08, to find out more about 'the activities of British television companies involved in programme selection and development' (p. 761). He asked them about the relationship between the 'creative' and 'non-creative' personnel in the companies they worked for with the aim of identifying 'the perceived differences in agenda between commercial and creative constituencies' (Roberts, 2010: 761 ). Roberts found that the interests of people in the 'creative' and 'non-creative' divisions of any given company were not so different – people were quite mobile in moving from role to role; the people in the 'non-creative' side of the industry (such as accountants and managers) had chosen their careers because they wanted to work in the culture industries and considered themselves to be creative minded. The differences between Tunstall's findings and Roberts' highlight several changes in the television industry over the intervening 30 years. Employment patterns have become much more flexible, the labour force is more casualized and there is an absence of any clear career structure for new entrants. The media more generally no longer operate along the factory system of specialization which led to the development of the Hollywood studio system or the bureaucratic model of management which dominated the BBC for most of its life.

When Paul du Gay and his colleagues investigated the Sony Corporation in their classic study, *Doing Cultural Studies: The Story of the Sony Walkman* (Du Gay et al., 1996), they saw how the philosophy of the corporation was significant in designing and developing an important predecessor to the iPod, the Walkman. They observed the means by which the corporation executives left the designers to carry on unimpeded by their intervention beyond being given a brief. We have seen subsequently how the development of the internet by Tim Berners-Lee came about in large part because he was given a lot of freedom to design and develop his own product (Berners-Lee, 1999). Likewise the Microsoft Corporation prides itself on having a particular kind of work environment which encourages design innovation on the part of its employees. In a post-Web 2.0 media environment, this trend has continued. Today, the design and development of some new products takes place completely outside of any formal employment structures. There is a new kind of industry worker coming to the fore, the *user entrepreneur*, who designs and develops new media and cultural products independently of any company. In the following case study, an article published in *Research Policy*, Stefan Haefliger, Peter Jäger and Georg von Krogh used a combination of methods to investigate the user entrepreneurs who helped form the Machinima industry (Haefliger et al., 2010; www.machinima.com; Lowood and Nitsche, 2011).

## Case Study

**Stefan Haefliger, Peter Jäger and Georg von Krogh, 2010. Under the radar: industry entry by user entrepreneurs. *Research Policy*, 39: 1198–213.**

This study, published in the journal *Research Policy*, looks at the development of a new form of film-making which exploits games software features to create new texts – *machinima*.

> Defined as 'shooting film in a real time 3D environment' … Machinima is (1) a production technology, and (2) the name for the genre. It is deeply rooted in the gaming culture where gamers … experienced the need to record, edit and distribute proof of their gaming skills on film to demonstrate their proficiency as gamers. (p. 1200)

The development of new products usually occurs from the design and development of new products by major corporations but machinima first developed as something fun for gamers to do before it became an industry in its own right. The 'user entrepreneurs' interviewed in this study identified entrepreneurial opportunities in the process of using a product (in this case games) and subsequently went on to develop and market them. Recognizing that machinima had not followed the typical pattern of product development, Stefan Haefliger and his colleagues interviewed industry insiders to find out what was the motivation behind the development of machinima and when and how it became commercialized.

A total of 26 subjects were interviewed during 2006–07, involving personnel from seven different machinima companies including both *Machinima.com* and *Rooster Teeth Productions*. Comprehensive desk research on the machinima community and the video games industry was carried out in addition to interviews and ethnographic observation.

When interviewing professional people from a small community such as the machinima producers, it may not be necessary to anonymize interviewees and, in this case, all participants are listed in table A2 of the paper (p. 1212). In this study, professionals are talking about their role in the development of a successful new media form and are very willing to contribute. The authors' goal is to develop a model for understanding how 'entrepreneurship' takes place in an environment where users are themselves the innovators and where the usual divide between 'audience' and 'producer' has been breached. They relate their knowledge of this community of 'user entrepreneurs' and of theories of entrepreneurship to demonstrate a new style of innovation. They label the process of developing products behind the backs of the official entrepreneurs as working 'under the radar'.

One of the problems researchers of the industry report is the lack of willingness of industry insiders to be interviewed. Haefliger et al. report no such difficulty in securing interviews, nor with observing people in their workplaces. People seemed willing to talk and quotations are attributed to participants by name and role. This may be a factor of the openness of the games industry, of the new media or of a younger generation. The sample of machinima creators they have interviewed are all currently working in the games or machinima industry and these are, by definition, successful; had they interviewed the people who were *unsuccessful* or who had never had one of their products 'commercialized', it might have been a different story. There are many problems with drawing conclusions from such a selective sample which goes to the heart of industry research – people do like to talk about themselves, but are happier to do so if they have had happy experiences with a positive outcome. Haefliger et al. may well have identified a new form of 'under the radar' commercialization; they may also have found a group of successful, self-congratulatory entrepreneurs who exploit the efforts of naïve young people who work for nothing developing new software. The problems of exploitation at work are endemic in the media and cultural industries. Many people are attracted to these professions and, with the weakening power of trades unions and a supply of good, enthusiastic workers the cost of labour has been falling. Today we find that large numbers of people – students like the readers of this book – are encouraged to work as interns for little or no money. The economics of employment and the weakening power of the unions has left many workers in the sector defenceless against poor working practices and low or even non-existent pay (Deuze, 2009; Napoli, 2010).

Some interesting work has been done in the area of media production and identity, especially in research conducted from a feminist or queer perspective. For example, Frances Cresser, Lesley Gunn and Helen Balme (2001) investigated 'women's experience of publishing online and how they perceive the construction of online identities and the politics of their publications' (p. 458). They interviewed 39 female authors published in e-zines during August and September 1998. The interviews were structured at first, and followed up by more informal exchanges which solicited more textured and in-depth responses.

## INTERVIEWS ABOUT THE PAST

Interviews with industry insiders are sometimes difficult to come by, but it can be easier to find subjects who are retired or who have left the industry. One such person was Monty Margetts, the presenter of an early television cookery programme, and the subject of an oral history study by Mark Williams (Williams, 1999). Oral history involves interviewing people about their past experiences and memories. It was developed as a research method by historians to study social history – it is a very loose form of interview where the subject is given freedom to speak freely as he/she wishes. Oral history has been used as a means of recording survivor testimony, for example the witness statements of Holocaust survivors. The United States Holocaust Memorial Museum in Washington is home to a large database of oral history testimonies. Oral history is a technique well suited to allowing people to speak freely in order to elicit opinions and information that *they* wish to give and which the interviewer might not be able to anticipate.

Consider the following case study: Stuart Goosman's oral history of men in Baltimore and Washington who had made up the 'doo-wop' bands of the 1940s.

---

## Case Study

**Stuart L. Goosman, 2005. *Group Harmony: The Black Urban Roots of Rhythm and Blues*. Philadelphia: University of Pennsylvania Press.**

Stuart L. Goosman uses oral history as a major part of his research into doo-wop bands in the 1940s and 1950s in the African-American neighbourhoods of Baltimore and Washington (Goosman, 2005). Goosman is interested to explore the relationship between *race* and *culture*, specifically in the American music industry during the height of segregation. How did black musicians respond to the racism and discrimination of a white-controlled music industry? Did growing up in segregated cities influence young men

---

to create a particular kind of music? What were the determinants behind the growth of the doo-wop bands such as the Cardinals and the Orioles? Goosman explores how this particular musical form grew up as a genre which integrates Tin Pan Alley with blues music. His research encompasses a range of methods including library research conducted at the Library of Congress and the Afro-American Newspapers Archives and Research Center in Baltimore, USA (www.afro.com).

Goosman uses 'the interpretive lens of oral histories provided by individuals who performed or participated in post-World War II secular black group vocal harmony' (p. ix). The book is structured around interviews conducted in 1989 and 1990. By using oral history Stuart Goosman's research allows the men who were there at the beginning of doo-wop to tell their stories and to give meaning and context to the music and archive material.

The singers who formed these groups report that they found a great sense of liberty in their work. They tell Goosman of the joy they gained in expressing themselves through singing with others. Singing gave them a sense of empowerment and control which they did not feel they could have attained through any other means. The oral history interviews put life into the story of the rise of a musical genre which was important in shifting the representation of black people in post-war America. Goosman demonstrates how black American artists articulate themes of integration and segregation, identity and difference, economic necessity and the joy of creativity.

> The story of group harmony illustrates the connection between human experience and music making and these two historical and extant human actions, which have largely shaped black music in the United States – celebration and resistance. (p. 21)

This research challenges the prevailing idea that black music grew up in Detroit and Chicago by tracing the origins of this important genre of music to the street culture of Baltimore and Washington in the 1940s and 1950s. Goosman brings to light a rich, neglected aspect of America's musical history through the authentic voices of the men who made the music.

While archive history relies on what has been collected and saved, and interviews rely on people's reports of their behaviour, attitudes and opinions, the oral history interview relies on what has been remembered and can be recollected by human beings. Oral history will differ from written history in significant ways. As we saw in Chapter 1, oral 'ways of knowing' have different criteria for 'truth'. It takes a political leap sometimes to accept, when using oral history, that the subject's authority over their own recollections is paramount.

The convention is to fully respect the reports of your subject. You do need to be well prepared before the interview, so make sure that you read around the subject and understand the main debates and issues from the perspective of the media historian. As with any fieldwork, make sure you have a well-developed research question before you conduct the interview. It is most unprofessional to waste people's time unless your interviews have a clear focus. Draw up a list of questions or main points that you want to cover in advance, and, if possible, give your subjects notice of the kinds of things you are going to ask them so that they also can be prepared. Even if you are interviewing people who are well known to you, such as a close relative, they will realize that you are serious and will, in turn, take your project seriously if they can see that you have done your homework. When you treat your interviewees with respect and consideration, they are more likely to treat you in the same manner.

Begin the interview by asking your subjects to clarify relevant facts – their job title, periods of employment and so on. Don't expect them to know government legislation or the specific dates of historical events. Don't argue with or contradict them. In oral history, you give absolute respect to the person recounting the past. Make sure you record your interview, and keep to the subject. Try to let your interviewees do most of the talking – you should only chip in for clarification or to keep them on the subject.

Oral history allows the subjects to define the topic and to speak about their own experiences with minimal intervention from the interviewer. When conducting your own oral history research you may need to prompt your subject to talk about specific things related to your object of analysis, but the interviewee should be able to define the talk. Questions or general topic areas should be given to the subject in advance so that they can have a chance to think about it.

## Conducting your own interviews

The first question lots of people ask when conducting interviews is 'How many interviews should I do?' For *Television Producers* Jeremy Tunstall interviewed a large number of producers – some 254 in all; Haefliger et al., in the study above, interviewed 26 people, while Williams (1999) interviewed just one. In the time frame most readers of this book have for their project a large set of interviewees would not be possible. It rather depends on what you are trying to say: Haefliger et al. are talking about a relatively specialized sector of the games industry and talking about a specific activity. Tunstall wants to make generalizations about the television production industry as a whole. Mark Williams' oral history focused on one television performer, Monty Margetts, in his study of women in early American television (Williams, 1999). The culture industries are great for 'case study' research in an interview with one key worker could be all you need.

Organizing an interview can be very time-consuming and you usually only get one shot at it, so you must prepare well in advance. When researching the culture industries, the people you are talking to are professionals and are unlikely to want to criticize their company or industry. Don't expect anyone to 'spill the beans' – most industry people will not be willing to talk about the negative side of the business to an outsider. When conducting research into the Hollywood film and television industry, John Caldwell found that the higher up in an organization a person was, the less likely they were to veer from the bland corporate speak you would find in the company publicity (Caldwell, 2008). It is quite likely that students will be given the official line on any controversial events from most employees within the media, or any other industry.

When conducting interviews with industry professionals you need to be aware of the status they have relative to you. Harriet Zuckermann describes how 'difference in rank' was a significant obstacle in her attempts to interview scientists who, as Nobel Laureates, were members of 'an ultra-elite'. She found that her interviewees put themselves in a role where they were evaluating her performance as a professional and as an interviewer. 'They saw themselves as judges and saw me as the object of judgment' she says (Zuckermann, 1972: 175). Tine Ustad Figenschou looks at the problems she faced as a 'young, female, Western researcher' interviewing 'senior, male, Al Jazeera officials' who she often found to have patronizing and misogynistic attitudes (Figenschou, 2010). When studying the Hollywood film industry, Sherry Ortner (2010) found a reluctance to talk among the Hollywood workers; and John Caldwell, looking at the same industry, elected to base his research on the 'below the line' workers in Hollywood film and television – they were more likely to talk, freer, less allied to corporate world view and more equal in rank. For Ursula Plesner, researching '*sideways*' caused as many problems when she interviewed journalists and sociologists who were colleagues of equal social status to the researcher; she found that interviewees wanted to negotiate a relationship with the researcher and concludes that, in the interest of good research, it is better to develop a confrontational research approach when dealing with people of equal status. The 'agent provocateur', after all, can often get people to reveal their true thoughts about a situation (Plesner, 2011).

So, when you are designing your study, try to anticipate what the likely response is going to be and whether this is going to be helpful in answering your research question. Before you begin your interviews you should always discuss with your supervisor what form the interviews should take. As an ethical consideration, every university will have guidelines for researchers who are dealing with people, sometimes called a 'human subjects panel' or an 'ethics committee'. Before you go 'into the field' interviewing people, you should make sure that your work does not compromise the well-being of any of your subjects, and find out what the procedure is at your university or college for ensuring your work is always conducted ethically.

## Stages in conducting interview research

### Select your interviewees carefully

You must target the right people, and get permission to interview early in the project. Don't assume that people will talk to you – some people get lots of requests to give interviews to undergraduates and are too busy to do so. Interview as few people as is necessary to conduct your study; interviews are very time-consuming for both interviewer and interviewee, so make sure that you don't waste people's time. Aim for the right level of person: if you are interested in the adoption of new technology, you will want to speak to a person in the company interested in that area; if you want to find out about employment policies, you should interview someone in human resources. Don't assume that you have to interview the chief executive officer of a company to get reliable information. If you are using personal contacts, take advice from them about the appropriate procedure you should follow to request an interview as this may differ from one industry or industry sector to another.

### Conduct background research

Find out as much as you can about the structure of the industry and the company, and about the roles of the people you will be interviewing, well in advance. Make sure you understand fully the location of any industry worker you will be interviewing within the organization and the status of their company or organization within the industry overall. Be up to date with any current legislation and familiarize yourself with the main debates in the industry by reading recent copies of relevant trade journals.

### Planning the interview

Draw up a list of questions or topic areas. Be ready to go with the flow, but make sure you know precisely what information you want and what questions are likely to elicit this. Practice the questions in advance so that you don't need to read them and be prepared to speak with written notes for prompts.

### Conducting the interview

Be prepared and look prepared. Try to establish a rapport with the subject. Be friendly and courteous; shake hands with the interviewee and smile; thank the interviewee for agreeing to talk to you at the beginning and end of the interview. Never use academic jargon in an interview. If subjects use a term that you don't understand, apologize and ask them to explain. Make sure you record your interview – practise using the recorder in advance if it is one you have not used before, and make sure you have spare batteries and media with you! It can be very embarrassing if your equipment breaks down or you run out of space during an interview. You should always get permission before you record an interview and before you turn the recorder on, and you should explain why you need to record the interview. Refer to your list of questions or topic areas, but don't read from it. Listen carefully to the responses and try to conduct a natural conversation – this will elicit more interesting and spontaneous conversation from your interviewee.

## Take notes

Even though you are recording the interview, you should still take brief notes during the interview. It will help if you tick off the topic areas as they are covered or jot down a question while the person is talking so you don't interrupt.

## Transcribe the interview

A transcript of an interview is very helpful if you are going to analyse it in detail. But it is very time-consuming to type up an entire interview – professional researchers would employ an administrator to do this. There are transcription services available if you wish and you can afford it, but these are not always necessary. If you do transcribe the interview, the transcript should be included as an appendix and will not contribute towards the final word count (see Chapter 7 for a discussion of appendices).

## Reflect

The most important stage of the interview is to reflect on what your subject has said. Does he/she say anything surprising or unexpected? Does the interviewee support or refute your research question? Do you need to reconsider your research question? Have you got some fresh ideas you need to follow up? The basis of all analysis is comparison, so compare the actuality with your expectations. If you have more than one interviewee, think about the comparisons between them: what areas do the subjects agree on and where do they differ? How can you account for these similarities and differences?

Interviews can elicit rich and complex information which can form the basis of your project. They are very useful, too, in ethnographic research of industry, where the in-depth interview can be accompanied by observation. When we come to consider interviewing audiences in Chapter 6 we will discuss some of the various questionnaire protocols in more structured questionnaires and focus groups. The next section of this chapter looks at ethnographic research and how we can use observation of people in the field alongside interviews to study people in the media and cultural industries.

# ETHNOGRAPHIC RESEARCH

Ethnography is an approach to research which derives from *anthropology* – the study of people and relationships in communities, historically of non-Western people.

> Ethnography usually involves the researcher participating, overtly or covertly, in people's daily lives for an extended period of time, watching what happens, listening to what is said, and/or asking questions through formal or informal interviews, collecting documents and artifacts in fact, gathering whatever data are available to throw light on the issues that are the emerging focus of the inquiry. (Hammersley and Atkinson, 2007: 3)

It is a method which has been increasingly used to study the working practices in the media and cultural industries, reflecting a greater interest in the dynamics of the workplace. Bronislaw Malinowski is considered by many to be the founder of modern anthropology, famous for his work with the Trobriand Islanders (Malinowski, 1997 [1932]). In media and cultural studies, however, one of the most important progenitors of the ethnographic approach is Clifford Geertz (1973). In his book *The Interpretation of Cultures*, Geertz advances the idea of anthropology as a 'thick description' of social life. This concept has been applied to the workplace within cultural and media studies, resulting in a rich body of work exploring the workplace from an ethnographic perspective – see, for example, Schlesinger, 1987 [1978]. A key concept deriving from anthropology is that of 'making strange' those things which would otherwise seem ordinary and everyday; to get behind the social systems at stake in our 'normal' routines and interactions. This is a fundamental characteristic of much cultural-studies methodology. Often researchers get a better understanding of an industry when they are part of that industry or when they can *participate* in the routines of the industry as if they were members of that community. Participant observation is a method which derives from ethnography and is used by scholars conducting fieldwork, usually living among distant peoples to understand their way of life. Participant observation requires a mixture of involvement and detachment, and scholars need to be able to judge from the situation just how involved or detached they need to be. Ethnographers may spend several months, or even years, building the trust which will enable them to learn about the lives of their subjects, as did Daniel Everett whose work we discussed in Chapter 1 (Everett, 2008). In our area, most industry-focused participant observation is conducted within corporations or companies by people who already work there or who have very good contacts, and the fieldwork is conducted over several months, such as Philip Schlesinger, (1987 [1978]). However, it is also possible to conduct observation of great value in a shorter period, as Anthony Cawley does in his study of the online newsroom of the *Irish Times* which comprises our case study on pages 109–110 (Cawley, 2008).

Ethnography meshes well with the idea of studying culture in the sense that Raymond Williams means it when he talks about a 'way of life', and it has been used with great success to study domestic consumption (see, for example, Lull, 1990; Moores, 1993; Morley, 1980; 1986; 1992; Morley and Silverstone, 1991; Silverstone, 1994) – see Chapter 6 pages 191–196 for further discussion. Applying this anthropologically based method to working practices gives us a different set of opportunities and challenges. People are at work for a purpose (to make and sell a product of some kind) their roles and intentions are more readily laid out, and they usually have a 'job description' – all of which helps to define the situation in which they operate; however, the roles of people as 'audiences', usually in a domestic environment, are more flexible and less readily defined. Hortense Powdermaker wishes to study the 'social system' in operation among Hollywood workers. She says:

> A social system is a complex co-ordinated network of mutually adopted patterns and ideas which control or influence the activities of its members. (Powdermaker, 1951: 3)

The 'social system' is likely to be a primary object of analysis in any workplace ethnography. By watching people as they go about their everyday routines, the ethnographer is able to identify patterns and behaviours which can be related back to theoretical ideas discussed in the academic literature. Observation is typically supported by in-depth interviews with key workers to elicit their understanding of the situation. Thus there are two different research techniques involved in the ethnographic method: 'participant observation' – where one joins in with the group which one is studying, often observing from a point of view of membership (as Henry Jenkins does in his 1992 study of fans, discussed in Chapter 6); and 'in-depth interview' – where key subjects are interviewed, typically in the workplace. In the workplace ethnography the 'participant observer' may participate in the routines of work, and may even be a co-worker of the subjects. Interviews may be formal, at appointed times and to given questions, or informal – occurring as part of normal conversation in the course of a working day or anything in between. The researcher needs to blend in and be as inconspicuous as possible, and this means following the workplace norms as far as possible.

Hortense Powdermaker was one of the first scholars to turn an anthropological lens on the creative industries. After a long career studying the South Sea Islanders she turned her attention on the 'Hollywood dream factory' in 1946 which provides a classic case study in ethnographic research.

## Case Study

**Hortense Powdermaker, 1951. *Hollywood, the Dream Factory: An Anthropologist Looks at the Movie-Makers*. Boston: Little, Brown and Company.**

*Hollywood, the Dream Factory,* is a ground-breaking and insightful study of the Hollywood film industry in its prime. 'The purpose of this study,' says the author, 'is to understand and interpret Hollywood, its relationship to the dreams it manufactures, and to our society' (p. 11). Hortense Powdermaker spent a year in Los Angeles getting to know the Hollywood film industry and conducting participant observation and interviews while officially employed as a part-time visiting professor of anthropology at the University of California in Los Angeles (UCLA) in 1946–47.

> I went there to understand better the nature of our movies. My hypothesis was that the social system in which they are made sig nificantly influences their content and meaning. (p. 3)

Powdermaker believes that any form of art, including the films produced in Hollywood, are shaped and conditioned by their 'particular history and system of production'. In order to understand this process, she uses the anthropologist's technique of immersing oneself completely in the lives of one's subjects, and she lived as much as she could in their culture: attending parties, visiting studios, offices and workplaces. The fact that she did not work in the industry was viewed by Powdermaker as a strength: 'I had no ax to grind in a situation where everyone was very busy grinding his own' (p. 4).

The interviews themselves took careful planning and before going to conduct an interview she always had 'a detailed outline of the problem' under investigation. However, in order to ensure the smooth flow of conversation, she always left this at home and took no notes during the interview except what she calls 'statistical' ones. When the interview was over she would drive her car round the corner and write up her recollections of the conversation in a notebook which she would then record into a dictaphone when she got home to be transcribed later by her secretary.

About 300 people were interviewed in total, including producers, directors, writers and actors. Interviews were held in a variety of settings: people's offices, homes, in cafeterias and restaurants. 'All human beings love to talk about themselves and are flattered at having their opinions taken seriously' (p. 6), she observed. Hollywood people made particularly good interviewees because, she says, 'The level of frustration was very high and frustrated people love to talk' (p. 6). In addition to the interviews,

Powdermaker thoroughly researched the industry, reading the *Screen Writers Guild* files, the MPAA production code, and all the industry trade papers, singling out *Variety* as the 'most important single source of printed information' (p. 6).

Powdermaker's final conclusions about the *Hollywood Dream Factory* are pretty negative. The conflict between 'creative' and 'commercial' imperatives which one would find in any cultural industry seem to have been largely resolved, in Powdermaker's analysis, with the commercial parties the clear victors – the *artists* in Hollywood work under the near-total direction of the *businessmen* who have very little understanding of art or culture.

> The social organization of Hollywood has ... permitted the businessmen to take over the function of the artists and to substitute his values for theirs. The movies are the first art form of any kind, popular, folk or fine, to become a trust. (p. 316)

She argues that Hollywood has 'mechanized creativity' and that:

> It is only an exceptional executive who does not give the impression that he would have been equally satisfied as a tycoon in any other industry. (p. 316)

The critical stance taken in Powdermaker's book was quite shocking, the industry vehemently rejected her findings and she was excoriated in the press. The extent to which her findings resonate with the work of Marxist scholars, Theodor Adorno and Max Horkheimer, has been noted by Kelly Askew (Askew, 2002). There is some evidence that Horkheimer and Adorno were in Los Angeles during the time that Powdermaker was conducting her research, although there does not seem to be any evidence that they ever met. Askew has observed of Powdermaker's similarity to the Marxist scholars of the Frankfurt school:

> Together they shared and promoted a view of the film world as a crass and brutal industry thinly disguised as art that used its technological advantage to objectify viewers and impose on them politically numbing cultural formulae. (Askew, 2002: 4–5)

No wonder the Hollywood film industry has been so impenetrable to researchers ever since! Little surprise, then, that John Caldwell (discussed above, pages 89–90) was obliged to focus his study on the 'below-the-line' workers.

One recurrent application of ethnography to the media industries has been to the study of news (Cottle, 2007). Many scholars have observed newsrooms, using methods similar to Powdermaker's, but from the perspective of the political economist rather than the anthropologist. An important motivation for many scholars of the media is to consider its role in relation to the political realm (see, for example, Gaye Tuchman (1972; 1980) and Michael Schudson (2003) and discussion by Simon Cottle (2007)) – the idea of the press as part of our 'public sphere' (Habermas, 1989) with a special responsibility for keeping the public informed in order to have a healthy democracy.

A classic of communication theory, and one of the earliest studies of the operation of the press, is David Manning White's essay from 1950 on the work of the 'gatekeeper' in the newsroom of a local daily newspaper in the US (White, 1950). He observed the working practices of the desk editor, who he called 'Mr. Gates' during one week in 1949 as he read the press agency reports coming in to the newsroom via the telegraph. It was Gates' job to decide which stories were to be written up and published in the newspaper, and which ones rejected; White found that Gates' decision-making was subjective and lacking any systematic criteria of newsworthiness. He concluded that the role of the 'gatekeeper' was powerful in determining the content of the newspaper. The label of the 'gatekeeper' has since been frequently applied to news workers in television news (Berkowitz, 1990) and elsewhere (see, for further discussion, Shoemaker, 1991; Shoemaker and Voss, 2009).

Philip Schlesinger was quite unique in applying ethnographic methods to the study of the British Broadcasting Corporation's newsrooms in the 1970s (Schlesinger, 1987 [1978]). His study of the BBC was completed in 1977 using methods derived from ethnography to produce a study based on 'theoretically informed observation of the social practices of cultural production' (p. xxxii). Schlesinger observes the extent to which theories of news production are reflected in the operation of the BBC's radio and television newsrooms at Broadcasting House and at the television news Television Centre in London. Schlesinger's study took place over about four years and he interviewed 95 members of staff. *Putting Reality Together* is one of the first studies to take a theoretical perspective on the activities of media workers and is a foundational text in British cultural studies. An important finding of this research was that, despite the highly politicized environment, the newsroom is a place where politics are routinely denied. Few scholars picked up on the lead made by Schlesinger, whose work was particularly poorly received by the media. There have, however, been several recent studies applying ethnographic methods to the workplace, particularly to the newsroom (see, for example, Wardle and Williams, 2010). Chris Paterson and David Domingo (2008) have edited a good collection of case studies using ethnography to study newsrooms around the world during the period of the introduction of online news services. This book has a good introduction discussing the advantages of ethnography as a research method for investigating the workplace (Paterson, 2008). Our next case study is an essay from this collection looking at the online newsroom of the *Irish Times.*

---

## Case Study

**Anthony Cawley, 2008. News production in an Irish online newsroom: practice, process and culture. In Chris Paterson and David Domingo (eds), *Making On-Line News: The Ethnography of New Media Production.* New York: Peter Lang, pp. 45–60.**

Anthony Cawley conducted his ethnographic study of the online newsroom (*Ireland.com*) of the *Irish Times* for a three-week period in August 2001. The *Irish Times* dates back to 1859 and 'holds a reputation for impartial quality journalism akin to the *Guardian*'s standing in Britain or *The New York Times* in the United States' (p. 49). In 1994 the *Irish Times* began their first website and in the late 1990s introduced an online edition, *Ireland.com*. They recruited an online editorial team to run the new service, which worked independently of the newspaper with separate offices and different terms of employment. At the time of Cawley's research *Ireland.com* employed 57 full-time staff, including technical, marketing and editorial.

Cawley's goal in this study is to examine:

> the relationship between the old organization and the new organization, between the old media form and the new media form, and the strengths and conflicts that come from their close and direct relationship. (p. 45)

From his observation, Cawley finds that the online journalist fulfils all the tasks that any other journalist would: writing copy, interviewing sources, reviewing the press releases. In addition, online journalists also edit their own copy, upload it onto the internet, take their own photos and upload those, too. As Cawley observes, 'the traditional demarcation of news production does not apply' (p. 47).

Cawley finds that print journalists could be dismissive of their online colleagues, who are often marginalized in meetings, for example by being addressed as 'online' rather than by name, as is the case with the other journalists. It becomes clear to Cawley that print journalists have greater kudos within the organization.

The biggest change in working practices at the time of Cawley's study is the shift to a more televisual way of working as audiovisual content is added to the web; Cawley wonders how journalists will manage this new

*(Continued)*

---

*(Continued)*

transition. The ethnographic study could not have predicted the external changes in the economy which resulted in 40% of the full-time staff being fired in 2001 as the *Irish Times* contracted its online operations and shifted to a subscription service. The video services which were being toyed with in 2001 were handed over to a Swedish company in 2006 which provided the content to *Ireland.com TV* (p. 59). By the time Cawley's essay was published in 2008, he concludes:

> Despite the new video service, and some 13 years of development, the website remains primarily a text-based news-service dependent, heavily, on the content of the newspaper. (p. 59)

The opportunities and challenges of the internet seemed not to threaten the hegemony of the traditional print room in 2001.

Anthony Cawley's study is an example of how ethnography works to create what Clifford Geertz refers to as a 'thick', that is, detailed and complex, description of an environment at a particular time and place. By the time the essay came to press, some years after Cawley's initial fieldwork, the relationship between the online and print versions had changed; no doubt the relative status of each at the *Irish Times*, in keeping with other newspapers, continues to change as print rooms are closing across the UK and in the US. The dynamic rate of change within the media industries ensures that the situation is in constant flux – this should not dishearten you, but should remind us that all research is 'historical' even if it is 'contemporary history'. Events may well have overtaken your findings before you commit them to paper. As researchers it is our duty to be as truthful as we can about the situation which we find, to record for posterity the changing situation and to make generalizations from our specific studies to the broader industry.

It is possible for students who wish to study the patterns of behaviour and activities in the workplace to conduct a small-scale study, especially if they can use contacts that they already have. With Hortense Powdermaker, you need to have an interest in a media or cultural industry and 'its particular history and system of production' – this is your object of analysis. If you work in a media environment already, or you have a work placement, then this is an ideal time to conduct your own investigation into how the 'system' works. One of the biggest challenges to ethnographic research in the media and cultural industries is access. We have noted that media professionals are often antipathetic to academics, sometimes with good reason, and where proprietorial issues may be at stake and suspicion of the researcher can run very high. However, for people who already work in the industry, have good contacts or relevant work experience or internship, it may well be worth considering turning these into an object of analysis for your research.

## Stages in an ethnographic study

Ethnographic research of the media industries requires a high level of cooperation on the part of your target organization, so you need to make absolutely sure that you get the full permission of all the people involved. This includes relevant line managers and all the people you are going to be observing. Always remember to be very courteous and show full respect to everyone involved.

### Before fieldwork begins

You need to be well prepared before you begin your fieldwork in order to get the best out of your research. Read the relevant trade papers and the main-stream papers to find out as much as you can about the relevant industry and the location of the company or department within that industry. Use your target organization's own website and that of any relevant trade organizations to garner as much background information as possible. Write a description of the industry showing how your target company fits in. Draw an organizational plan of the company (use their annual reports and/or public information such as their website or the industry press to help you) and think about how the area you are going to study fits in with the whole. Design your study carefully, writing a detailed plan and a schedule. Get permission, in writing, to conduct fieldwork from the relevant people in the organization and arrange exactly what days you are going to be observing well in advance.

### During fieldwork

Always be prompt and efficient during fieldwork. Take your cues on how to dress and behave from everyone else. Introduce yourself to everyone on the first day, and try to schedule a time with all subjects individually, at their convenience, to talk to you about their work. Find out about people's roles by asking questions politely when your subjects are not busy. Try to engage people in conversation in quiet periods or away from the work environment, as for example around the coffee machine. Be flexible and friendly in your approach, bearing in mind all the time your reason for being there. While others might have axes to grind, as Powdermaker says, you *don't* – so listen and smile even if and when people say things you don't like or find objectionable. You have a responsibility to get the most from your subjects and they will usually feel more free to talk if you don't challenge them.

111

## Note-taking

Take notes as you go along. Make your writing as unobtrusive as possible – if possible, leave the room to write your notes. Don't sit with your phone on and type comments into the phone while you are speaking to people; be discrete. Note the details of key relationships and any decisions made. Who does what? Identify key roles and observe how and why things are done. Keep your notes brief and frequent. At the end of each day, make notes in your diary about what happened. Spend time after each period of fieldwork relating your observations to your research question. Before you go back to the field again, look through your notes from the previous visit and try to fill in any gaps. Make provisional analyses and sort your notes as you go along – you may need to redefine your research question as you go along, so be flexible and open minded about what you find and don't be too concerned if you don't find what you were looking for.

## After fieldwork

Spend some time reading through your notes and diary, and think carefully about what you have found. Reflect on your experience and write up the stages in your thinking during the observation period. After you have carefully reflected on your experience, you can begin to write your findings. Include what you found as well as what you did not find and discuss any areas where you could have done better. Write down your mistakes – it is better to reflect on them than to pretend they never happened. You will learn more from this experience if you think seriously about where you went wrong. Go back to the literature which formed your research question and see if you have different ideas about the theory after having done your fieldwork. Reflect also on the method you undertook – could you have found out more if you had behaved differently? Maybe if you had looked at a different department or been given different access, you could have made some more interesting observations – these are the kinds of thing which are worth commenting on. When you come to writing up your dissertation, you may want to include a diary or log of your visits as an appendix, but the bulk of what you write will be your interpretation and analysis of what was going on, not a simple chronology of what happened. As with all projects, write it up with reference to the theories and writings which informed your original research question. For more guidance on conducting ethnography see Mike Crang and Ian Cook's book *Doing Ethnographies* (2007). Chris Paterson and David Domingo include a number of interesting examples of ethnography from around the world in their edited volume, which also includes a terrific essay on the topic of 'Why Ethnography?' by Chris Paterson (2008). In Chapter 6 we will look at the use of ethnography for studying audiences and consider the different responsibilities of the researcher to their subjects in conducting research on members of the public.

## METHODS AND APPROACHES
## DISCUSSED IN THIS CHAPTER

Of course, there are many more ways of researching the media and culture industries than we have space to discuss in this book. This chapter has examined four such methods: *archive research*, *discourse analysis*, *interviews* and *ethnography*. The choice of which method to adopt rather depends on your research question, as I trust you will have realized by now. Although we have discussed them separately, the methods discussed in this chapter could be used in conjunction with one another to address the same question. Indeed, some of the case studies and examples we have discussed do precisely that – for example John Caldwell's study of the television and film industries in Los Angeles, which combines all four of these methods to analyse the culture of the workplace. We can have a look at the opportunities and challenges offered by each of the methods discussed in Figure 4.2.

Access is a key problem for many of the methods discussed, be it access to materials or people. Access to personnel is a particular problem in researching the media and cultural industries, as we have seen in this chapter and as Sherry Ortner found when she tried to interview Hollywood producers (Ortner, 2010). Access to material artifacts can be difficult, although increasing amounts of information are available on the internet. There are vast archives which are available to you, and the speed at which material is put on the internet outstrips the researcher's capacity to keep up with it. You will find that proprietorial information such as product research will not be freely available; and some materials are liable to be withdrawn without notice. If you have a good archive close available at your university, or locally, these make excellent resources. Interviews are a valuable research method for finding out an insider's perspective. Student researchers may find it difficult to get access to people in the culture industries unless it is through personal contact. If you already know people working in an industry who are willing to talk, this is a good method but don't rely on getting access to key industry people. The oral history approach is terrific if you do have access to people with interesting experiences to convey. Ethnography is a great way to research people's behaviour in their own environment, but there are always ethical issues to be addressed in conducting research on people in any situation. However, the workplace is where people are on display anyway and there are less concerns about researchers conducting this kind of work in such public places than in the home, where subjects may feel more compromised. Participant observation has the advantage of allowing you to use your work experience or internship as a research site. Ethnographic observation has an advantage over interviews in that the researcher aims to be 'invisible' and as inconspicuous as possible and may avoid some of the 'experimenter

**FIGURE 4.2** A comparison of the opportunities and challenges of selected methods for researching the media and culture industries

| Method | Opportunities | Challenges |
|---|---|---|
| **Archive Research** | An excellent way to utilize local or specialist *archive resources.*<br><br>If you are using a virtual archive, there is the benefit that your research can be done from your computer.<br><br>Your university library may subscribe to relevant archives.<br><br>You may identify documents which have not been studied before. | There may be difficulties of access – you may have to travel to physical archives.<br><br>You may need to pay to access some archives – make sure you budget for any costs.<br><br>Items in physical archives are not always available for viewing – be sure to check you can access all relevant items in advance of any visit.<br><br>Your object of analysis is limited to what has been archived or collected; much new media is not archived. |
| **Discourse Analysis** | A good method for analysing the *ideology* of the workplace, or of media producers, power relations and hegemony in culture. You can apply high-level theoretical concepts to your analysis; a good method for applying theoretical ideas.<br><br>Access to some kinds of industry discourse may be readily accessible. | Requires a high level of discursive skill on your part; you must enjoy writing.<br><br>Familiarity with the culture producing the discourse is required.<br><br>Beware of using corporate or proprietorial data which may be protected information. |
| **Interview**<br>**Oral History Interview** | The method to use if you are interested in people's *ideas, attitudes and opinions.*<br><br>For gathering *people's recollections* of the past; a nuanced method for identifying subjective insights.<br><br>Good for precise case-study work. | Access to subjects must be negotiated.<br><br>Beware the 'interviewer effect' (people telling you what they think you want to hear) or industry people towing the party line.<br><br>Issues of generalizability have to be addressed. You can often only talk about the experience of the person or people you are interviewing. |
| **Ethnography and Participant Observation** | The method to choose if you want to find out about *behaviour* – how people act in social situations. A good method for collecting data from a social situation.<br><br>Consider this method if you have an interesting work placement. | There are *ethical* problems in observing people at work: issues about observing people when they are unaware; getting permissions.<br><br>Issues around generalizability need to be addressed. |

effects' which can result in interviewees telling the investigator what they think they want to hear, or what they want them to be told.

Even if the production end of the communication chain is not your main focus, it is important to locate your object of analysis within the economic materiality of media production. All research projects can benefit from some research into the relevant industry. In the next chapter we consider some methods you can use to study texts which the culture industries produce before going on in Chapter 6 to consider some methods for researching audiences.

# FURTHER READING

Deacon, David, Michael Pickering, Peter Golding and Graham Murdock, 2007. *Researching Communications: A Practical Guide to Methods in Media and Cultural Analysis.* 2nd edition. London: Bloomsbury Academic.

This is a good, inclusive textbook on research methods in media and cultural studies. Of particular relevance to this chapter are: Chapter 2, 'Dealing with Documentation' (for a good discussion of archives and access to them) and Chapter 11, 'Being an Observer' (a discussion of different applications of ethnographic methods to the study of media workers and audiences).

Hesmondhalgh, David, 2007. *The Cultural Industries.* 2nd edition. London: Sage.

Hesmondhalgh provides a thorough and interesting overview of some of the main contemporary debates facing the culture industries; this book is particularly strong when he discusses concepts of conglomeration and the impact of digital technology on the media.

Holt, Jennifer and Alisa Perren (eds), 2009. *Media Industries: History, Theory and Method.* Chichester, West Sussex: Wiley-Blackwell.

A terrific collection of essays relating to the current state of research in the media industries.

Paterson, Chris and David Domingo (eds), 2008. *Making Online News: The Ethnography of New Media Production.* New York: Peter Lang, pp. 1–11.

An international survey of ethnographic studies looking at the introduction of digital technologies to newsrooms. Highly recommended case studies.

Priest, Susanna Hornig, 1996. *Doing Media Research: An Introduction.* Thousand Oaks, CA/London: Sage.

This book provides an excellent overview of some of the main methods of researching the media. See Chapter 2, 'Anthropology and the Range of Human Experience' for a good description and rationale of ethnographic methods.

Below are some links to journal articles relevant to researching the media and culture industries.

Philip Napoli's articles presents a Marxist analysis of the role of the audience in the new media economy.
Napoli, Philip M., 2010. Revisiting 'mass communication' and the 'work' of the audience in the new media environment. *Media, Culture and Society*. **32** (3): 505–516.
http://mcs.sagepub.com/content/32/3/505.full.pdf+html.
Brenton J. Malin's case study of the production of the hard-boiled detective series, *The Shield*, provides an interesting exploration of ideas of masculinity within the post-broadcast era television industry.
Malin, Breton J., 2010. Viral menhood: niche marketing, hard-boiled detectives and the economics of masculinity. *Media, Culture and Society.* **32** (3): 373–389
http://mcs.sagepub.com/contents/32/3/373.full.pdf+html.
The Sami people are a minority culture in Northern Scandinavia and Russia. In this article Sari Piekikäuinen uses interviews and ethnographic study to research Sami journalistic culture.
Piekikäuinen, Sari, 2008. Broadcasting indigenous voices: Sami minority media production. *European Journal of Communication*. **23** (2): 173–191.
http://ejc.sagepub.com/content/23/2/173.full.pdf+html

## TAKING IT FURTHER ... ON YOUR OWN

*Identifying potential research topics using trade journals*

Select a trade journal of relevance to a media or cultural industry in which you are most interested, for example, *Broadcast, Campaign, Variety* or *MediaWeek*. Look through the latest issue and conduct a brief content analysis of the main stories (See Chapter 5, pages 140–143 for discussion of content analysis). Consider which topics are currently of greatest concern to your chosen industry. Next, you should find an edition from the past – 10, 20 or 30 years previous. Conduct the same exercise identifying which themes and issues are of greatest concern in your chosen journal from the past. Can you identify any changes in emphasis? What is the biggest change you notice? What is the biggest similarity between past and present coverage? Write a single page report on your findings and consider whether you might like to pursue any of the ideas arising from this for your dissertation. How could you design a study to investigate the changes which have occurred in the industry between these two times?

# TAKING IT FURTHER ... IN CLASS

*Identifying research topics from shared knowledge
of the field in class*

Look at the list of possible topics to investigate when researching the media or cultural industries on page 80 above. Working in small groups of three to six, select a media or cultural industry of particular interest to your group, such as television, the internet or advertising. Drawing on your knowledge of the industry concerned, identify an example of an *object of analysis* relevant to your chosen industry for each of the eight different topic areas in the list. Each group should then decide which would be the most fruitful to pursue, and make a presentation to the whole class of your topics. In their presentations, students should identify: a specific *object of analysis*, an appropriate *research method* and a *theoretical paradigm* they would apply to that topic.

Follow-up activity: Write a single-page research proposal on an area of researching media or cultural industries.

# TAKING IT FURTHER ... BEYOND THE CLASSROOM

*Making the most of local resources*

Identify what resources are available locally in relation to the media and cultural industries. As a class you could identify as many different resources as you can in your area. These might include a local history archive, a newspaper collection at a local library, or an art collection held by your university. Make a presentation to the class about the different local resources and the opportunities they offer to the media and cultural scholar. After selecting the most promising, make arrangements to take the class to visit and, if possible, arrange a talk by an archivist or curator.

Follow-up activity: Write a research proposal on an original topic based on the location you have visited.

# 5 RESEARCHING TEXTS: APPROACHES TO ANALYSING MEDIA AND CULTURAL CONTENT

## Aims and Objectives

- In this chapter we demonstrate how media and cultural texts have been investigated by previous scholars.

- We offer some guidance on conducting your own research into methods of textual analysis. In the first part of this chapter we focus on the following three research methods:

  - semiotic analysis

  - content analysis

  - discourse analysis.

- We then consider a set of research approaches which all address the content of the media according to 'type'. These are:

  - genre study

  - auteur analysis

  - star study.

- Some guidance is offered on further reading.

- Finally, this chapter provides some follow-up activities for you to do on your own or in class.

## INTRODUCTION

The previous chapter considered some of the ways we can research the media and cultural industries. Now we turn our attention to the products of those industries; the artifacts and events which they produce. The analysis of media content is one of the most productive areas of research in our field, and work focusing on the films, television programmes, music, advertisements and so on constitute the lion's share of research in media and cultural studies. Concern with the media as a set of texts engages us with key debates which relate back to ancient times, taking us to the territory of *aesthetics* – the study of the beautiful. It leads us to ask – what makes a terrific movie? How do photographs work? What is the power of a great painting? The study of media texts necessitates an engagement with issues of *representation*. We consider what obligations media and cultural workers have to produce texts which reflect society fairly. We might ask questions such as 'Are disabled people depicted fairly in the media?' and 'How do the media cover student riots and unrest?' Do these things matter? Why/not? We may think, too, about the extent to which the media may be living up to their role as the guardians of a healthy 'public sphere' – we might consider how newspapers fulfil their role as the 'Fourth Estate' or the extent to which we can identify the operation of the public sphere in today's media landscape.

Analysing texts can allow you to investigate a wide range of hypotheses about the nature of media and cultural artifacts. The methods discussed in this chapter can be used to draw out latent themes within texts and make connections between them. If we want to find out about the production of texts it is necessary to use the methods discussed in Chapter 4 (exploring ways of studying the culture industries). If you want to find out about how texts are received and understood by their audiences, you will find more guidance in the following chapter, Chapter 6, which examines the research of media and cultural audiences.

## HOW TO RESEARCH MEDIA AND CULTURAL CONTENT

Some of the richest methods of analysis are discussed in this chapter, including some of the foundational approaches of our field of study. In this chapter we are going to focus on some of the most well-used methods which are available to students. Some are probably familiar to you from your previous studies, such as semiotics – one of the fundamental analytical tools available in media studies. Figure 5.1 below, some methods for researching media and cultural texts, shows the methods we will discuss, their typical object of analysis and the case studies we will be presenting.

*Semiotics* involves the close analysis of texts for detailed analysis of meanings and was popularized in cultural studies by Roland Barthes (see for example, Barthes, 1967; 1973; 1981; 1984; 1987; 1990). It is to Roland Barthes that we turn for a classic case study: his famous essay, 'The Rhetoric of the Image' (1984) which explores how meaning gets into an image; while the

**FIGURE 5.1** Some methods for researching media and cultural texts discussed in this chapter

| Method | Object of Analysis | Case Studies |
|---|---|---|
| **Semiotics** | The implications and meaning of a text or set of texts; the *ideological* content of a media message; how media messages relate to cultural myths. | Roland Barthes, 1984. Rhetoric of the image. In *Image, Music, Text.* Translated by Stephen Heath. London: Fontana, pp. 32–51.<br><br>Richard K. Popp and Andrew L. Mendelson, 2010. 'X'-ing out enemies: *Time* magazine, visual discourse, and the war in Iraq. *Journalism,* 11(2): 203–21.<br><br>Marcia A. Morgado, 2007. The semiotics of extraordinary dress: a structural analysis and interpretation of hip-hop style. *Clothing and Textiles Research Journal,* 25(2): 131–55. |
| **Content Analysis** | *How much* of something occurs in a set of texts; quantities of media phenomena such as the amount of coverage devoted to a particular news story or the number of television programmes of a particular genre. | The Glasgow University Media Group, 1976. *Bad News.* London: Routledge and Kegan Paul.<br><br>Jeffery P. Dennis, 2009. Gazing at the black teen: con artists, cyborgs and sycophants. *Media, Culture and Society,* 31(2): 179–95.<br><br>James Curran, 2000. Literary editors, social networks and cultural tradition. In James Curran (ed.), *Media Organizations in Society.* London: Arnold, pp. 215–39. |
| **Discourse Analysis** | *Discourses* or modes of talk contained in media texts; the analysis of the ideology or belief systems inherent in the text. | Kari Andén-Papadopoulos, 2009. Body horror on the internet: US soldiers recording the war in Iraq and Afghanistan. *Media, Culture and Society,* 31(6): 921–38.<br><br>H. Samy Alim, Jooyoung Lee and Lauren Mason Carris, 2011. Moving the crowd, 'crowding' the emcee: the coproduction and contestation of black normativity in freestyle rap battles. *Discourse and Society,* 22(4): 422–39. |
| **Genre Study** | A group of texts of the same kind or genre, for example, documentary, game show, reality television. | Jane Feuer, 1982. *The Hollywood Musical.* London: Macmillan/British Film Institute.<br><br>Jessica Ringrose and Valerie Walkerdine, 2008. Regulating the abject: the TV make-over as site of neo-liberal reinvention toward bourgeois femininity. *Feminist Media Studies,* 8(3): 227–46. |
| **Auteur Study** | A group of texts by the same 'author' or creator. | Thomas Elsaesser, 2011. James Cameron's *Avatar:* access for all. *New Review of Film and Television Studies,* 9(3): 247–64. |
| **Star Study** | The study of a star persona which may be advanced through texts in which that star features or in 'extra-textual' discourses such as fan websites, television chat shows or review magazines. | Richard Dyer, 1987. *Heavenly Bodies.* London: British Film Institute. |

image of a single magazine cover is the subject of our more recent case study by Richard K. Popp and Andrew L. Mendelson. Popp and Mendelson examine the meaning of the single letter 'X' when written in blood over a photograph on the cover of *Time* (Popp and Mendelson, 2010). Semiotics can also be applied to the fashion system (see, for example, Barthes, 1990) and an article in the *Clothing and Textiles Research Journal*, by Marcia A. Morgado investigates the semiotics of 'hip-hop' style (2007).

*Content analysis* is an excellent method for measuring representations in the media, and our 'classic' case study dates from the 1970s; it is a key work in studies of the news – *Bad News* by the Glasgow University Media Group (1976). This study uses the quantitative method of content analysis to identify and challenge the institutional bias in television news coverage in the UK. *Bad News* was the first in a series of publications by the Glasgow University Media Group (for example 1980; 1982; and Philo, 1996; 1999). Our next study also counts representations on television: Jeffrey Dennis conducts a content analysis of black characters on children's television programmes (Dennis, 2009); while our third case study looks at the content of the book reviews in the British press (Curran, 2000b).

*Discourse analysis* is a method which analyses particular kinds of *talk* or *discourse*. Our first case study in this section looks at the discourses included in, and surrounding, images of extreme violence posted on the internet by US soldiers serving in Iraq. Kari Andén-Papadopoulos' study of 2009 shows how the various discourses involved in these violent images may serve diverse functions (Andén-Papadopoulos, 2009). Our second case study in discourse analysis takes as its object of analysis the 'rap battles' which occur in a Los Angeles hip-hop community; this research by H. Samy Alim, Jooyoung Lee and Lauren Mason Corris (2011) shows how oral culture is still an important part of the social, cultural and musical lives of young Americans. Their research examines discourses relating to race, identity and black normativity in the linguistic stand-offs between an African American and a Latino emcee.

A large section of research into media and cultural texts revolves around categorizing texts as belonging to particular 'types'. I refer to these methods as *typological* because of this quality of classifying content according to specific types, be it 'genre', 'auteur' or 'star'. This is a form of research involved in exploring how meaning is produced, received and interpreted in texts. In this section we present four case studies: Jane Feuer's 1982 classic genre study *The Hollywood Musical*; Jessica Ringrose and Valerie Walkerdine's study of the television genre, the makeover show (2008); Thomas Elsaesser's study of the film *Avatar* as the product of the film director and 'auteur', James Cameron (Elsaesser, 2011); and another classic of film studies, Richard Dyer's *Heavenly Bodies*, in particular his chapter on Paul Robeson (Dyer, 1987). In the following sections we discuss each of these research methods in turn, offering case studies, examples and further guidance for conducting your own research.

# SEMIOTIC ANALYSIS

Semiotics is one of the main methods used by students of media and cultural studies in their dissertations. It provides a very fruitful way of analysing media texts and cultural content and has been used to study everything from photography to fashion. The field of semiotics can trace its origins further back to the Swiss linguist Ferdinand de Saussure (1857–1913) and to the American philosopher Charles Sanders Peirce (1839–1914) (Peirce, 1958). It was Saussure who first proposed that many of the ways in which language is used could be applied to other forms of culture in his 'Course in General Linguistics' which he delivered between 1906 and 1911 at the University of Geneva. A version of the course was reconstructed by Saussure's students from their lecture notes and was posthumously published in 1916 by the Parisian publisher, Payot. This was later revised and it is the 1972 Payot edition which forms the basis of the most common translation in English by Roy Harris (Saussure, 1983). Saussure's work shifted the theoretical paradigm for the study of language to embrace a new field of linguistic analysis – semiotics – also sometimes known as 'semiology', meaning 'the science of signs'. Most scholars in the nineteenth century had focused on the *history* of languages and *aetiology* – seeking the origins of words. Saussure argued that the history of language was less important to what words mean than the way words related to one another as part of a *structure*. The mode of research he proposed, examining elements (words) in a system (language) through their relationship to one another is often referred to as *structuralism*. Saussure held that the relationship between a word and its meaning was *arbitrary*. Saussure argued that words were 'signifiers' referring to concepts but having no ontological relationship to the 'signified'. The connection between the signifier and the signified was the product of *convention* and the structure of the language. Meaning came, Saussure argued, not from the origin or source of the word, but from its *relationship* to other words – from its place in a linguistic structure. In the *Course in General Linguistics* (1983) Saussure proposed the application of a scientific, as opposed to a historical, study of language which he calls 'semiology'. Saussure believed that there were several different 'sign systems', of which language was 'simply the most important' (Saussure, 1983: 15). He therefore proposed that:

> It is ... possible to conceive of a science *which studies the role of signs as part of social life*. ... We shall call it *semiology* ... It would investigate the nature of signs and the laws governing them. Since it does not yet exist, one cannot say for certain that it will exist. (Saussure, 1983: 15)

Perhaps the person who has done most to ensure that semiology does exist is Roland Barthes who applied many of the ideas of semiotics to the study of a wide range of other areas of culture (Barthes, 1967; 1973; 1981; 1984; 1987; 1990). Roland Barthes writes in his introduction to *Mythologies*:

> I had just read Saussure and as a result acquired the conviction that by treating 'collective representations' as sign systems, one might hope to go further than the pious task of unmasking them and account *in detail* for the mystification which transforms petit-bourgeois culture into a universal nature. (Barthes, 1973: 9)

For Barthes, and other semioticians who followed, a primary goal is to reveal the ideology of 'petit-bourgeois culture'. Umberto Eco, the Italian philosopher and writer, also built on Saussure's work, popularizing semiotics in the 1970s and 1980s primarily through his work, in *A Theory of Semiotics* (Eco, 1978), *The Role of the Reader: Explorations in the Semiotics of Texts* (1984) and *Semiotics and the Philosophy of Language* (1986). It was in large part the translation of work by Barthes and Eco into English which popularized the ideas of Saussure in British and North American academia in the 1970s and 1980s and which put semiotics and structuralism at the heart of media, cultural and communications studies.

The study of linguistics, and in particular etymology and meaning, goes to the heart of thinking about how we know anything, as we saw in Chapter 1. Semiotics unravels the processes by which texts and images are ideologically loaded. It is an interpretive method we can use to unpack the processes by which ideology is in operation in our media and culture. Judith Williamson's book *Decoding Advertisements* is a study of the semiotics of advertising in women's magazines which also applies theories of psychoanalysis, ideology and feminism (Williamson, 1978). Williamson is particularly indebted to the work of the French psychoanalyst Jacques Lacan and his discussion of 'the mirror phase' – that is, the moment in child development when the infant becomes aware of itself when looking in the mirror. Prior to this stage, children have no sense of their selves as separate from their mothers, or indeed the rest of the world. During the mirror phase the child recognizes a self which is both *itself* and yet *different*. The infant fantasizes about the 'imaginary other' as being more able, more powerful than herself. Lacan believed that we return to this state of the *imaginary* when we are at the cinema – in the dark, alone with our thoughts (Lacan, 1968). We enter the imaginary when we identify with the characters on screen and we are that person riding that horse, making love with that guy, singing that song ... In her analysis of advertisements, Williamson argues that a similar process takes place in advertisements – we are presented with a perfect 'other'. Advertisements are part of an ideological apparatus in which an 'imaginary' self is being sold to us; we are being given a subject position of a particular kind through our reading of the advertisement. In this way the 'signs' in the advertisement – the pictures and words which we can recognize from the real world – construct an ideological message which we imagine to have been our own original thought.

One of the central preoccupations of Roland Barthes is '*How does meaning get into the image?*' (Barthes, 1984: 32). And that is the key to semiotics: it is about how the producer of an image uses the existing structure of meaning to ensure that the product means something, and how we, as readers, extract the meaning. Semiotics breaks down the content of texts into their component parts and relates them to broader discourses. A semiotic analysis provides a way of relating specific texts to the system of messages in which they operate. It provides the intellectual context to the content: it addresses the ways in which the various elements of the text work together and interact with our cultural knowledge to generate meaning. Semiotics is about revealing the processes by which ideology is normalized and made to seem universal. Because it is an interpretive method, semiotics is not reliable in the traditional social science sense – another analyst who studied the same texts may well elicit a different meaning! But this does not devalue semiotics, because it is about enriching our understanding of the texts. Semiotic analysis is usually applied to images or visual texts (Berger, 1998a; Bignell, 2002; Rose, 2007). This method involves analysing the smallest units of meaning – '*semes*' – and relating them to the ideological structure which organizes meaning. Semiotics has been applied to the study of photography (Ramamurthy, 1997), advertising (Williamson, 1978), shopping (Miller, 1998), wrestling (Barthes, 1973) and fashion (Barthes, 1990; Garber, 1992).

## Case Study

**Roland Barthes, 1984. Rhetoric of the image. In *Image, Music, Text*. Translated by Stephen Heath. London: Fontana, pp. 32–51.**

This key text in the history of semiotics is one which anyone interested in analysing visual images, especially advertisements, should study in detail. Barthes' short essay applies the theory of semiotic analysis, developed by Saussure for the study of language, to the study of images. Barthes chooses to analyse an advertisement because of the purposeful, deliberate nature of the messages advertisements contain – they are always 'motivated' in that they have a purpose – to sell you something! As he says:

> If the image contains signs, we can be sure that in advertising these signs are full, formed with a view to the optimum reading: the advertising image is *frank* or at least emphatic. (p. 33)

The advertisement discussed in this essay is from a French magazine for a brand of Italian foods (pasta, sauce and cheeses) trading as 'Panzani'.

Barthes pulls apart the various meanings of the advertisement looking first at the literal meaning, or *denotation*, and second at the *connotations*. At the denotational level, the advertisement shows a string shopping basket with packets of Panzani pasta, sauce and Parmesan cheese as well as fresh produce (tomatoes, green peppers, onions and mushrooms). The denotation is of groceries displayed in a still life composition. The image *suggests* much more, though, and it is the *connotational* level which interests Barthes. For him, the advertisement connotes 'Italianicity'– the pasta and produce to make a sauce, and the red, yellow and green of the produce reiterating the idea of *Italy* through reference to the colours of the Italian national flag. The relationship of *language* of the visual codes in relation to the images is important, and Barthes examines the relationship between the linguistic codes – the words written in the copy and on the produce – and the images. The connotation of 'Italianicity' is reinforced by the Italian-sounding name of the company, Panzani.

For Barthes, images are *polysemic* – they have multiple meanings and are open to diverse interpretations. But Barthes also maintains that images are rarely presented to us without words of some kind accompanying them and that this accompanying linguistic code serves to limit the potential meanings of the text. Barthes shows that the language used – the words narrow the potential meanings of the image.

This essay demonstrates the relationship between the *denotative* and *connotative* codes of analysis; between what is *displayed* and what is *implied*. It shows how semiotics can be used to unpack the meanings which underpin the power of the image; how analysis of the cultural codes which are being triggered by the image can explain how the meaning gets into the content of the media.

I would recommend anyone interested in finding out about the range of work which can be done with semiotics to dip into Barthes' *Mythologies* (1973) as a starting-off point. Here you will find essays on 'The Face of Garbo', 'Striptease', 'Toys' and 'The World of Wrestling' among many others, each one a short study in the practice of semiotic analysis. One scholar who has applied Barthes' insights to contemporary cultural artifacts with tremendous grace and style is Dick Hebdige – see, in particular, his essays 'Object as Image: The Italian Scooter Cycle' and 'The Bottom Line on Planet One: Squaring up to The Face' (both in Hebdige, 1988).

The application of semiotics as a method relies on the consideration of a number of binaries. In the discussion of Barthes' essay in the case study above, we can note the importance of the paired concepts of denotation and connotation. In any semiotic analysis it is necessary first of all to identify the signs being presented at a *denotational* level. In other words, one should begin by *describing* what any given text *shows*, *demonstrates* or *depicts* – including consideration of any text, figures, images and so on. Once this has been established the analytical work of determining what these signs *connote* can begin. The analysis of the connotative value relies on your cultural knowledge, for example, that colours in the Panzani advertisement suggest the Italian flag. Barthes shows how the connotations are the product of a *myth* or ideology of Italianness circulating in French society. It is only by first of all isolating the *denotational* that we can locate the operation of the myth in the signification of media content. This is where the meaning is most important – in the ideology beneath/behind the sign, deeply embedded in the mythological underbelly of which the sign is a mere carapace.

Key to any semiotic analysis is an identification of the process by which the sign stands in for something else; the semiotician must unveil the processes by which one thing means another and to persuade the reader of the veracity of the interpretation. In our next case study, the ideological work at play in the use of just one symbol – the letter 'X' – in the cover art of one issue of *Time* magazine brings a fascinating insight into the realm of the unspeakable, the unsayable and the unsignifiable.

## Case Study

**Richard K. Popp and Andrew L. Mendelson, 2010. 'X'-ing out enemies: *Time* magazine, visual discourse, and the war in Iraq. *Journalism*, 11(2): 203–21.**

This research article from the academic journal *Journalism* takes as its starting point the death of Abu Musab al-Zarqawi, reportedly head of Al Qaeda in Iraq, following a US air strike on 7 June 2006. Popp and Mendelson want to find the latent meanings behind the image of al-Zarqawi which later graced the cover of *Time* magazine showing a full-page photo of al-Zarqawi's head with a large red 'X' overlaid; the 'X' is uneven, as if roughly painted and dripping in blood. Popp and Mendelson want to know: how does this image work?

> The purpose of this article is to examine the discursive frames staked out by *Time*'s 21 June 2006 al-Zarqawi coverage and thus trace the development of a visual trope and examine the way the magazine has deployed it. (p. 204)

Popp and Mendelson show how the image draws on a series of cultural codes, including the collective memory of the society, and the institutional history of *Time* to create a complex meaning and to 'advance neo-imperialistic interpretations of the war' (p. 204). They conduct a historical analysis of the way the same blood-red 'X' has been used in other issues of *Time*, and a comparative analysis of the way the same subject (the death of al-Zarqawi) was covered in *Time*'s rival publication, *Newsweek*.

Popp and Mendelson research the other occasions on which the 'X' has been used on the cover of *Time* and are thus able to identify what messages the 'X' brings from the history of the magazine. They find that this powerful sign was first used over a photo of Adolf Hitler in 1945, after the fall of Berlin. The 'X' was not used again until 1988 to illustrate a story on medical advances against cancer, and was later used in relation to Slobodan Milosevic in 1999 and Saddam Hussein in 2003. Protests were made to *Time* against the 'visual equivalence' of Hitler and these two latter-day tyrants. When used in relation to al-Zarqawi, Popp and Mendelson argue that the editors of *Time* were drawing on the history of their magazine and the memory of their readers to create a connotation which could not be verbalized. Popp and Mendelson claim that: 'Pictures are able to make a rhetorical statement that might be unacceptable to utter verbally' (p. 205). By drawing on imagery used in relation to Hitler, they linked the current war in Iraq with World War II. The 'X' is used as a representation of unspeakable evil, and Popp and Mendelson show how this fits in with a particular discourse of the war being advanced by military and government officials with a clearly identifiable, personalized enemy. It seems that the sign of the 'X' over the photo of al-Zarqawi is redolent of many meanings; not least that there are clear cut distinctions between 'good' and 'evil' in the very complicated war in Iraq, and that al-Zarqawi is undeniably 'evil' and the US, consequently, 'good' – the image makes the war a 'just' cause.

The semiotic analysis undertaken to investigate the meaning of the single magazine cover above necessarily involves the researcher in locating that sign within a specific discourse. Semiotic analysis is not finished until it relates its analysis back to the cultural codes and connotations which are being referenced by the sign. The work is to consider how the codes contribute to the creation of particular ideologies – in this case a militaristic one which is legitimizing a 'war on terror' through articulating codes previously used to describe a war against fascism and totalitarianism in 1939–45.

While the case study above, by Popp and Mendelson, explores in detail the meaning of a single sign, our next case study looks more broadly at the operation of a particular system of signs working in a specific style of dress. Marcia A. Morgado's essay owes much to the work of Dick Hebdige's book *Subcultures: The Meaning of Style*, an important landmark in the history of semiotics and a great contribution to our understanding of the relationship between dress and subculture (Hebdige, 1979). Marcia Morgado's essay is not in a media or cultural studies journal, but in a journal aimed at people in the clothing and textiles industry – including academics. She does not assume any knowledge of semiotics, which makes the essay a readable introduction as she offers a neat description of semiotics as a method and includes a useful 'guide to concepts'. Morgado's work also relates well to our field of study as it has clear links with the work of Roland Barthes (particularly his book *The Fashion System*, 1990).

## Case Study

**Marcia A. Morgado, 2007. The semiotics of extraordinary dress: a structural analysis and interpretation of hip-hop style. *Clothing and Textiles Research Journal*, 25(2): 131–55.**

> The outrageous characteristics of hip-hop style, its simultaneous appearance as high fashion, antifashion, and mass fashion, the controversy it engendered, and its apparent semiotic richness led me to design a study through which to make 'sense' of the dress form. (p. 147)

Fashion, by its nature, is in constant shift and Morgado locates her study clearly in the late 1980s and early 1990s when 'gangsta rap' and hip-hop was at its peak. As a lecturer in fashion, Morgado found hip-hop style interesting and fun, but was surprised to find that others did not appreciate it in the same way and were even outraged by the style. She set out to 'identify the structural features that supported hip-hop style as a semiotic system … and interpret those features so as to make sense of the contradictory and incendiary nature of the style' (p. 134).

The sources she used to identify the elements of the fashion system included academic books and journal articles on hip-hop as well as personal observation and information garnered from her students on a fashion theory class in 1993 and 1994. From these sources she identified the 'pertinent signifiers' – those features which were consistently mentioned such as baggy and droopy trousers; clothes worn 'back-to-front' and 'excessive belt lengths'. These become her objects of analysis – the items on which she is going to direct her analytical attention.

Morgado describes the next stage, during which she began to unpack the paradigmatic structure:

> Paradigmatic structure was coaxed from the hip-hop semiotic system by considering signs in the hip-hop system in relation to features and expectations associated with conventional dress. An initial binary opposition designated conventional–unconventional was established to facilitate the analysis. (p. 141)

From this comparison she is able to identify particular kinds of opposition, for example, that in hip-hop culture 'undergarments' are visible. This is contrary to the conventional dress code which determines that 'underwear is private; it is not for public display' (p. 141). This 'suggests that the paradigmatic structure includes invisible–visible, inside–outside, and private–public'. Some of the signs do not fit into the fashion system at all:

> Alarm clocks are not items of dress in the conventional system. These are household furnishings. Category boundaries are transgressed when clocks are worn as decorations, and the practice makes the wearer look foolish. In terms of paradigmatic analysis, the clocks suggest the opposition jewelry–home furnishings and sense–nonsense. (p. 141)

The opposition to conventional dress becomes a dominant theme in the semiotic analysis of the hip-hop style and in Table 3 of the article she presents a list of some of the rules of conventional dress which hip-hop style violates.

She argues that hip-hop is a form of 'extraordinary dress' which is intended to provoke intrigue and interest. This new term, 'extraordinary dress' is such that: 'the novelty of the form invites observers to question it, to propose its meaning, or to otherwise attempt to understand it' (p. 148). Semiotic analysis here allows for a rich, detailed analysis of just why hip-hop fashion is so 'extraordinary'.

Fashion is one of those sign systems in which we all engage everyday when we get dressed. So much so that nudity is more of a statement than wearing clothes. Marcia Mordago argues that 'the rules of ordinary dress are naturalized to the extent that they are largely invisible while simultaneously being perfectly obvious' (2007: 149).

Semiotics has been used to study a range of visual material, some of which are discussed in Theo van Leeuwen and Carey Jewitt's *Handbook of Visual Analysis* (2001) and also in Gillian Rose's book *Visual Methodologies* (2007). Rose discusses the application of semiotics to the study of visual images of 'others' – non-Western people (Rose, 2007). Rose summarizes the work of Catherine Lutz and Jane Collins who took as their object of analysis nearly 600 photographs of non-Western people featured in *National Geographic* magazine between 1950 and 1986 (Lutz and Collins, 1993; 2002). They showed how the 'other' was constructed in these images and are able to demonstrate that *National Geographic Magazine* has a consistent view of non-Western people wherever they are from. This shows the Western-centred nature of the magazine which reduces difference between people even as it seems to be celebrating global diversity.

## Stages in a semiotic analysis

There are no rules about which precise texts one should focus on or how many texts are necessary. In the case studies above, Popp and Mendelson looked at just one cover of one magazine, focusing on the meaning of a single symbol, the 'X', while Marcia Morgado looks at a whole school of fashion, the 'hip-hop' style and its meanings and implications.

*Define your object of analysis.* The first thing to do, then, is to define your object of analysis. This might be something which strikes you as very important and misunderstood or something which is intriguing. Think about why it is interesting or intriguing. Ideally there should be some puzzle or problem you feel driven to explain. Consider how this relates to the different theoretical paradigms for thinking about media and culture.

*Gather the texts.* Whether your object of analysis is magazines, television programmes or films, gather together all the texts you are going to study before you begin your analysis. The exact number depends on the depth and breadth of your research and the importance of the semiotic analysis for the rest of your project. (Is semiotics the only method you are going to use, or are you using it as one among a few methods?) You need to immerse yourself in the subject and give yourself time to think about how the chosen text signifies.

*The analysis.* When you conduct a semiotic analysis you are interested in drawing out the cultural assumptions at play and the processes by which not just meaning, but ideological intent, has got into the text. Identify the denotation/connotation pairing: What is denoted or *shown*? What is implied or *suggested*? How do the signs operate to make us form this connection? What cultural codes are being orchestrated? What knowledge is 'taken for granted' and what 'goes without saying? What value judgements are being made, hiding as assumptions?

*What is it explicitly saying?* The first stage of your analysis is to describe the content of the texts or images very carefully. Carefully identify all of the elements or semes which comprise the *denotational*. What is the setting? Is it urban or exotic? Domestic interior or wild countryside? How many models are there? Describe their pose. Separate out the linguistic message (the words) from the visual imagery and describe each as precisely as possible. You need to identify exactly what is included: discuss the text and its relationship to image; is colour used? How? Try to stick to description of the *literal* image and text, or what is *denoted* by the images.

*What is it implying? Or what does it* really *mean?* The next stage allows you to begin to discuss the meanings and implications of each separate sign individually and then collectively. Here you are considering the connotations of the texts. What is the relationship between the linguistic signs and the images? How do the two codes of signification work in relation to one another? Does reading the words give you a different interpretation of the images than just looking at the images alone, or are the words reinforcing the images?

*How is it utilizing what I already know?* What kinds of *cultural knowledge* do you need to understand the text? How are the images drawing on our cultural knowledge to help us to create particular kinds of meaning? Are the cultural codes those one would expect?

*What ideological positions is it reinforcing/assuming?* What can you say about what the texts or artifacts you have studied *mean*? To paraphrase Barthes: *what has meaning got into the text?* Moreover, what is the ideological position being advanced by the articulation of some (and not other) codes?

*Relate to theory.* What theoretical approaches have you had to draw on to conduct your analysis? For example, you might look at the representation of the riots in London in August 2011 and consider how ideologies of race, class and gender intersect. How can you draw out hypotheses about your findings? What other codes and conventions do they draw on that we had not anticipated before we began?

There are good descriptions of semiotic analysis in the work of Asa Berger (1998b); Jonathan Bignell (2002); and Marcel Danesi (2002). Semiotics is a deconstructive method frequently used to challenge mainstream ideas, mores and values. Barthes' work, removed from us in time, may appear to have lost some of its political edge to us now, though the work of Popp and Mendelson, addressing a more recent topic, more clearly demonstrates a counter-hegemonic role. Semiotics is often used for counter-cultural agitation, for example in the work of Canadian group Adbusters. The public understanding of semiotics is seen in the work of artists such as Banksy who toy with the accepted ideological meanings of images and meanings in their work.

## CONTENT ANALYSIS

Semiotics can be combined to good effect with the next method we are going to explore. Content analysis is one of the most direct methods of textual analysis which can be applied to a range of media and cultural artifacts. This approach involves counting phenomena in texts (Berger, 1998a; Deacon, Pickering, Golding and Murdock, 2007b; Krippendorff, 1980; Rosengren, 1981; Weber, 1985). Because it involves counting and adding phenomena, content analysis is often referred to as a '*quantitative*' research method. However, in making decisions about *what* to count and how to classify our material, content analysis relies very much on interpretive judgements and is equally '*qualitative*'. We need to decide what it is we are going to count, and how to decide what is included in our study and how to create categories for these. It is because of this 'qualitative' aspect that content analysis is considered by one of its leading exponents, Klaus Krippendorff (1980), to be primarily a *symbolic* method: it is used to investigate symbolic material (media texts). Within media studies, content analysis has been used to study media texts – newspaper stories, television coverage of specific issues, film content and more besides. The method has also been used in social science research, primarily to investigate 'qualitative' data such as open-ended surveys. Content analysis, then, is a method of analysing textual material and summing the occurrences of specific phenomena such as specific words or images.

The Payne Fund Studies, in the 1930s, used content analysis to research the representation of 'violence' and 'romance' in the cinema, as we saw in Chapter 2. In the 1970s it was widely used to investigate representations of violence and to support arguments that there was 'too much' violence on television (Barker and Petley, 2001). The reporting of violence on television in the Surgeon General's Report of 1972 used content analysis of television programmes to demonstrate dangerous and corrupting levels of violence on television, while the 'Cultural Indicators Project', established by George Gerbner looked at the effects of violence on television, and was predicated on content analysis purporting to prove there was an excessive amount of violent content on television. It has been used by critical and 'administrative' scholars to equally good effect. For example, Theodor W. Adorno, one of the Frankfurt-school scholars discussed in Chapter 2, employed content analysis to study the 'philosophy of irrationality' in the advice given in the astrology column of the *Los Angeles Times* (Adorno, 1994).

In the UK the most famous proponents of content analysis are those at the Glasgow University Media Unit Group (www.glasgowmediagroup.org). This group was a pioneer in the analysis of news with their classic work, *Bad News* (Glasgow University Media Group, 1976). The Glasgow University Media Group comprises a group of British scholars who have been most consistently engaged in the analysis of media content, although the range of methods used extends far beyond content analysis (Eldridge, 1993; Glasgow University Media Group, 1980; 1982; Philo, 1996; 1999).

Our next case study looks at the first major study to be published by the Glasgow University Media Group, *Bad News* (1976) – a study of television news content.

# Case Study

**The Glasgow University Media Group, 1976. *Bad News*. London: Routledge and Kegan Paul.**

The Glasgow University Media Group's *Bad News* applies content analysis to television news coverage of industrial relations in the 1970s. It was one of the first to apply empirical methods to the study of the media content. The research team were using the most sophisticated research technologies available at the time, including the video cassette recorder (only domestically available a couple of years earlier) and the recently launched software system SPSS (this was in the days of mainframe computing and punch cards). Originally scheduled to gather data over one year, the study was cut to six months because the researchers underestimated the amount of material they would collect and the amount of time it would take to conduct the analysis.

The Glasgow University Media Group looked at the differences in media coverage of management and labour representatives in the reporting of industrial relations. The researchers categorized hundreds of hours of television, using story categories such as 'economics', 'city' and 'human interest'. The work was very labour-intensive, time-consuming and demanding of resources. During the 1970s, computers were still in their infancy and were considerably more cumbersome than now, so data had to be entered by hand, using punch cards. In addition to the content analysis, the team also interviewed some television news workers and carried out participant observation in newsrooms.

The project was particularly focused on the coverage of industrial action at a time when there were many strikes in Britain. In order to get a picture of the 'contours of coverage', the team categorized industrial news coverage for the period January to May 1975 according to various industrial sectors (for example, aerospace, textiles or mining). Using industrial data, they collated the number of strikes occurring in each of the industrial sectors and compared these figures with the number of stoppages reported in the news. They found that there was 'no consistent relationship' between the number of official recorded stoppages and the number covered on the television news. This, the study concluded, was accounted for by what it claimed to be a concentration on 'unscheduled interruptions to production and consumption patterns' (p. 204).

The Glasgow University Media Group found strong evidence of ideological bias at the heart of television news. *Bad News* argues that television reportage lays the blame for industrial unrest with the workers; the researchers consider it to be harmful and socially divisive for the media to focus on the people taking action as the villains of the piece while treating management as authoritative sources removed from the causes of the action.

*Bad News* and the subsequent volumes *More Bad News* (1980) and *Really Bad News* (1982) are now considered foundational studies in the field, and any study of media content, especially if the primary concern is with news, should refer to these important texts. The Glasgow University Media Group continues to be involved in studying media content by a range of methods (Eldridge, 1993; Philo, 1996; 1999). There is much to be learned from the experience of the Glasgow University Media Group in terms of the method of content analysis, including its strengths and its dangers. The methods employed by the group have grown increasingly diverse and more sophisticated since the publication of *Bad News*, but this research remains a key text in the history of media studies and an essential piece of background reading for anyone interested in conducting content analysis.

Content analysis has been used to study radio, television, magazines, newspapers and music. Newspapers make good subjects for content analysis as they are often digitized and therefore searchable. This means it is easier to count phenomena, as long as they are coded accurately. David Deacon discusses the different kinds of analysis permitted by databases such as LexisNexis which include all news coverage (Deacon, 2007). The advantages and disadvantages of using these 'digital newspaper archives' are discussed by Deacon. Noah Arceneaux and Amy Schmitz Weiss (2010) looked at newspaper coverage of the social networking site *Twitter* from 2006 to 09. They identified their sample by using the search string: '*Twitter* and microblogging' on the LexisNexis database (p. 1268). In 2006–07, when *Twitter* was launched, there were only a handful of articles using these words; by 2008–09 there were hundreds – amounting to over 1,100 stories in the first three years of the launch. A sample of about 20% was taken for analysis, selected using 'purposeful sampling' (Lindlof and Taylor, 2002). Their analysis revealed that coverage of *Twitter* as a new medium did not differ significantly from coverage of previous new media forms such as the radio and the telegraph.

Television programming is the subject of content analysis in Eli Avraham and Anat First's study of the representation of the Arab population of Israel on television – 'Television news coverage of the Arab population in Israel during conflict' (Avraham and First, 2010). Content analysis enables you to conduct your primary research and come up with your own facts and figures to use as evidence in your argument. You may count the number of stories, the number of images or the occurrences of mentions of a particular subject, using categories which you define in advance. These categories should come out of your theoretical paradigm and be supported by reference to the themes of the relevant literature.

One use of content analysis is to provide evidence to argue for the under- or over-representation of particular phenomena. This has been the case for studies of how well different ethnic and social groups are represented in the media. Jeffery Dennis was concerned about the representation of black and

Latino characters on children's television and decided to follow it up in the case study we present next from *Media, Culture and Society*.

## Case Study

**Jeffery P. Dennis, 2009. Gazing at the black teen: con artists, cyborgs and sycophants. *Media, Culture and Society*, 31(2): 179–95.**

From his knowledge of children's television, Jeffery P. Dennis has a hunch that there is something different in the way black and white boys are depicted:

> White preteen and teenage boys save the world a dozen times a day; they win athletic trophies; their plans succeed; their romantic overtures receive enthusiastic responses. Black preteen and teenage boys conduct computer research, concoct schemes that go wrong and gaze at unrequited crushes. (p. 179)

Is this verifiable? Dennis uses content analysis to test his hypothesis that black and white children are represented differently by gathering some statistical evidence regarding the differences in the representation of children and adolescents of different ethnic groups on television.

The *object of analysis* for this study is the characters played by black youngsters on fictional programmes produced by the three major global children's channels: Disney Channel, Nickelodeon and Cartoon Network. Dennis identifies 26 programmes across these three channels which contain human characters and, after excluding those which do not contain any black juvenile characters, there are 12 shows remaining, including *That's So Raven, Just Jordan, Kim Possible* and *Ed, Edd n Eddie*. He sampled 112 half-hour episodes of these shows broadcast in the spring of 2007.

Content analysis requires the coding of variables according to criteria determined by the researcher. Dennis takes care to describe how he codes each character according to four *independent* variables: *race, character type* ('star', 'regular' or 'occasional'), *gender* and *age*. The *dependent* variables relate to the qualities which have been given to the characters by the television programme. Dennis identifies these as: *role, physique, sexual orientation* and *romantic prowess*. These latter are subject to coding by sub-categories so that under the category 'role' the characters are further defined as 'dangerous', 'attractive', 'harmless' and 'background/other'. One aspect of 'dangerous' is 'streetwise' and, while 33% of black female characters were coded as such, none – not

*(Continued)*

*(Continued)*

one – of the 20 boys could be categorized as 'streetwise'. Black male characters do not use street slang, even when white boys do, and this use of 'conventional English' helps to confirm the idea that the black juvenile characters are uniformly 'harmless' (p. 186).

Dennis cites the literature which shows that black men are usually seen as a threat and that the stereotype of the black man is of a strong athlete:

> The black male body is a particular source of racist disquiet; its strength and power threatens the 'naturalness' of white male conceptions of superiority, so it must be erased, or at least tamed and made docile through athletic competition. (p. 186)

But most of the black boys here are shown as 'Brains, nerds or tricksters' and only two (20%) are ever shown participating in sport. The black boys were not shown as muscular and 35% were coded as 'fat'. The effect of this may be to counter the stereotype of the adult black men as 'players', but it also serves to render black characters 'uniquely undesirable'.

Dennis maintains we should be concerned for the children who watch these television programmes, for he has demonstrated that:

> The target audience are seeing ... black male youth who are soft, passive and malleable, who are ineffectual, who are humorous sidekicks but never leaders; never powerful, never destined for futures as politicians or professors of economics; never beautiful, never objects of desire. Meanwhile white male youth are regularly displayed as active, agentive, as uniquely desirable, as uniquely qualified to save the world. (p. 192)

Dennis discovers that, in an effort to neutralize the perceived dangers of black youngsters, the programme makers have created a whole class of somewhat neutered characters. The producers shy away from having black male figures being sexually attractive in a heteronormative way, which leads to dramas which actually offer a wider range of sexual role models for the youth, including the possibility of homosexual relationships. Dennis would not have been able to make his case so convincingly without the numerical data to support his argument. The method has enabled him to identify some unexpected findings and to create a more nuanced interpretation of what is happening in youth television than would otherwise be the case. Dennis is able to make convincing and persuasive arguments about television programming and the representation of black youth as a consequence; arguments which may be generalizable to the way black youngsters are represented more widely in the media.

Content analysis is useful for looking at patterns of representation of any phenomenon, but has been used widely to measure representations of social groups within the media. For example, the lesbian and gay activist group Stonewall (www.stonewall.org.uk) used content analysis to examine how gay and lesbian people are represented, or not represented, on youth television in the UK (Stonewall, 2010). Meanwhile Philip Bell analyses the covers of the Australian women's magazine *Cleo* to discuss the strengths and limitations of content analysis (Bell, 2001). Dmitri Williams and colleagues investigated representations of gender, race and age in their content analysis of 150 video games from nine different platforms (Williams et al., 2009). Content analysis can also be used to very good effect in conjunction with other, more interpretive methods, such as semiotics (discussed earlier in this chapter) or interviews (considered in subsequent chapters). Peter Beharrell's analysis of how the British papers covered HIV and AIDS is illustrative of the way semiotics and content analysis can be combined to create a nuanced and sophisticated account of news coverage of a particular issue (Beharrell, 1993). This research combines content analysis of press coverage of HIV and AIDS with careful ideological analysis of the news. Beharrell charts the history of how much coverage of HIV/AIDS there has been in the press, measuring stories in column inches. Subsequently, he investigates the more nuanced changes in attitudes towards AIDS and HIV. This research unravels the different ideological positions of the press and investigates shifts in their various agendas. The following case study by James Curran, combines content analysis with interviews to investigate the work of the literary editors of the British broadsheets to identify the differences between what the editors claim they are doing and the actuality of their coverage.

## Case Study

**James Curran, 2000. Literary editors, social networks and cultural tradition. In James Curran (ed.), *Media Organizations in Society*. London: Arnold, pp. 215–39.**

A powerfully persuasive example of how content analysis can be combined with interviews is James Curran's insightful study of literary editors in the British press. Curran had a hunch that the reviews pages of the leading newspapers were favouring particular genres and authors and were therefore excluding other kinds of books. Literary editors are the 'key gatekeepers' in the publishing industry: the people who determine which books get reviewed, and by whom. Curran wanted to discern 'how the literary editors do their job and how their judgements reflect and influence the hierarchy of knowledge in our society' (p. 215).

*(Continued)*

*(Continued)*

For this study, 22 interviews were conducted in total: 11 in 1986 and another 11 in 1999. When editors were asked about the process of selection, Curran found that two alternative explanations were offered. On the one hand, the editors claimed that books 'select' themselves for coverage and that the editors are merely responding to the events in the publishing industry. On the other hand, they also claimed that the editors' decisions are determined quite instinctively.

The editors see their job as alerting the public to books that are important, yet when Curran analysed the range of books reviewed, he found that *science and technology* books were seriously under-represented. Less than 2% of the space was devoted to books in these categories. *Social science* and *politics* were also under-represented. Content analysis revealed that the most frequently reviewed books were in the categories of *biography*, *literary fiction*, *history* and *general humanities*. Curran presents detailed tables showing the distribution of book review space in national newspapers (p. 219) and in weekly magazines (p. 220). Curran argues that the bias he reveals is the product of the education and background of the editors themselves. He found that the vast majority of editors interviewed had degrees from Oxford or Cambridge universities, and that of these, virtually all had degrees in the arts or humanities, mostly in English or History. The editors choose to commission reviews of books of interest to them and select in the areas about which they are most knowledgeable. Although the editors would define science and technology books as important in interview, the content analysis revealed that they did not accord them importance in terms of space. Curran draws attention to contradictions between the claims made by these particular cultural workers about their work, and their actual output. As he says, 'Subjective impression, however informed, is not as reliable as systematic analysis based on careful measurement using social-science procedures' (p. 218).

Content analysis is a persuasive method which can generate reliable, replicable data. It is flexible, creative and relatively easy for a beginner researcher to undertake. It has been used more often by colleagues in the communications tradition and less so in media and cultural studies, with the very notable exception of the Glasgow Media Group. Conducting your own content analysis is very straightforward and requires only a basic level of mathematical skills. It is a very adaptable method, and most media and cultural texts are amenable to content analysis. The results can be readily presented in tables which are easily read, making it very accessible and comprehensible.

The disadvantages are that it can be insensitive; sometimes content analysis can be a bit of a blunt instrument. For example, in studies of violence on television, scholars have often simply counted acts of violence without distinguishing between acts of vengeance, justice or acts committed by a mythical beast against a farm animal. The method is only as sophisticated as the categories which the researcher defines – so researchers have to be very careful to base their coding scheme on theoretical criteria. Content analysis is often criticized for being too descriptive, and this is a weakness to which the beginner researcher is especially vulnerable: make sure that your hypothesis is well developed and that your categories operationalize it sufficiently to avoid this pitfall. Content analysis is sometimes criticized for lacking reliability; for instance, the way you categorize material does not cohere with how somebody else would do it. There are tests of 'inter-coder reliability' which researchers use to try to eliminate the coder's bias. The most typical method is to ask two researchers to code the same data and then to compare the results – this is too time-consuming and expensive for most students (see Krippendorff, 1980, for more detailed discussion). I would advise students to show their categories to their supervisor before they begin coding the material, and get their tutor's agreement on categories and definitions.

## Computer aided qualitative data analysis software (CAQDAS)

The main weakness of content analysis to date has been that it is very laborious: coding hundreds of column inches of newspapers or hours of television programmes can be very time-consuming. The counting, classifying and analysis of your texts is made considerably easier with the help of 'computer aided qualitative data analysis software', or 'CAQDAS', computer packages such as Atlas.ti (www.atlasti.com), NVivo (qsrinternational.com) and MaxQDA (www.maxqda). The various CAQDAS programs which are currently available can be of enormous benefit; find out if your university has a site licence for any of these, or get hold of a student copy. Most of these were developed for the analysis of qualitative data in the social sciences; media scholars have been slow to adopt the tools. But they are very powerful, allowing you to upload and analyse media in a variety of forms including text, video and photography. Two good examples of recent research using CAQDAS are Jen Birks' essay on newspaper campaigns published in *Discourse and Communication* (Birks, 2010) and Jaco van Sterkenburg and colleagues' examination of the representation of race in sports media (van Sterkenburg, Knoppers and De Leeuw, 2010). Another example of the use of computer-aided design in the analysis of media content is Valérie Gorin and Annik Dubied's study of the coverage of celebrities in the French media (Gorin and Dubied, 2011). Gorin and Dubied looked at a sample of 3,875 articles from 54 French-language newspapers and magazines, including tabloid and broadsheet, published between November 2005 and March 2006 (Gorin and Dubied, 2011). The analysis of such a large data set would have been impossible without the aid of a large army of graduate students or a CAQDAS tool.

## Stages in a content analysis

### Identify your chosen medium and form

The first decision to make regards your general area of interest. Are you going to look at a particular genre, a medium or a single text?

### Read widely

Look at previous work focused on the medium in which you are interested. You should try to find previous content analyses focused on your object of analysis to discover how previous researchers have addressed your topic. But don't be shocked if you cannot find anything exactly on your theme. Your literature review should include books and articles on the medium as a whole. For example, if you are studying the celebrity Gok Wan, you may find little on the man himself, but there are several books and articles about television make-over shows, about celebrity in general and about gender identity and popular culture, all of which could provide valuable sources of information and theoretical perspectives. You should also examine previous work using content analysis, whatever the medium, to find out more about how and why this method has been applied.

### Establish your hypothesis

Make sure you have a clear hypothesis for your content analysis: be sure that you know what you want to find out. Your hypothesis should emanate from your reading, so be sure that you know how it fits in with the published literature.

### Define your object of analysis

Isolate the material you are going to study and think about how your selection will help to test your hypothesis. State which texts you are going to study and why. You need to think about how many texts you are going to examine. It should be a large enough sample to be representative and yet small enough to be manageable. Six issues of a magazine will provide plenty of material to code, and three half-hour episodes of a television programme should be sufficient if you are conducting a detailed content analysis. If in any doubt, go ahead and conduct a provisional analysis on one text using your provisional categories and then decide, first, how many you have time to analyse and, second, how many it is necessary to analyse to convince the reader of your case. You should always confirm with your supervisor that you have set yourself about the right amount of work to do according to the criteria laid down by your institution, so check with your tutor before you proceed.

## Define your categories

Decide what categories of content you are going to be counting in your analysis and define them clearly. Ask yourself what you are going to be actually counting in your content analysis. If it is 'occurrences of black models in fashion magazines', decide how you are going to define 'black'. Sometimes you will need to rely on your own cultural knowledge to determine whether particular items fit a category. Defining your categories as carefully as possible in advance will help; for example, if you are looking at representations of old and young people in television advertisements, define what you mean by 'old' (e.g. 'looks over 55 to me') and 'young' (e.g. 'looks under 25 to me'). Also, decide what you are going to do when the inevitable happens and the text you are analysing contains a phenomenon that you do not know how to categorize. For example, how do you code the age of the Jolly Green Giant? You will need an 'other' category for most media and cultural texts, but in your test you should make sure that there aren't too many elements which fall outside your coding scheme.

## Create a coding sheet to record your findings

Designing the coding sheet will help you to think about the categories themselves; it is a useful exercise in making sure that you fully understand the texts you are studying. The coding sheet needs to be in the form of a grid with the objects of analysis on one axis and the categories you are coding them into on the other. Make sure that you have all the information you will need. Make sure the categories reflect the variables you are going to discuss. For example, if necessary, you could put 'black' and 'Asian' in the same category if you are interested only in whether models are white or not. However, if you want to make a comparison between the representation of Asian and Afro-Caribbean women, you will need to code them as a separate category. As a general rule, be as specific as you can in the early phases, and when you want to make conclusions, you can aggregate the groups. If you have coded all non-white models as 'black', you will not have the opportunity later to dis-aggregate them into 'Asian' and 'Afro-Caribbean'. You will need to create a coding sheet which you can use for each separate text.

## Test your coding categories

Try out your categories on a small sample to see if they work. You will save yourself a lot of time by testing your coding categories as early in the process as possible, and they may need to be revised in the light of what you find. If need be, don't be afraid to abandon your hypothesis and come up with a new one more suited to the actuality of the texts. You may find that you need to revise your hypothesis and/or your coding categories several times before you get them right. Keep a careful record of all these changes and ensure that you discuss them in your 'methods' section in the final essay – it is very important to show the reader how your ideas have developed.

## Collect your data

Once you have tested your categories and are confident that the coding sheet you have designed will get the information you need in order to answer your research question, you should go ahead and collect your data. Have a separate sheet for each of the texts you are analysing. Be very careful and methodical and make a note of any exceptions or particularly difficult decisions.

## Sum your findings

Add up how many occurrences of each category there are and convert these to percentages. Organize your findings in a table or pie chart so you can easily identify patterns in the data.

## Interpret your data and relate back to your research question

Now you can begin to make conclusions about whether or not your hypothesis is borne out by the data. Be honest with yourself. It is not a worse project if your hypothesis turns out not to be true: remember that the way you execute your study is more important than the conclusions you are able to draw at this stage. Perhaps you have proven your hypothesis unreservedly – if so, great. It is more likely that you will have not completely found what you were looking for – even better. You learn more (and so does the reader) when you reflect on how and why things did not go according to plan. Reflect on what you could have done otherwise and how you would have done things differently with the benefit of hindsight. Have you answered the question – partially or wholly?

## Present your findings

Whether your hypothesis is proven or not, you need to present your findings neatly, using appropriate tables and charts. Show how you conducted the content analysis by including discussion of how you carried out each of the above stages. Use published studies such as the case studies discussed in this chapter as models of how to present your own work.

## Discussion

Finish your study by discussing the strengths and weaknesses of content analysis as applied to this question. Consider how you might have conducted the study differently; would you have reached different conclusions? Show that you have learned from the experience.

Analysing media using content analysis is a fairly straightforward method which can produce some very sophisticated results. You need to have a well-articulated theoretical argument underpinning your work which will be evident in the way you create the coding categories you are going to use for your work. The coding has to be carefully conceptualized in order to produce reliable results and in order for you to be able to demonstrate the extent to which you have addressed your research question or hypothesis. It is a method which you could use as part of a broader discourse analysis or in conjunction with a semiotic analysis. The next method we are going to explore is discourse analysis, which is more obviously interpretive.

# DISCOURSE ANALYSIS

Thinking about texts as the product of particular kinds of *discourse* provides one of the leading forms of media textual analysis. Discourse analysis comprises a highly interpretive set of methods relying on your skills of rhetorical analysis to be successful. There are many different kinds of discourse analysis, ranging from conversational analysis (exploring syntax and semantics) to the analysis of visual discursive practices such as maps or photographs.

Within communication studies, 'discourse analysis' may refer to a set of analytical practices focusing on the study of interpersonal communication, mainly the spoken word. In this section we discuss the work of H. Samy Alim et al. (2011), which applies the tools of linguistic discourse analysis to 'rap battles' which are part of the street culture of Los Angeles. The verbal interactions between the principal interlocutors, and between them and the assembled audience, are carefully transcribed and analysed in this discourse analysis of a particularly lively performative form of linguistic communication.

Within cultural-studies paradigms, the idea of discourse analysis has somewhat different connotations, deriving as it does from the work of Michel Foucault. For Foucault discourse is very much entwined with power and with ideological hegemony. Foucault's work relies on the identification of power structures and ideological forces at work in everyday practice and communication. As Gillian Rose says, 'the notion of *discourse* is central to both Foucault's theoretical arguments and to his methodology' (Rose, 2001: 136). Discourse is the location of power and the means of the articulation of ideology. Discourse, again, according to Rose, 'refers to groups of statements which structure the way a thing is thought, and the way we act on the basis of that thinking' (2001: 136). Discourses help to structure social relations – for the media generates both subjects and subject positions – and we are addressed as having a particular subject position. Readers (or viewers) are positioned in relation to the text in a specific way; the text has power to position the reader – for example to speak or to be spoken to, to write or to read, to create or to consume.

We discussed discourse analysis briefly in Chapter 1 under the rubric of Aristotle's rules about rhetoric. At the end of Chapter 1 one of the follow-up activities required you to look at the news and identify the rhetorical devices of logos, pathos and ethos (see page 24). Discourse analysis is a form of rhetorical analysis and you could begin a discourse analysis by examining the different rhetorical tropes that Aristotle identified which roughly correspond to logic, empathy and credibility respectively. Aristotle was discussing how to construct an effective argument; how to be a persuasive communicator. The skills of creating a good argument lay in balancing these elements, and we can use these same categories as analytical tools to dissect the content of media messages.

We saw in the previous chapter how we can apply discourse analysis to the corporate messages of the culture industries. We looked at John Caldwell's work on the discursive practices of the film and television industry in Los Angeles (Caldwell, 2008; 2009). We also looked at the 'white wedding' industry so neatly analysed in Chrys Ingraham's book *White Weddings* (2008). Ingraham's work shows us how the wedding industry promotes discourses of 'heteronormativity' through multiple media forms associated with the wedding 'event'. In her study, Ingraham also analyses media texts which are about weddings, including situation comedies such as *Friends* and films like *Four Weddings and a Funeral*. Both of these case studies in Chapter 4 provide excellent examples of discourse analysis.

One of the main ways discourse analysis has been used in media studies is to investigate the construction of (dominant) ideologies through the news media (see for example, Bell, 1991; Bell and Garrett, 1998). News reportage is one of the most ideologically loaded elements of the media. It uses discursive tropes and story construction to render the messy reality of the world into interpretable form for us. In so doing, it is inevitable that ideological input is incorporated; and equally inevitable that this ideological input should be forcefully and regularly denied. Narratives are not just the product of 'fiction' – factual media also creating 'narratives' (Garrett and Bell, 1998; Nichols, 1991; van Dijk, 1988). The news is structured around 'stories' and story elements as much as any theatrical performance (Bell, 1991; Bell and Garrett, 1998). Narrative is a component of just about every media and cultural form to a greater or lesser extent. The drive to narrativize is present in human responses to the world – we can't help ourselves; we interpret the world through narrativization. Narrative also conveys the ideology of a culture, and it is one of the means by which values and ideals are reproduced culturally.

One element of discourse analysis is the identification of the mode of address: the position from which the discourse is being made and the assumed identity of the person or persons who are being addressed. The following case study explores the different modes of address and discursive construction of attitudes towards violence of soldiers in a war zone. Kari Andén-Papadopoulos' essay on 'body horror on the internet' analyses the violent images posted on the internet by US soldiers stationed in Iraq and Afghanistan on sites such as *NowThatsFuckedUp.com* and on *YouTube* and *MySpace*.

## Case Study

**Kari Andén-Papadopoulos, 2009. Body horror on the internet: US soldiers recording the war in Iraq and Afghanistan. *Media, Culture and Society*, 31(6): 921–38.**

In 2004, *NowThatsFuckedUp.com* (NTFU) was set up 'as a website for amateur pornography in which male users shared sexually explicit images of their wives and girlfriends' (pp. 925–6). The relationship between pornography and violence is disturbingly evident in Andén-Papadopoulos' discourse analysis of this website. When American soldiers posted overseas had difficulty accessing the site from abroad, they were encouraged to send pictures of themselves in Iraq and Afghanistan to prove that they were serving US soldiers. Some posted images of the base and their friends; others of more harrowing scenes of injured civilians or scenes of battle. Andén-Papadopoulos examines the verbal and visual discourses of these postings looking at how the soldiers differently address three distinct interlocutors: their fellow soldiers, the American public, and less directly, the 'enemy'.

The photographs are gruesome and horrific depictions of real injuries and fatalities in a war zone. Among the images taken are several showing the severed heads of 'insurgents':

> This continuous posting of visuals with repetitive variations on a motif that the soldiers themselves callously call the 'headshot', indicates a mode of pathological fixation in which the acts of taking and circulating these atrocious photographs function to reproduce traumatic war experiences in the form of a compulsive acting out. (p. 928)

The relationship between the images and the accompanying text is analysed and comments such as: 'That's gotta hurt' or 'Give that man a

*(Continued)*

*(Continued)*

Tylenol' show a high level of callousness but also serve as a form of self-protection, by which the posters distance themselves from the atrocities depicted. Some of the comments show an appreciation of the way NTFU shows war as it 'really is' rather than the sanitized official representation one sees on the network news. This is a quote from one of the men posting:

> For me, to be able to come to a site where the story isn't white washed and the pictures are as real and gory as it gets, gave me some weird sense of hope that those who are now armless, legless, sightless, and outright dead, are given a place here to be known and respected. (The Trip)

For some, these images authenticate their experiences, and may well serve a therapeutic function. But for many, the traumas they have suffered ensure that the soldiers keep returning to the same kinds of images, in order to 'photographically repeat their traumatic experiences in a mode of compulsive and repetitive acting out' (p. 931). The idea that the images can serve a didactic function, explaining the realities of war to the people back home, is also a recurring theme.

Andén-Papadopoulos shows that these sites cannot be dismissed as simply 'war pornography'. This analysis shows more complex uses for the site and suggests that open forums, including sites such as NTFU, can allow for an alternative to the dominant views of the military and state-controlled media outlets.

Discourse analysis reveals the diverse subject positions people using NTFU adopt. It illustrates a valuable strategy of discourse analysis – the identification of subject positions and the role of discourse in placing speakers in relation to a) their interlocutors and b) the real world. Soldiers using this website are given the power to offer a definition of their situation – to 'show' themselves in a war zone. If they take this opportunity to define their own subject position in ways which others might find reprehensible, that is perhaps because the voices of soldiers serving in a war zone are more often muted by the apparatus of both the state and the military. The discourses of the soldiers on the front line are seldom heard, for a good reason, some of which are immanent in Andén-Papadopoulos' essay.

Other work focuses on more conventional discourses in the media, such as those conveyed in broadcast programmes, for example, Debra Smith's analysis of the ideology of 'fatherhood' proposed by two very different black male role models: Snoop Dogg and Rev. Run. Both feature in reality television shows about their own families and both have different attitudes to fatherhood (Smith, 2008). Smith analyses the construction of attitudes towards fatherhood evident in their language and behaviour towards their own children in *Snoop Dogg's Fatherhood* and Rev. Run's *Run's House* – two television programmes of the same genre but with very different ideologies of masculinity.

Discourse analysis is also applied to conversation and to spoken language. One of the cultural forms which still uses the spoken word, which one might call 'oral culture', are rap battles, part of hip-hop culture studied by H. Samy Alim and colleagues and which provides the basis of our case study below. This article is from *Discourse and Society*, a good academic source for finding examples of different approaches to the study of discourse.

---

## Case Study

**H. Samy Alim, Jooyoung Lee and Lauren Mason Carris, 2011. Moving the crowd, 'crowding' the emcee: the coproduction and contestation of black normativity in freestyle rap battles.** *Discourse and Society,* **22(4): 422–39.**

This study explores the vocabulary and language used by rappers in South Central Los Angeles, the heart of gangland culture. The researchers are interested in the extent to which rapping is a part of 'black' culture and want to investigate how the 'rap battle' is constructed as a 'black space'. Historically, research into rap battles has focused on the way rap reinforces particular ideas of black masculinity. The research on hip-hop shows that the form is almost exclusively for black performers. Although there are non-black rappers these are often marginalized within the hip-hop community and are rarely the subject of academic concern. Alim et al. label this phenomenon 'black normativity'.

In this project, the researchers are concerned to see how the idea of 'black normativity' is addressed as a theme in the rap battles between a black emcee, Flawless, and a Latino one, Lil' Caese. The investigators look at the way in which race is articulated and not articulated; how the emcees use the crowd and also how they respond to the crowd. The research focuses on the performances of hip-hop emcees and has the aim of:

> ... illustrating how hip-hop emcees perform and are performed into racial and ethnic identities in freestyle rap battles. (p. 424)

They base their discourse analysis on video-taped recordings of the rap battles which took place on the street corner outside the open mic

*(Continued)*

*(Continued)*

venue, Project Blowed. The recorded battles are transcribed, and the speech and the actions of the emcees and the audience participation are notated. The authors then subject the transcripts to very close scrutiny, examining each word and gesture in detail. Racialized language and stereotypes are closely considered for evidence of 'black normativity':

> (by) ... examining instances in which the black emcee racializes the Latino emcee by drawing on stereotypes of Mexicans ... [we] show how the Latino emcee sometimes participates in his own racialization and, at other times, opposes this process with the support of the audience. (p. 423)

When the audience object to Flawless's use of racial stereotypes of Mexicans in his attack on Lil' Caese it is observed that Flawless shifts his focus to critiquing his opponent's street credibility. The researchers show the importance of the interaction of the audience with the main interlocutors in the rap battles. The article demonstrates how racial identity is itself contingent and subject to negotiation and contestation, how the crowd moves the emcee away from racial stereotypes, and how the battle provides a location to challenge 'black normativity' in rap.

Discourse analysis of the kind conducted by Alim et al. is careful, detailed work. Their study is based on many months of observation and a detailed knowledge of the scene. The transcriptions require a thorough understanding of the kind of language used, and the interpretation a sophisticated knowledge of street slang. Discourse analysis requires considerable time from the researcher and a high level of expertise about the object of analysis.

## Stages in a discourse analysis

Discourse analysis requires the selection of a 'text' or 'object of analysis' which touches up an area of interest to you theoretically. The theoretical approach may be deductive – you may have a clear idea that you wish to apply, for example, a Marxist analysis of the television programme *The Secret Millionaire*. Alternatively, perhaps more usually in discourse analysis, you may have a text which you are interested in which has an interesting mode of address or has a strange style which you want to study more. First of all then, you need to select your text; define the limits of it clearly and justify the selection in terms of your academic interest.

Second, you need to completely immerse yourself in the object of analysis and really get to know it well. If it is a television programme, you need to watch it several times. The details are very important in discourse analysis – you must have a very good knowledge of the nuances of language, gesture and expression, which you can only acquire through close study. Consider how these specific discourses relate to the others of the same category.

The third stage is one of analysis – identify the interlocutors and their 'subject positions'. Who has the power to contribute to the discourse? What are the limits of their participation? Within which frames is the discourse constituted? Identify what is at stake in this discourse and how you can relate your findings back to the theory. Some good sources of further advice on discourse analysis include Rose (2007) and Tonkiss (1998).

## TYPOLOGICAL METHODS OF ANALYSIS

In this section we are discussing a cluster of methods which consider texts as belonging to a certain *type*. We will consider *genre*, *auteur* and *star study* as three approaches to the analysis of media and cultural content. All have their origin in film studies, but can readily be applied to many other forms of media artifact or cultural event. Rhetorical methods such as these can be used to explore the relationships among different types of text. The most obvious example of a typological analysis is that of *genre*, and this is where we begin our discussion of typological methods.

## GENRE STUDY

One of the best-recognized means by which media and culture is classified is by genre (Altman, 1999; Neale, 1980). Hollywood films have traditionally been classified and marketed according to genre, and readers will be familiar with the categories of the western, musical or thriller. Steve Neale's book *Genre* (1980) was an early study of genre in film, and Neale has subsequently written widely about genre in cinema (1999; 2002). But we might also think of genres in music (jazz, rock, punk, dub) in television (situation comedy, documentary, quiz show) and literature (spy thriller, chick-lit, romance). The term *genre* has origins in art history, where it is used to refer to popular paintings (as opposed to literary or high-brow ones), a fact which gives genre the connotation of being low-brow. It is a term still used in the publishing industry to distinguish mass-market books from literary ones. Genre is a term thus associated with popular, working-class culture.

One of the key ways in which films have been developed and marketed is along the lines of genre. The classic Hollywood films are frequently classified generically: musical, western, romantic comedy, film noir – all these are terms which describe a genre (Schatz, 1981). Genres come and go in fashion although perhaps the only genre which never seems to go out of style is the comedy, perhaps because it is so flexible, as Neale and Krutnik demonstrate (Neale and Krutnik, 1990). The western is an archetypical genre, largely because of the strong iconography, distinctive *mise-en-scène* and close relationship with the myth-making function of the West in the American imagination. One of the most influential books on the western is Will Wright's *Six-Guns and Society* (1979), the epilogue of which includes a highly insightful discussion of the importance of methodology and the role of the scholar in bringing meaning to light.

Hollywood studios have been mass-producing films of specific types in order to help create marketable products since the earliest days. One of the first studio films, *The Great Train Robbery* (directed by Edwin S. Porter in 1903), was produced and marketed to cash in on the success of the western novel. The western has antecedents in the comics and dime novels of the nineteenth century, which were themselves marketed according to genres popular at the time (Wright, 1979). Genres are largely the product of the studio system in the classical Hollywood era during approximately 1930–60 (Balio, 1976; Bordwell et al., 1985; Neale and Smith, 1998), when studios produced films of each genre – westerns, comedies, musicals, etc. – to ensure maximum audiences in their cinemas overall. Some studios specialized in particular genres; for example, MGM was known for the musical and Warner Brothers for the gangster movie.

Genre is a *semiotic* category in that there are codes and conventions which films of a genre share. Elements such as location, visual style and *mise-en-scène* each contribute to the coded system by which films can be classified. For example, horror movies include key iconographic elements such as the isolated house, screaming youngsters and shaky camera work. The posters use a 'gothic' text and feature the colour red often in the shape of dripping blood – all key semiotic signifiers of the horror genre.

Genre is also a *narrative* category: the boy-meets-girl structure of the romance is an invariable deep structure of any movie of the genre. The plot will vary according to the precise obstacles preventing the boy and girl getting together, but we know they will in the end and we are rarely disappointed. 'If you've seen one, you've seen 'em all', we may hear people say of romance, gangster or horror films. The gangster movie has to have the stake-out, the chase scene, the 'execution', the betrayal – all are narrative conventions which have grown up over the years, and which are developed and worked on by subsequent film-makers. Altman says:

> The pleasure of genre film spectatorship thus derives more from reaffirmation than from novelty. People go to genre films to participate in events that somehow seem familiar. (1999: 25)

Another pleasure of the genre film is in seeing how each key element, or 'set piece', is reinterpreted or reinvented for contemporary mores and values. The western came to maturity during the 1940s and 1950s with films such as *Shane* (1953) and the great westerns directed by John Ford, including

*Rio Grande* (1950) and *The Searchers* (1956). The western was also a television genre during the 1950s and 1960s, and television drama became the more typical vehicle for stories about the west as the cinema declined in cultural significance. In the 'post-Hollywood' era, the western has become more parodied. *Unforgiven* (1992), Clint Eastwood's take on the western, is a deconstruction of the classic western. The remake by the Coen Brothers of the classic western *True Grit* (dir. Ethan and Joel Coen, 2010) indicates a shifting interest in the western. It stars Jeff Bridges reprising the role of Rooster Cogburn played by John Wayne in the original (dir. Henry Hathaway, 1969). One of the reasons for the longevity of the western is its association with the mythic aetiology of America itself. The conquest of the West, the relationship between civilization and nature, between the indigenous people and the 'frontier' continue to concern Americans in various forms (McMahon and Csaki, 2010).

While auteur criticism (discussed below) links films to the psychology of the director, in genre criticism it is more likely that the film will be seen as a product of its time. For example, the British gangster film of the 1990s is read as an allegory of Thatcherism by Claire Monk (1999a). British gangster movies have different sets of preoccupations and themes than their Hollywood counterparts, in large part because of the different cultural location of the villain in the two societies (Chibnall and Murphy, 1999).

A genre which grew up with the gangster movie in the 1930s is the musical. Set in a similar milieu – the excitement of urban life – the musical is in some ways the inverse of the gangster film. Instead of the rise and fall of the hood, the musical tells the story of the fall and rise of the star. Our next case study, Jane Feuer's study of the Hollywood musical, provides a classic example of the method of genre study.

## Case Study

**Jane Feuer, 1982. *The Hollywood Musical*. London: Macmillan/British Film Institute.**

This analysis of the Hollywood musical charts the history of the genre starting with its origins in the music hall and popular theatre. Recurrent themes are identified and analysed with careful and detailed illustration from over 100 musical films. Feuer argues that the musical has much in common with 'folk art' of a pre-industrial era, yet it is a mechanical medium in which the relationship between the audience and performers is temporally and spatially remote. According to Feuer, the musical works to reconstruct the sense of community we have lost in the industrial age

*(Continued)*

*(Continued)*

by recreating that lost spirit of camaraderie on the screen. She claims: 'The Hollywood musical becomes a mass art which aspires to the condition of a folk art, produced and consumed by the same integrated community' (p. 3). Feuer presents the case that the musical genre has changed and adapted through time – she creates a roughly chronological categorization of the main subgenres of the musical.

According to Feuer, the musical genre has a kind of life cycle: it begins as an outcrop of the musical stage. It develops as a means of showcasing performers – the stage element is present in early musicals of the 1930s to justify the singing and dancing. During the 1950s, it develops into a genre where the singing and dancing can just occur as part of ordinary life, and no one notices that it isn't normal. This is the heyday of the MGM musical and the Freed production unit which produced such wonderful films as *Singing in the Rain* and *Meet Me in St Louis*. But eventually the genre becomes about making a film about putting on a show, and then a film about films about putting on a show, before finally becoming a self-referential joke. Feuer is able to generalize from the musical to genres in general and to argue that there is a tendency for genres to follow a similar life cycle and to become self-parodic in time.

The musical has undergone something of a comeback subsequent to the success of several theatrical shows, such as *Mamma Mia!* (1999). A number of films are in production which exploit the success of current stage shows in London's West End or on Broadway, New York, such as *Wicked*, *Jesus Christ Superstar* and *Jersey Boys* (all scheduled for release in 2014), and *Les Misérables*, *Annie* and *Carousel* (to be released in 2013). These films return to the origins of the musical, which in the early years were filmed versions of theatrical shows. Perhaps the musical, having expired out of self-parody, is now having a literal 'renaissance' and we will see the life cycle begin again.

There have been many different theories put forward to explain the changing pattern of genres. Martin Rubin (1999) argues that the thriller has gone through three distinct phases: formative, classical and modern. These three broad categories might be applied to any number of genres. Hansen et al. cut the cake a slightly different way when they argue that there are five stages in the history of a genre, as follows:

1 experimental

2 classical

3 parody

4   deconstruction

5   post-modernism.

*Source*: Hansen et al., 1998: 179.

We can see how the contemporary western plays with the ideas and expectations of the genre, displaying a 'post-modern' attitude, as in *Cowboys and Aliens* (2011) which plays in a somewhat direct way with notions of the western and the monster movie using the *mise-en-scène* and many of the themes of the western and introducing to this the troubling presence of the aliens. The genre of the film noir has been imitated in the game, *L.A.Noire*, which takes many of the same elements of the classical Hollywood genre of the noir film and puts them into a video game.

Genres can transfer from one medium to another. Many genres of film and television are derived from radio (such as the game show) or magazines (for example, product reviews such as the *Gadget Show*). Jessica Ringrose and Valerie Walkerdine's essay from the journal *Feminist Media Studies* looks at the genre of the television 'make-over' show, such as *What Not to Wear* (Ringrose and Walkerdine, 2008). This case study is an example of the application of feminist theory to the study of a new television genre which has its roots in the make-over features of women's magazines. Whereas the magazine features would typically be concerned mainly with cosmetics, the make-over show, as a variant of the 'lifestyle' genre, attempts to work on the body, the psyche, indeed the *person* being featured.

## Case Study

**Jessica Ringrose and Valerie Walkerdine, 2008. Regulating the abject: the TV make-over as site of neo-liberal reinvention toward bourgeois femininity. *Feminist Media Studies*, 8(3): 227–46.**

Programmes such as *You Are What You Eat* (Channel 4), *Get Your Dream Job* (BBC3) and *Spendaholics* (BBC3) are low-budget documentaries in which members of the public (usually working-class women) subject themselves to transformation into 'generalized and normalized bourgeois feminine subjects' (p. 227). Ringrose and Walkerdine examine how the women featured are at first constructed as 'to be reviled' before being transformed by the skills of various fashion advisors, make-up artists, dieticians and fitness trainers.

*Abjection* is a term they borrow from the work of Julia Kristeva (1982) to refer to someone or something which is 'outside' or 'other'. In our

*(Continued)*

*(Continued)*

society, working-class women are dismissed variously as 'tarts', 'chavs' or 'slappers' – figures that are 'other' and 'abject'. Ringrose and Walkerdine integrate feminist psychological theory with class analysis in their discussion of 'the classed dynamics of *abjection*'.

The paper describes an episode of *Get Your Dream Job* (BBC3) in which an unemployed single mum arrives for a job interview at a funeral parlour in the following attire:

> A bubble gum pink suit and matching pink Timberland boots, white blond hair with inches of black roots and giant gold hoop 'ghetto' ear-rings. (p. 239)

In three days she is 'transformed' into a 'credible candidate', a fact proven by the estimate of passers-by that she was a 'professional' making 'over £30,000 a year'.

> The show ... positions consumption of the right products along with the right personalized coaching as offering a path toward respectability, a proper job, and ultimately material security. (p. 239)

The article takes a feminist psychoanalytic approach to investigate the myths underlying the construction of femininity in the make-over genre. Judith Butler claims that gender is not a biological given but is a social construct which is *performed*. Gender roles, Butler argues, are culturally prescribed and determined; through acting out and responding to cues from those around us, we gradually internalize the socially prescribed gender norms (Butler, 1990). Ringrose and Walkerdine apply Butler's ideas to the process by which the women on these shows are taught a very particular kind of femininity. These programmes perpetuate the notion that by adjusting one's *performance* these working-class women will be able to achieve greater success. The failure of the social, economic and political system (Giddens, 1991; 1998) is transferred onto the individual who is compelled to understand their lack of employment, decent diet or dress sense as a personal pathology.

A standard narrative trope of the genre is when, towards the end of the programme, the women are shown footage of their earlier selves and are expected to look back in horror at how fat/gauche/ridiculous they were. The narrative is suitably resolved when the women are able to look in the mirror at a new, more successful self. Ringrose and Walkerdine analyse how the premise of the genre contributes to an ideology in which women (especially working-class women) need to be worked on, worked over, improved, and turned into models of bourgeois femininity.

a geek, a scientist fascinated by imagery and by the underwater expeditions of Jacques Cousteau. It is the water theme which Elsaesser identifies as coming through the personal narrative and into *Avatar*. For the world which he has created for the Na'vi bears more similarities to an underwater world than an outer-space one – especially in relation to the movements of the creatures. So the auteur's story resonates with that of the world projected; we recognize this world as the product of a science nerd with a strong interest in science fiction art.

Third is the element of 'true lies'; of keeping the reader aware of the story-telling; projecting the artifice while also denying it through the narrative. Thus the central trope of the film – that the military–industrial elite are stripping the land to obtain 'unobtainium' is a key figure of this contradiction.

> 'Unobtainium', in short, is the name for that which links and joins what cannot be brought together, and thus it is the signifier of *both* the gap *and* of the cognitive switch needed to bridge the gap. (p. 258)

The 3D technology which the film uses is the same technology that is used by the scientists in their quest for the unobtainium. The film makes apparent the shared technology of the movie 3D with the real use of 3D graphics in US military operations. Elsaesser asks whether this is evidence of the 'military–entertainment complex' succeeding the 'military–industrial complex'.

The reader is obliged to make their own interpretation from the 'switches in reality status' of the film.

> Since the message is fundamentally self-contradictory, unraveling its meaning results in a higher 'ontological commitment' on the part of the viewer to his or her particular interpretation – a commitment that works in favor of the affective bond formed within a given film. One could even say that a double bind situation gives the illusion of 'empowering' the spectator, an impression confirmed by the film's reception history. (p. 260)

Certainly, it is these ambiguities and uncertainties, double-binds and twists of identification that engender a kind of engagement which, Elsaesser argues, are elements of the control James Cameron exercises over the film as 'auteur'.

The work of the *auteur*, then, can be analysed in the control the director has over elements of the narrative structure, the *mise-en-scène* and the ideology of the film. Elsaesser seems to be reinforcing the idea that the phenomenon of the auteur is still alive and well even as he critiques the mythology of the auteur.

## Auteurs are everywhere

Auteur analysis has not only been applied to the cinema, of course. The idea of the *auteur* originates in English literature where the author has long been the primary means of categorizing and studying literature. The questioning of the 'great man' theory of literature and of the canon came about in the 1960s at the same time that the film critics were applying notions of authorship to the movies. The idea of the auteur is not unique to high cultural forms, but can be applied to other forms, too. Auteur analysis has been applied to the study of television, where sometimes the auteur is the writer of the drama, like Dennis Potter (*The Singing Detective, Pennies From Heaven, Karaoke*) or Jimmy McGovern (*Cracker*). In other instances, it is the producer who is selected for the accolade, as is Steven Bochco, the producer of *Hill Street Blues* (1981–87). This famous American police series shows the humanity of police officers in what is arguably the first of modern police dramas. *Hill Street Blues* paved the way for contemporary television police dramas such as *NYPD Blue* (also a Bochco show). Evidence of Bochco's authorial control can be seen in the fact that when he and Michael Kozoll were asked by NBC to do a police series, they agreed only on condition that they could have complete artistic control.

David Marc and Robert J. Thompson examine the role of the television producer, including Steven Bochco, in *Prime Time, Prime Movers: From 'I Love Lucy' to 'L.A. Law' – America's Greatest TV Shows and the People Who Created Them* (Marc and Thompson, 1995). Marc and Thompson place their enquiry firmly in the realm of the auteur when they pose the question: 'Who is the author of television?' Marc and Thompson argue that, despite the highly industrial nature of modern media production, 'the artistic act still thoroughly depends on the conscious effort of the individual creator' (1995: 4). The individual creator in the case of television is the producer, and *Prime Time, Prime Movers* presents brief biographies of over two dozen producers of American television. The selection is based on a subjective measure of the 'greatest' American television shows; the importance of the producer is based on the implicit claim that this role is the single most important one in the production of a television programme. They include in their list the producers of the most important situation comedies, dramas and soaps. The historical producers are Norman Lear (*All in the Family, The Jeffersons, Archie Bunker's Place*); Sherwood Schwartz (*Gilligan's Island, The Brady Bunch*) and Jack Webb (*Dragnet*). Among the more recent producers, they discuss the documentary maker Ken Burns (*The Civil War, The Story of Jazz*), the situation comedy producer Diane English (*Murphy Brown*) and, of course, Steve Bochco, whose *Hill Street Blues* reinvented the television police series, and who also created *L.A. Law, Doogie Howser, M.D.* and *NYPD Blue*. This study contrasts significantly in approach with Jeremy Tunstall's study (1993) of British television producers discussed in Chapter 4 (see pages 93–94). For here the focus is on the television shows as a function of authorial intent by the producers, whereas Tunstall's concern is with the cultural economy of the workplace.

Where you think that a set of texts (films, radio programmes or songs) have been shaped by the influence of a single author (despite being mass-produced), you could use auteur analysis. You need to show that the common characteristics are the product of the single authorial voice (and not of some other shared characteristic such as production company or star vehicle). Typically, auteur study involves an element of psychological attribution: asserting a link between the psyche of the auteur in question and the themes of her or his work.

## STAR STUDY

Leo Lowenthal called the star the 'idol of consumption' and argued that modern society favours these over the 'idols of production' – the engineers, architects and scientists who were the heroes of the modern era (Lowenthal, 1961). In what we might now call a 'post-modern' age, celebrity is bestowed on people for the least achievement or misdemeanour; the nature of the idolatry is reduced; we may say that the modern celebrity is nothing more than the target of gossip and tittle-tattle. In many media forms it is the performer, celebrity or star who is the locus of the product's identity and marketing strategy. The *star* is one of the main means by which films have been classified and marketed under the classical Hollywood studio system and ever since. Richard Dyer wrote a foundational work on the study of stars in his book *Stars* (Dyer, 1982) but it is from his second book on the subject, *Heavenly Bodies* (1987) that we take our next 'classic' case study, focusing on his chapter on the great African American actor and activist, Paul Robeson.

---

## Case Study

**Richard Dyer, 1987. Chapter 2: Paul Robeson, Crossing Over, *Heavenly Bodies*. London: British Film Institute. pp. 67–139.**

As a young man, growing up in the early part of the twentieth century, the African American Paul Robeson was a gifted scholar (with a stellar record at Rutgers University during 1915–19 and subsequently at Columbia Law School, where he was the only African-American graduate student) and a great athlete (playing football for the national team the All-Americans). During his career his achievements in music, theatre and film were all celebrated. He is best known for his renditions of spirituals and

*(Continued)*

---

*(Continued)*

was lauded as 'the greatest singing star of the age' while his performance as Othello was considered to be superb. He worked with black film-maker Oscar Micheaux (*Body and Soul,* 1924), with avant-garde film-makers in the 1930s and in the musical *Show Boat* (1935).

Dyer focuses on the period 1924–45 in Robeson's career and asks: 'How did the period permit black stardom?' The explanation Dyer offers is that Robeson's image was able to elicit different interpretations, to provide different meanings from a black and white perspective.

> What I want to show is that there are discourses developed by whites in white culture and by blacks in black culture which made a different sense of the same phenomena: Paul Robeson. (p. 70)

Dyer shows how Robeson changed the lyric of *Old Man River,* the African American spiritual which made him famous. He altered the language to reflect his own education and diction but also shifting the meaning so that the song becomes about freedom and resistance rather than about resignation to one's fate. The song as originally written was about the great Mississippi river being indifferent to the fate of the slaves who toil on its banks. Robeson changes the meaning of the song by changing a single line in which his character refers to the Mississippi as being '*de ol' man dat I like to be*' to '*the old man I don't like to be*'. The 'Uncle Tom' attitudes of acceptance of slavery in the original has been transformed. The rendering of the song into standard English makes a political statement, too, as Robeson refuses to suppress his education and play the foolish black man.

One of the strategies employed was to show Robeson as the typical black man who does not actually *do* anything. In white discourses, black people may be shown as the object of history – people to whom things are done – but not as the subjects of history – agents who make things happen. In the representations of Robeson, the potential power of the black man is contained. The examples of the photos from *Sanders of the River* (1935) and *King Solomon's Mine* (1937) depict him in stereotypical 'African' roles stripped of any agency or sexuality.

However, the pin-ups, and especially the photographs by Nicholas Murray, do advance an erotic image of the black man. These are nudes which display what contemporary commentators called his 'pure beauty' in the 'heroic mould'. The poses are reminiscent of those of the statues of antiquity and focus on the sinews of the body and the texture of the skin. The emphasis on the form, says Dyer, 'is both a way of producing potentially erotic images while denying that that is what is being done' (p. 121).

162

Dyer concludes that Robeson:

whose body ... finally does nothing, contained by frames, montages, narrative, direction, vocal restraint. He was a cross-over star because (and as long as) he so hugely em-body-ed, in-corp-orated this historical functioning of black people in Western representation and economy. (p. 139)

The star is a product of its time; the relationship of the star personae to the norms and values of the time and place in which they operate is a theme of Dyer's work. The star system is often viewed as a product of the Hollywood cinema, yet in the case of Robeson the star persona was developed and conveyed through plays, singing, posters and pin-ups. Star study necessarily includes discussion of the performances which comprise the main work of the person involved. However, the star image is developed beyond the products of the industry. It is also in the billboards, interviews, essays and articles which you might find in the newspapers, on the internet or in the movie magazines. Stars are featured players or principal performers in a film. But they are more than that – there is much paraphernalia of literature and publicity devoted to building a star image. Stars attend gala awards, premieres and openings; they appear on chat shows and game shows; they give interviews to magazines and television programmes – all of these activities contribute to the construction of the star image. It is this *public persona* of the star that you could access in your analysis. Star studies are not concerned with the real Johnny Depp or Selina Gomez – they are concerned with the image of 'Johnny Depp' or 'Selena Gomez' as saleable, realizable commodities. The primary analysis for such work involves looking at the many places where stars are figured. The primary sources for star studies includes the following:

- media products (films, tv programmes, etc.), in which your star appears;
- posters and advertisements for their work;
- interviews and appearances on television;
- press coverage and stories in the print media;
- official and unofficial fan literature and websites;
- (auto)biographies and books.

Most scholars working in this area today owe a great deal to Dyer's work, a debt acknowledged by Susan Holmes in her study of film stars on British television (2001). This essay is an analysis of the star image of Joan Crawford in the British television programme *Film Fanfare*, which ran on ABC television in the UK from 1956 to 1957. She also uses as a primary source contemporary magazines, especially the popular general interest magazine *Picture Post*. She shows how major movie stars, such as Crawford, engaged in a renegotiation of their star identity by appearing on *Film Fanfare*. Holmes discusses the shifting relationship between film and television at the time and shows how Crawford's star persona was also changing at this time. Her secondary research, then, would have involved an investigation of the status of the two signifying industries and the state of Crawford's career at the time. Holmes finds that, 'while the central paradox of stardom, that of being constituted as ordinary yet extraordinary, was partly modeled on conventions established by other media, television reshaped it within the specificity of its textual form' (Holmes, 2001: 186).

The rise of celebrity culture is a phenomenon which has seen the focus on performers in other media rise to fame. Some rise to fame for no very good reason; television programmes such as *Big Brother* have created 'celebrities' from ordinary people. Performers on shows like *American Pop Idol* and *X-Factor* have been brought to levels of great fame and notoriety by a press eager to find cheap copy. Popular books and biographies also feature stars of the sporting world whose images, too, are constructs of the media, such as Tiger Woods (Cole and Andrews, 2001). Stars such as Frank Sinatra attract a huge number of popular biographies; he is also the subject of an academic study by Chris Rojek (2004). Rojek argues that the star persona of Sinatra was so influential that he became a 'celebrity icon', a figure able to 'embody complex and contradictory relations within society, articulating images of belonging, recognition, identity and resistance' (Rojek, 2004). We might compare this role with contemporary music performers such as the late Amy Winehouse or Eminem – both white performers with complex relationships to black culture. The field of star and celebrity studies is a growing field of research with some notable collections by P. David Marshall (2006), Sean Redmond and Su Holmes (2007), and Jessica Evans and David Hesmondhalgh (2005) and some monographs by Paul Willis (2005) and Chris Rojek (2001) among others.

Your star study could focus on stars you particularly admire (or loathe – but it is a good idea to have some strong feeling). Think about their career and what stage they are in. Select three to six different elements – a performance on television, an interview in a magazine, an album – and analyse what they are saying about themselves and their public personae. Star study involves archive research, textual analysis and semiotic analysis to be fully successful. Along with 'genre' and 'auteur', 'star' is one more means by which media products can be classified and analysed. You may find yourself using semiotics, content analysis and/or discourse analysis in your star research. Indeed, each of the 'typological' approaches we have discussed in this section are thematic rather than methodological categories, and one cannot be too prescriptive as to how you research them.

# COMPARISON OF RESEARCH METHODS DISCUSSED IN THIS CHAPTER

In this chapter we have compared some of the main methods of analysing texts, as seen in Figure 5.2. Each of these methods has a large and growing literature; I hope I have been able to introduce you to some of the key texts in this material. There is a strong tradition of researching media and cultural texts which you can draw on, providing you with a sound theoretical base on which to build your own studies. At the same time, there are always new things happening so you can find your own examples and add your own interpretations. A big advantage of working with media texts as your object of analysis is that you are able to draw on your own knowledge and enthusiasms. You can apply the skills and expertise you have learned on your course to contemporary culture.

**FIGURE 5.2** Comparison of the opportunities and challenges of some methods for researching media and cultural texts

| Method | Opportunities | Challenges |
| --- | --- | --- |
| Semiotics | Simple and direct, this method requires few resources and the objects of analysis are all around you! | Not as easy as it looks! This method relies on a great understanding of the underlying myths operating in society. |
| Content Analysis | Can gather original data quite quickly and easily; allows one to use some powerful analytical CAQDAS tools. | Can be quite time-consuming; need to have an object of analysis which can be conceptualized in terms of quantifiable phenomena. |
| Discourse Analysis | Allows the inclusion of a wide range of material; great method for applying your rhetorical skills. | Need high level of interpretive skills and sophisticated handling of writing. |
| Typological Research: Genre Study Auteur Study Star Study | These methods allow you to consider the text in relation to audience interpretations and understandings and industry marketing. These methods require a level of general knowledge of your chosen object of analysis. | Multifaceted methods which require multiple skills – you must be able to analyse texts and also to examine a wider range of information in the extra-textual literature which surrounds the media and cultural products and contributes to their identity as belonging to the specific 'type' under investigation. |

One of the key advantages of semiotic analysis is that it demands relatively few resources. It is possible to conduct a semiotic analysis of only one text or image, as Popp and Mendelson do in our case study on page 126–127 above. Because the method is *interpretive*, it does not have to be 'reliable' in the sense of being applied to a large number of texts. It is a method which is based on rhetorical analysis (as the title of Roland Barthes' essay suggests) and it must generate an argument which is *persuasive*. The essential factor in semiotic analysis is that you need to understand what myths are at play in order to appreciate the ideological power of the signs. It can help if you are part of the interpretive community using the relevant media to be able to fully understand the conventions in operation. Semiotics can very usefully be combined with other methods of analysis. It is particularly fruitful to combine semiotic analysis with content analysis. You could use content analysis to determine how many of a certain kind of image exist in a given set of texts, and then use semiotics to analyse a smaller selection in more detail. This combination would give you some breadth (looking at a range of images) and depth (analysing a small sample closely). For example, you might conduct a content analysis of the genres of music broadcast on selected radio stations across peak week-day evenings to ascertain what kind of music gets the most coverage in terms of number of plays. Then you could use this data to determine which is the most popular genre (let's say it is rap) and then conduct a semiotic analysis of one or two of the most frequently played tracks of this kind. Content analysis works very well with semiotics to give you a quantitative overview of the content under discussion. One of the advantages of content analysis is that it gives you statistical data which can help build a very persuasive case and provide quantitative evidence which can be convincing. It is, however, only as good as the codes you have designed and so you do need a good knowledge of your object of analysis and a high level of analytical skill to be able to design a good coding schema. It can be very time-consuming but new methods using CAQDAS and other kinds of software are opening up content analysis to new applications and I expect to see this method used a lot more widely in media studies in future. Discourse analysis is a very rich and sophisticated method which has the benefit of enabling you to apply your theoretical knowledge in interesting ways. Discourse analysis will challenge you to develop your skills of rhetorical analysis both in deconstructing your chosen object of analysis and also in your ability to write about it. The typological methods I have described above – looking at genre, auteur and star – each provide very interesting methods of researching the media. They are more of a topic than a method and in studying any of these you may well use all of the methods described above.

The methods described in this chapter are all suitable to the research and analysis of texts alone or in combination. Although it is sometimes tempting to think you can do everything in your dissertation, I would advise you to begin by doing just one of the above and test it in a small-scale study on just one part of your object of analysis. When you have written about 1,000 words on just one small piece of your research, then reconsider the scale and scope of your project. It is better to do one thing really well than to try to do several things and not fully accomplish any of them.

Of the three main elements in the communication chain – production, text, audience – it is texts which have attracted the most critical and popular interest. Yet in order to fully understand any media or cultural text it is necessary to understand its position in relation to the bigger picture. If your main focus is on the products of the media industry, you should still spend some time researching the location of that text as an economic/material product and consider its relation to the industry which produced it, as we discussed in the previous chapter. You must also always consider who the audience is. How is the text received and understood? How do people use media and culture? These are some of the questions we will address in the next chapter.

## FURTHER READING

Berger, Arthur Asa, 1998. *Media Research Techniques*. Thousand Oaks, CA/London: Sage.
Arthur Asa Berger's very useful textbook includes in Chapter 3 an example of how content analysis can be applied to the comics pages of newspapers. Berger guides the reader through the technique of content analysis and provides a very good summary of both the advantages and disadvantages of the method.

Bertrand, Ina and Peter Hughes, 2005. *Media Research Methods: Audiences, Institutions, Texts*. London: Palgrave Macmillan.
This very good textbook includes a particularly useful discussion of narrative and discourse analysis in Chapter 10, 'Gathering and Analysing Textual Data'.

Bignell, Jonathan, 2002. *Media Semiotics: An Introduction*. 2nd edition. Manchester/New York: Manchester University Press.
Jonathan Bignell's *Media Semiotics* is an excellent analysis of the application of semiotics and includes a terrific discussion of Roland Barthes, with sections on applying semiotics to advertising, women's magazines, newspapers, television news and drama, and cinema.

Deacon, David, Michael Pickering, Peter Golding and Graham Murdock, 2007. *Researching Communications: A Practical Guide to Methods in Media and Cultural Studies*. 2nd edition. London: Bloomsbury Academic.
This collection of essays provides a good survey of several methods and includes lots of good, practical guidance on conducting your own research. The chapters on 'Counting Contents' (pp. 117–37) and 'Analysing Texts' (pp. 138–192) are particularly relevant to the themes of the above discussion.

Krippendorff, Klaus, 1980. *Content Analysis: An Introduction to Its Methodology.* Beverly Hills, CA/London: Sage.

This remains a standard in content analysis and a definitive guide to the method. Chapter 14, 'A Practical Guide', gives a step-by-step account of doing content analysis at a more advanced level.

Rose, Gillian, 2007. *Visual Methodologies: An Introduction to the Interpretation of Visual Materials.* 2nd edition. London: Sage.

This set of essays provides some good examples of how to analyse visual media and is particularly strong on discourse analysis – see especially Chapters 6 and 7 which consider two different categories of discourse analysis.

Storey, John, 2009. *Cultural Theory and Popular Culture: An Introduction.* 5th edition. Harlow: Pearson Education Limited.

John Storey is an excellent writer; he explains the principles of semiotics and discourse analysis particularly well in Chapter 6, 'Structuralism and Post-Structuralism'.

van Leeuwen, Theo and Carey Jewitt (eds), 2001. *Handbook of Visual Analysis.* London: Sage.

This wide-ranging collection of essays includes several good examples of the application of some of the research methods discussed in this chapter to a wide range of visual material including photography (Collier, 2001; Lister and Wells, 2001), magazines (Bell, 2001) and television (Iedema, 2001). There are chapters demonstrating how to apply content analysis, semiotics and iconography.

Two of our case studies using semiotic analysis are available to download via the Sage Website.

Richard K. Popp and Andrew L. Mendleson's study of the letter 'X' on the cover of *Time* magazine; and Marcia A. Morgado's semiotic analysis of hip-hop fashion.
Popp, Richard K. and Andrew L. Mendelson, 2010. 'X'-ing out enemies: *Time* magazine, visual discourse, and the war in Iraq. *Journalism.* **11** (2): 203–221. http://jou.sagepub.com/content/11/2/203.full.pdf+html.
Morgado, Marcia A., 2007. the semiotics of extraordinary dress: A structural analysis and interpretation of hip-hop style. *Clothing and Textile Research Journal.* **25** (2): 131–155. http://ctr.sagepub.com/content/25/2/131.full.pdf+html.

# TAKING IT FURTHER ... ON YOUR OWN

## Comparative content analysis of a magazine or newspaper

Ask a friend or relative who is a different age from you which is their favourite newspaper or magazine. Conduct a content analysis of this preferred reading. Decide on six to eight categories you will use to code the material and conduct a preliminary analysis, counting how many pages or fractions of pages, are devoted to each of your categories and then sum them. Then find an equivalent newspaper or magazine which you enjoy reading and see if you can use the same categories. What differences/similarities do you find? What are the strengths and weaknesses of content analysis as a method to compare media use between you and your subject? Discuss the findings with your friend or relative – what insights do they have on the process?

# TAKING IT FURTHER ... IN CLASS

*Semiotic analysis of advertisements: separating what is 'said' from what 'goes without saying'*

The tutor should select a range of advertisements from men's and women's lifestyle magazines – perfume or cologne ads work well because they are present in both kinds of magazines and are selling something intangible (a scent). Working in small groups or pairs, students analyse one advertisement. First of all identify all the 'denotative' elements. At this stage they must describe the image and text, avoiding any reference to connotations or implications at all. They report back to the whole group, sticking strictly to the denotational level – what it *shows*. In the second phase identify what each separate denotational element identified above implies or suggests – here work to determine the 'connotative' elements. When these have been unpacked, students reconstitute what the image means – how meaning gets into the image by reference to the double-layered analysis of denotation and connotation. Finally, having established how the denotational and connotational elements of the message work together, students discuss the 'cultural codes' necessary to understand/unpick the deeper-level meanings of the advertisement. What cultural myths does it tap into, for example, around gender, beauty or exoticism? How do different cultural competences enable different readings of the ad? What is the ideological message of the ad and how is it encoded?

# 6 RESEARCHING AUDIENCES: WHO USES MEDIA AND CULTURE? HOW AND WHY?

---

## Aims and Objectives

- This chapter discusses some of the ways audiences have been understood and researched.

- We aim to prepare students to take account of the particular issues raised when researching people.

- We discuss the opportunities and challenges provided by selected approaches to audience research. In this chapter we concentrate on the following research methods:

  ○ surveys and interviews

  ○ focus groups

  ○ ethnography

  ○ oral history.

- Some suggestions for further reading are offered.

- Some activities are suggested for you to take it further with your studies, on your own, in class and beyond.

---

## INTRODUCTION

In previous chapters, we have discussed how we can study *texts* and *industries*. Now we turn our attention to the third major area of analysis: *audiences*. In media and cultural studies, the term 'audience' is used in the everyday sense to refer to the people who attend a particular performance or who view a film or programme on television. But we also use the term to refer in a broader sense to people who are exposed to, or who respond to, media culture. Indeed, in its broadest sense, the term 'audience' is almost interchangeable with 'society', for it is used to refer to the many ways in which the media relate to the broader social world. In this sense, all people in a society constitute a potential audience for any media product. In the following discussion, we will be considering audiences in this inclusive sense and thinking about methods of researching people's particular relationships with the media.

Several kinds of research are undertaken into audiences by organizations, institutions and individuals. People who produce media artifacts, government regulatory bodies, lobby groups and politicians are just some of the many people who study audiences. Governments need to know if people are being informed about issues; programme-makers need to know whether people like their programmes; advertisers need to know what magazines their target audience read; and regulators need to keep up to date with public manners and mores. All kinds of agencies, public and private, make it their business to find out what kinds of media are used, when, where and how.

This chapter introduces you to some of the special issues that arise in the study of people when they are constituted as audiences. We look at some questions of ethics and consider how you need to be especially sensitive to issues of privacy, safety and well-being when you research 'human subjects'. We consider what is meant by an 'audience' and how this idea has changed with each successive new technology, most particularly how new computer technology has shifted the relationship between producer and consumer to create a new brand of audience member who is also a 'prosumer'.

## METHODS DISCUSSED IN THIS CHAPTER

We saw in Chapter 3 that your research method should always be selected to suit your object of analysis. The methods discussed here cover the range of approaches from the more objective to the instrumental. Much research is bureaucratic (see discussion in Chapter 2), but professional research commissioned by industry will also include more subjective forms of research, such as the focus group which has become a mainstay of all audience researchers.

In this chapter we investigate the research methods most suited to the student or beginner researcher. Figure 6.1 lists the approaches we will concentrate on here: surveys and interviews, focus groups, ethnography and oral history.

The first method we consider is probably one with which you are very familiar; *surveys* are a widely used research tool ideally suited to finding out about people's *attitudes and opinions.* Surveys in the form of questionnaires or interviews are among the most favoured research instruments for the social scientist. Our first case study is a classic study by Ien Ang (1985) who

**FIGURE 6.1** Methods for studying audiences discussed in this chapter

| Method | Object of Analysis | Case Studies |
| --- | --- | --- |
| Surveys and Interviews | People's own thoughts and responses to questions; people's opinions and attitudes. | Ien Ang, 1985. *Watching 'Dallas': Soap Opera and the Melodramatic Imagination.* London: Methuen.<br><br>Andrea Millwood Hargrave, 2000. *Delete Expletives?* London: The Advertising Standards Authority, British Broadcasting Corporation, Broadcasting Standards Commission and the Independent Television Commission.<br><br>Lisa M. Tripp, 2010. 'The computer is not for you to be looking around, it is for schoolwork': challenges for digital inclusion as Latino immigrant families negotiate children's access to the internet. *New Media and Society*, 13(4): 552–67. |
| Focus Groups | The attitudes, opinions and beliefs of people in a group. | Andrea Millwood Hargrave, 2000. *Delete Expletives?* (as above).<br><br>Tim Healey and Karen Ross, 2002. Growing old invisibly: older viewers talk television. *Media, Culture and Society*, 24(1): 105–20. |
| Ethnography | The observed behaviour of people, either alone or in groups. | Daniel Miller, 2011. *Tales from Facebook.* Cambridge, UK/Malden, MA: Polity Press. |
| Oral History | People's recollections of the past; especially of past behaviour and attitudes. | Shaun Moores, 1988. The box on the dresser: memories of early radio and everyday life. *Media, Culture and Society*, 10: 23–40. |

used a very simple kind of survey to develop a sophisticated argument about the pleasures Dutch people enjoyed in watching the culturally reviled American television soap opera, *Dallas*. The second case study was funded by the British television industry to investigate public mores and standards in relation to the sensitive issue of swearing and abusive language on the television. Millwood Hargrave's research *Delete Expletives?* uses both surveys and focus groups in her research (Millwood Hargrave, 2000). The *survey interview* is also used by Lisa M. Tripp in her study of the use of the internet in Latino families (Tripp, 2010). The *focus group* is a technique often used in marketing to test brands and by political pundits before launching new policies or campaigns. Tim Healey and Karen Ross's research into older people's opinions of the way they are represented on television forms our case study in the use of focus groups (Healey and Ross, 2002). The third method we look at is *ethnography*, which we have already discussed in Chapter 4, when we considered investigating the workplace. Here we see how similar approaches can be applied to the study of audiences. *Ethnography* is a research method used in anthropology to observe the practices of different cultures. Daniel Miller is an anthropologist with a great interest in media use – our case study is Miller's exploration of the use of *Facebook* by Trinidadians (Milller, 2011). Our final method concerns how we can use people to capture knowledge of the past using techniques derived from the oral history movement. Shaun Moores' account of older people's recollections of the early days of radio is used as one of our case studies in this chapter (Moores, 1988).

In Chapter 4, *Researching Industries*, we considered some of the methods we could use to study the people who produce the media. Here we will find that there is some overlap when it comes to researching audiences. After all, we are still talking about researching people; some of the same ground rules apply whether the people we are investigating are creators or consumers, producers or audiences. The methods of interview and survey, for example, can both be used effectively to research media production or consumption. However, conceptually, the ways we think about producers and consumers of media artifacts differ in important ways. Mediated communication makes a distinction between the source and the receiver, meaning that producers of the media and culture are fulfilling a different function in the communication chain from the people who consume the artifacts and events. The earliest models of mass communication theory placed producers and consumers at different ends of the communication process.

The figure below shows the simple sender/receiver model of communication on which much previous research into media and culture is based:

Sender → Message → Receiver

Historically, this process has typically been considered as *linear*: originating with the producer creating a message and encoding it as a message that the reader can decode. This model has been built on and developed by scholars who say that feedback is important and that receivers have ways of telling producers what they want. This is a central idea to Stuart Hall's notion of encoding/decoding (Hall, 1981). The implication for the present discussion is that because messages originate with one group of people and are received by a different (albeit overlapping) group, conceptually each party has a very different relationship to the message. This necessarily suggests that different theoretical paradigms are required for understanding their relative roles. Thus, although the interview, for example, is a perfectly legitimate method of interviewing both producers and viewers, the exact way to go about interviewing each different group may well differ. Asking what producers think of a particular television programme, for example, will elicit different kinds of answers than asking viewers.

## WHY STUDY AUDIENCES?

We live in an increasingly mediated society and the rate of change in the media environment is unprecedented. In these days of globalization, we also are increasingly conscious of the rapid changes in media services. This awareness inevitably leads us to ask about the impact of the communication revolution on our lives. Questions about the impacts and influences of the media have driven research for the past century. Audience research puts human experience at the centre of our enquiry. Researching audiences for media and culture allows us to investigate the social uses of the media. By looking at how texts are received, we are able to understand the impacts, influences and effects of the media. Audience research also allows us to examine what people get out of the media, what people like (and don't like) and why.

## RESEARCHING MEDIA EFFECTS

One of the most controversial ideas in media studies, and one of the most widely debated themes, is the notion that the media have 'effects' (Barker and Petley, 2001; Gauntlett, 1995; Moores, 1993). Many people are attracted to studying the media because they have read or heard arguments that the media are powerful influences on our lives. In many newspapers, especially the tabloids, criminal behaviour is often linked with certain kinds of media habits. Sometimes, defendants try to use the media as an excuse, arguing that their actions were caused by media viewing. The film *A Clockwork Orange* was withdrawn by its director Stanley Kubrick because criminals said they had been influenced by it. In other cases, where apparently senseless behaviour is difficult to understand, people may attribute the cause of such actions to violent media. Often in the past, violent videos have been seen as the 'cause' of aberrant social behaviour; for example, in the reporting of the trial of the two children convicted of killing James Bulger, spurious links with the film *Child's Play 3* were made. There are many reasons why it would be convenient to blame the media for things which we don't – or don't want to – understand.

The media are often blamed for social ills to the detriment of identifying the real causes of the problem. In the past, politicians in the US and the UK have found it more convenient to blame various sectors of the media for social ills than their own policies and actions. It is easier to pass a law banning the representation of violence than to prevent violent conduct. But the real causes of violence in society – such as family instability, mental illness or poverty – are harder to solve. The idea that the media might play a role in making people behave badly has been well researched; there is no substantive evidence at all to support it. Criminal behaviour is most readily explained by poor background, poor parenting and a life of deprivation. The fact that people who watch violent videos might also be attracted to violence is a different matter.

There are media products which are designed to bring about change in people's behaviour. Anti-smoking campaigns, drink-driving campaigns and other public safety and health messages are purposefully designed with the goal of changing the attitudes and behaviour of the people who see them. Many studies have shown that the actual effect of these is very minimal: the best we can hope for is that they contribute to a gradual shift in cultural patterns. For example, we know that there has been a reduction in adult smoking over the past 20 years, but can we attribute this to anti-smoking messages in the media? I don't think anyone would be able to isolate a single factor which could be said to have caused this reduction, and, as an ex-smoker, I am unaware of anyone giving up smoking solely as a result of seeing a public information film. The impact of measures such as higher taxation and banning smoking in public places has had a considerably larger effect than any public information film. If purposeful messages designed to have 'effects' are so ineffective, then the argument that the media in general have deleterious effects becomes even harder to support. Many experienced scholars have attempted to study media effects and found very little hard evidence, as Barker and Petley demonstrate (Barker and Petley, 2001). It has been impossible to prove that the media have direct 'effects', and yet in popular discourse the myth persists to the contrary. Students of the media will find it nigh on impossible to prove that the media have effects – you are recommended to avoid this topic in your own work. When designing your own study, you could think about the ways audiences for particular programmes interpret the texts or what pleasure they derive from them. For example, we could study the way a particular group of people use the media as part of their social interaction. The uses that people put the media to are valuable means of understanding the relationship between the reader and the text. These kinds of 'pleasures of the text' are open to investigation by researchers who take the time to ask about them.

## THE ETHICS OF AUDIENCE RESEARCH

In each of the methods we consider in this chapter, your primary focus of analysis is *people*. Before we go any further, we need to consider the special ethical considerations in researching ordinary members of the public. Audience research typically falls within the rubric of what your university probably calls 'human-subjects research'. This means any form of research which involves using people as subjects in a research project. There are special rules and guidelines for dealing with 'human subjects' which your supervisor, or the chair of your university ethics committee, should be able to provide you with. As a general rule, though, you should never expose your subjects to any form of harm – physical or psychological. You should never embarrass or humiliate your subjects, nor should you do anything immoral or improper, or ask your subjects to do anything immoral or improper. You should always make sure you have obtained informed consent. There is very little justification for conducting research using children; likewise with the mentally ill or learning disabled. You should never show people potentially dangerous or pornographic material or break the law or allow your subjects to break the law. For example, if researching audience responses to violent video games, even if you know your 14-year-old cousin plays games for over 18s, you should not interview him about his use, as you would be deemed to be encouraging him. If in doubt, ask; if you can't get an answer, don't do it. Redesign your study if you think there is any chance that you might be in violation of human subjects' guidelines.

We said in the opening section of this chapter that, in the broadest definition of the term, any study of people constitutes a form of audience research. Consequently, potential subjects for audience research are all around us, and offer a valuable resource for the undergraduate researcher to exploit. Your friends, family, colleagues and neighbours all could be encouraged to participate in your research with a little charm and encouragement from you. In the following sections of this chapter, we are going to discuss some of the methods you can use to study audiences.

## SURVEY RESEARCH

The first method we are going to consider is one which is widely used in the media and cultural industries. While ethnography and methods of observation can be useful in finding out about audience behaviour, if you want to find out about people's ideas, opinions and attitudes, there is no substitute for asking them through survey research or interviews. Ien Ang was curious about the popularity of the American soap opera *Dallas*, despite it being considered lowbrow and being condemned by cultural policy-makers. In 1984, she decided to ask viewers what they liked about it, by putting an advertisement in a women's magazine and soliciting letters from *Dallas* viewers.

## Case Study

**Ien Ang, 1985. *Watching 'Dallas': Soap Opera and the Melodramatic Imagination*. London: Methuen.**

In 1984, Ien Ang placed the following advertisement in the Dutch women's magazine *Viva*:

> I like watching the TV serial *Dallas*, but often get odd reactions to it. Would anyone like to write and tell me why you like watching it too, or dislike it? I should like to assimilate these reactions in my university thesis. (p. 10)

At the time, there was a lot of public debate in the Netherlands (and elsewhere in Europe) about the status of American melodramatic series in European television. Ang wanted to find out why people liked these programmes, despite official pronouncements against such examples of American cultural imperialism. In response to her advertisement, Ang received 42 letters, the majority of which were from women or girls (three were from boys or men). This is hardly a representative sample, but rather a self-selecting group of people from among *Viva* readers – which itself is likely to be unrepresentative of the Dutch population as a whole. From a social scientific perspective, there may be some methodological flaws in this research. However, from the letters she received and her subsequent correspondence, Ang created a very rich study of the reasons why people like American melodramatic television. As she says, 'The central question is how these letter-writers experience *Dallas*, what it means when they say they experience pleasure or displeasure, how they relate to the way in which *Dallas* is presented to the public' (p. 11). This work has proved a classic in feminist media studies because of the way it gives voice to a marginalized audience and reaches an appreciation of the complexity of means people employ to understand the media.

Researching audiences by soliciting letters from them may not be a completely reliable method, but Ang's work made a significant impact on our thinking about what people like about television genres. By concentrating her analysis on viewers' reports of their thoughts and feelings, Ang was able to develop a theory of the 'melodramatic imagination'. This study is important because it focused on the (mainly) female viewers of soap operas. *Watching 'Dallas'* helped engender a shift in cultural studies and media studies away from exclusively considering the text, towards thinking about how audiences understand and interpret the media.

Putting an advertisement in an appropriate magazine is one way to target your subject group; it is a method used by Jackie Stacey in her study of fans of Hollywood film (Stacey, 1994). You might also consider sending emails or using *Twitter* or *Facebook* to contact your subjects. Ang conducted her work as part of her dissertation and thus had limited funds. A great deal of research into audiences is conducted by industry bodies, regulators or corporations with an interest in researching the media. Andrea Millwood Hargrave's study (2000) of people's attitudes to offensive language on television, for example, was funded by four different public bodies and therefore constitutes what we might call 'administrative research' into audiences. She was supported by public bodies with an interest in the outcome of her research. The questions she was asking were those which producers of television programmes needed to know – they must be aware of whether their products are offensive or are reflecting the norms and values of society. Likewise, Sonia Livingstone's book *Young People and New Media* (2002) is based on work funded by more than a dozen different companies and government agencies over several years.

There is a recurring interest in media-studies research to investigate harm or potential harm to children. Audiences are constituted as being 'at risk' by investigators who take it upon themselves to identify the processes by which this risk occurs. Fears about harm to children have existed since media studies began. We saw in Chapter 2 how fears about dangers to young people from cinema prompted the investigations by the Payne Fund in the 1930s. The Surgeon General's report of 1972 surveyed all the available data and information at the time in relation to young people's use of television and its impacts on them (Surgeon General's Scientific Advisory Committee on Television and Social Behavior, 1972). One of the criticisms of the Surgeon General's report was that it was laying the blame for perceived problems with youth at the time on the media. The general thrust of the report was that television was responsible for youth crime and 'juvenile delinquency'. It set out to 'blame the media' for the ills of society and thereby diminish their own responsibility. This work is continued in part by the *National Institute for Mental Health* (NIMH) which supports research into all aspects of mental health, including that of the impact of the media. See, for example, Doctor Jay Giedd talking about the impact of playing computer games on the brains of young people in this film from the NIMH website: http://www.nimh.nih.gov/media/video/giedd.shtml (National Institute for Mental Health, 2011). While government-sponsored research has often been undertaken in order to show the harm of the media, and to provide a critique of the media industries, academic research often has a different motive.

One project which aims to help us to understand the media use of children within the family context is represented in our next case study, by Lisa M. Tripp (2010). This is an example of a relatively small-scale project which used interviews as its primary data-gathering technique to study the way Latino families in Los Angeles use computers and the internet in the home.

## Case Study

**Lisa M. Tripp, 2010. 'The computer is not for you to be looking around, it is for schoolwork': challenges for digital inclusion as Latino immigrant families negotiate children's access to the internet. *New Media and Society*, 13(4): 552–67.**

There has been a great deal of research on the 'digital divide' (the difference between those who have access to computer technology and those who do not) and also on the 'participation gap' (between the infrequent and frequent – more confident – users of the internet). Lisa Tripp is interested in internet use in the family setting and draws our attention to a large number of studies which have explored how families negotiate internet use in the home (see, for example, Facer et al., 2003; Livingstone and Helsper, 2007; Seiter, 2005; 2008; Tripp and Herr-Stephenson, 2009). Tripp identifies a gap in the literature regarding the Latino community and decides to turn her attention to the low income, Spanish-speaking communities in Los Angeles. The research presented in this article in *New Media and Society* was conducted as part of the Digital Youth Project (Ito et al., 2009) 'a multi-site ethnographic study of young people's informal learning with new media' (p. 554). Tripp was one of three ethnographic researchers who worked on a media arts initiative in Los Angeles middle schools in 2005–06. The study discussed here focused on the families of one class of one school in which there were a large proportion of Hispanic or Latino students. Interviews were carried out in English or Spanish at the homes of the children with one or both parents and the child to identify the 'media ecology' of the household (Horst et al., 2009). The ethnographic phase of the research was conducted on a relatively small group of just seven families. Tripp justifies this small sample size as follows:

> The goal is not to represent 'Latinos' at large, but rather to speak to the diversity of the Latino experience in the US. (p. 554)

This research looks at how first-generation Latino parents negotiate with their children over internet use. It investigates how parents reconcile the (sometimes contradictory) information they receive about the need for children to access the internet to conduct school work, and the dangers their children may be exposed to while they are on the internet 'looking around'.

The parents interviewed had very traditional values which made them curtail their children's internet use and sometimes saw computers and/or internet connections as an expensive distraction. Tripp finds that the biggest loss to the children interviewed was in terms of socialization – she found that contemporary friendship networks are maintained and strengthened by using sites such as *MySpace* and *Facebook,* and when youngsters were denied this they feared being cut off from their friends and often felt isolated. While recognizing that this specific problem is likely to pass as internet access via mobile phone becomes more common, Tripp defends the value of her study by arguing that her work is:

> ... providing a glimpse into how families negotiated an interesting cultural and historical moment. At the same time ... the study also reflects wider social trends in how Latino immigrant families negotiated children's online participation. (p. 564)

Most social science research is based on people's reports of their actions in surveys or some kind of questionnaire (see Burns, 2000; Deacon et al., 2007a; Punch, 1998). Whether they use questionnaires, interviews or focus groups, researchers are not directly observing respondents to get their information, but are relying on reports of participants in the study. It is important to remember that the subjects are relaying information to the researcher about their world and are thus observing on the researcher's behalf. A key to making sure that respondents give accurate reports lies in the design of the questions asked.

## Questionnaire design

One of the most common ways of asking people about their opinions and attitudes is the survey questionnaire. A survey is used to compare a number of different people along the same variables. A variable is something which you can measure, and which differs between people, such as age or gender. The term simply means 'something that can vary' and is a technical term for something which you can measure. Every item on a survey is measuring a variable of some kind, whether it be age, gender or how many beers you typically drink on a night out.

The national census is a survey of all citizens in the UK carried out every ten years. The government gathers information on all households in the country in order to determine how to allocate resources and to monitor social developments. Elections are a form of mass survey – all voters are expected to say which candidate they want to represent them. Opinion polls are surveys which are used for various things, including predicting the outcome of an election. But in opinion polls, unlike the census or a general election, we don't ask everyone in the country what they think, but only a small sample of people. Organizations like MORI and NOP make generalizations based on these samples of how we will vote in a general election. However, the whole population is not surveyed until the election itself, and their predictions can be wrong. Opinion polls, like all forms of research involving asking people about things, cannot be protected from the possibility that people might not tell the absolute truth. Respondents may misreport in order to make themselves appear to be nicer, or more (or less!) experienced, capable or socially aware. Respondents may want to tell interviewers what they think they want to hear, skewing their answers accordingly. They might make something up to conceal the fact that they don't have a clue about what the interviewer is asking. People will often misreport to make themselves seem more important or knowledgeable than they really are. One of the problems with surveys is that people do not always tell the truth! When designing a questionnaire, you have to be aware of this possibility and take it into account.

Surveys are used in all areas of media and cultural research to find out people's opinions and attitudes. All of the major research companies and industries commission research. Ofcom, the regulator of broadcasting in the UK, commissions reports into public taste and preferences. A forerunner organization, the ITC, conducted frequent research into the standards and mores of the viewing public. For example, Guy Cumberbatch investigated the public's attitudes towards television in his book *Television: The Public's View* (Cumberbatch, 2000). In the following discussion of research questionnaires, we include examples from the ITC's Attitudes to Television Questionnaire (Independent Television Commission, 2001), which was the survey instrument used by Cumberbatch in his research.

## Types of questions

The type of question you want to ask depends on the kind of variable you are trying to get at. In the ITC survey, there are more than 50 questions using a variety of forms of question.

## *Binary questions*

Binary questions are those where there are two alternative responses. If you want to compare the ways men and women differ on a particular issue, for example, you will need to include in your survey instrument a question to identify the gender of your respondents. You may choose to code gender as having only two options: male or female. If operationalized like this, then gender would be a *binary* variable and require you to ask a binary question. You could also ask, 'male = yes/no?' and get the same information, but you would probably offend at least half the people. Sometimes you just want to know a simple answer to a yes/no question. For example, Question 2a on the ITC survey asks:

Have you bought or rented a new television set in the last 12 months?

1 YES

2 NO

*Source*: Independent Television Commission, 2001: 1.

Binary questions, then, are those where it is possible to give one of two responses, usually phrased as 'yes/no' questions.

## *Open-ended and closed-end questions*

In an open-ended question, respondents are asked to fill in their own responses, whereas in a closed-end question, the responses are given in the survey and respondents are required to indicate which is the appropriate response for them. If you wanted to know people's age, for example, you could ask, 'What was your age last birthday?' This is an open-ended question. However, the same question could be asked as follows:

Are you:

1  Under 18

2  18–24

3  25–40

4  41–65

5  66 or over?

In this case, you would not be able to do such fine analysis of the ages of your respondents. However, if you are interested in comparing the responses of 'old' people (whom you have defined as over 40) and 'young' people (whom you have defined as under 40), you will have ample detail with the above closed-end question format. The advantages and disadvantages of each type of question format are well discussed by Ranjit Kumar (1999).

## Using prompts

In conducting a survey, you may want to show your subjects identifiers of particular things. In media research, for example, people may be shown the logo of a television station along with its name to see if they can identify it. This method was used in the ITC survey of people's attitudes towards television. Subjects were shown a series of cards with the logo of all the television stations that were available in their area. First, the interviewers asked the subjects to tell them which channels they watched. Then, the respondents were asked questions about the stations which they had identified. For example: 'Which of these channels would you say you personally watch most often?' (Independent Television Commission, 2001: 4). The interviewer was instructed to ask, 'and which next?' until the respondent had identified four. The answers to these questions were then coded by the researcher conducting the survey interview.

## Constructing scales

Scales are used in survey research when sets of questions are used to develop a more complex picture of general attitudes. The Likert scale, named after the social scientist Rensis Likert, elicits from respondents the strength of feeling towards something (Babbie, 1989). For example, you might present your interviewees with a series of statements and for each one ask them to say whether they: 'strongly agree', 'agree', 'disagree', 'strongly disagree', or are 'neutral/don't know'. The ITC survey includes several questions using Likert scale questions. For example, Question 9a asks:

How interested are you in acquiring a satellite dish?

1 VERY INTERESTED

2 SLIGHTLY INTERESTED

3 DON'T KNOW

4 NOT THAT INTERESTED

5 NOT AT ALL INTERESTED

*Source*: Independent Television Commission, 2001: 11.

In her study of swear words, Millwood Hargrave (2000) uses a four-point scale for people to grade the offensiveness of words: 'very severe', 'severe', 'mild', or 'not swearing' (see Case Study on pages 186–187).

## Semantic differentiation

In a variation on the Likert scale, a semantic differentiation question gives respondents two opposite words and asks them to place their response on the continuum between the two. Survey questionnaires must be very carefully designed to elicit the required information. They have the advantage that information can be gathered in such a way as to be readily analysed by computer programs such as SPSS (Statistical Package for the Social Sciences).

## Sampling

A census asks questions of all the people in the country, and while we might want to find out what everyone in the country thinks about certain issues, that is not usually practical. In most cases, surveys are administered to a representative sample of people, and generalizations are made about how the rest of the population would respond. The government has a responsibility to represent all the people in the country, and they therefore survey everyone in the country and do not have to make generalizations based on their data. For example, the government can definitively say how many people of a particular religion live in a particular area – certainly more accurately than if you sampled all the people living in one street and multiplied that by the number of streets in a town. But you may not be interested in finding out what everyone in the country thinks. If you are interested in studying a particular community – for example, people who attend a particular club or regular film-goers – you are not interested in the opinions of the whole country. In this case, your population is all the people in that group; a sample is the subset that you are going to study. Thus, if you know that a particular club regularly attracts 500 people and you can get 50 people to answer your survey, you have sampled 10% of your population. This is a very good percentage on which to make generalizations. Samples should be random; otherwise, you will not be able to make reliable generalizations.

Many excellent undergraduate projects have been conducted by using questionnaires, and it is not difficult to design and administer your own small-scale questionnaire with some careful thinking and planning. You need to be aware of the different kinds of questionnaire and the different kinds of questions that one can ask (see Roger Sapsford, 1999, for more detailed discussion).

## Some common problems in questionnaire design

There are lots of problems that can arise if your questionnaire or interview schedule is not carefully designed. Below are some common problems in question design which can easily be avoided if you are aware of them in advance.

### Incomprehensible questions

Read your questions through carefully to yourself and then test them on others before you administer the survey. This will help to ensure that you do not have any questions which are simply not understood by your respondents.

### Double-barrelled questions

Questions which have two parts and which respondents may want to answer differently are 'double-barrelled'. Make sure that you avoid them, and that every question asks for a single response.

### Leading questions

Although you might prefer people to answer in a particular way, your survey should be designed so that it is impossible for respondents to guess what they are 'supposed' to say. You must avoid indicating in the question what the answer is supposed to be. For example, the question, 'What did you like about the film *Avatar*?' suggests that respondents did like it – your interviewee will be led to giving an answer which agrees with the question and not one which reflects his or her real belief.

## Speculative questions

Do not ask respondents to speculate on what might happen – for example, by asking, 'What do you think will be the impact of the internet on the film industry?' People may well feel that, because they want to please you, they should have an answer, but they may know nothing about the issue. It is best to avoid speculative questions altogether.

## Presumptuous questions

You should avoid asking anything which is presumptuous, that is, which assumes things about the person that you haven't established. 'What did you watch on television last night?' should not be asked unless you have established that the interviewee was watching television last night. Likewise, 'What kind of films do you prefer to go and see?' implies that people do go to the cinema, and it is therefore a presumptuous question.

## Longitudinal studies

There have been many studies of audience behaviour conducted over periods of time, and we call any such study into the long-term behaviour of respondents, longitudinal. The British Film Institute, for example, conducted an audience-tracking survey in the five years 1991–96. Some 500 respondents filled in questionnaire diaries about their television habits every day (Gauntlett and Hill, 2000; Petrie and Willis, 1995). This same sample was used by Robert Turnock (2000) in his investigation of audience responses to the death of Princess Diana on 31 August 1997. The BBC and other organizations also conduct longitudinal research into media habits. It is unlikely that readers of this book would be in a position to conduct longitudinal studies, but you should be aware of some of them.

## Reliability and validity

No undergraduate study is going to meet the standards of professional research methods which these tests are designed to measure. If you want to know more, there are several good textbooks on the subject, including those by Earl Babbie (1989), Robert B. Burns (2000), Keith F. Punch (1998) and Roger Sapsford (1999).

Survey research is an excellent way to investigate media and cultural audiences. However, students need to take great care in designing their studies and to recognize their limitations. The following case study uses focus groups and survey research to investigate audience attitudes to offensive language.

## Case Study

**Andrea Millwood Hargrave, 2000. *Delete Expletives?* London: The Advertising Standards Authority, British Broadcasting Corporation, Broadcasting Standards Commission and the Independent Television Commission (jointly funded research).**

Andrea Millwood Hargrave combined *survey research* with *focus groups* to understand how people from various backgrounds feel about sacrilegious or otherwise offensive language in the media. This research was funded by several bodies which have an interest in understanding the social mores and need to find out more about public opinion: the Advertising Standards Authority, the BBC, the Broadcasting Standards Commission and the Independent Television Commission. The researchers were required to determine public opinion with regard to swearing and obscenities on television programmes and advertisements, and in advertisements in magazines and on posters. Millwood Hargrave's team interviewed 1,033 people in their homes, asking for their attitudes towards vulgar and obscene swear words. Respondents aged over 18 in several different parts of Britain and from many diverse households were interviewed. They were given a list of words and asked to say how severe in offensiveness each word was from a choice of 'very severe', 'fairly severe', 'mild' or 'not swearing'. The researchers gave a score to each word so that 'very severe' was given three points: 'fairly severe', two; 'mild', one; and the category 'not swearing' was given no points. With this numerical value given to each response, it was possible to calculate a mean (average) score and use this to create the ranking shown in Figure 6.2.

The researchers found, perhaps not surprisingly, that 'cunt' is the word which causes most offence to most people. Because they also collected data on which groups respondents belonged to, and where they lived in Britain, they were able to correlate this information with the ranked data. Thus, they were able to report that respondents living in the south considered the term 'Jew' 'very severe' more frequently than respondents in the north of England. A similar survey had also been carried out in 1998, allowing the researchers to compare results obtained at two points in time and thus to analyse changes in standards. For example, attitudes towards words which insult people on the grounds of race, such as 'nigger' or 'Paki', had changed; people considered these terms of racial abuse more offensive in 2000 than they had previously. However, the relative status of words of profanity had not changed.

**FIGURE 6.2**  Ranked order of the ten most offensive words according to severity in 2000 and 1998

| | Year | |
|---|---|---|
| | 2000 | (1998) |
| Cunt | 1 | (1) |
| Motherfucker | 2 | (2) |
| Fuck | 3 | (3) |
| Wanker | 4 | (4) |
| Nigger | 5 | (11) |
| Bastard | 6 | (5) |
| Prick | 7 | (7) |
| Bollocks | 8 | (6) |
| Arsehole | 9 | (9) |
| Paki | 10 | (17) |

*Source*: Millwood Hargrave, 2000: 9.

# FOCUS GROUPS

There are often advantages to interviewing people in groups in an informal setting which allows subjects to respond in an open way to questions posed by the investigator. Whereas surveys tend to be delivered via pen and paper or electronic questionnaires either alone or one-to-one with an investigator, focus groups bring together groups of people with a researcher working to facilitate discussion around a particular issue or question. The method is widely used in public opinion research, in marketing and advertising to ascertain people's point of view on issues ranging from the presentation style of a prime minister to the taste of a particular brand of chocolate. Focus-group research on the media tends to address questions of audience taste and preference and is a good method for getting an understanding of people's responses, attitudes and beliefs about certain topics (Krueger and Casey, 2009; Morgan and Krueger, 1998; Morrison, 1998).

Millwood Hargrave used focus groups as a follow-up to her survey research to ascertain how people responded to swearing and offensive language on television. She was sponsored by the television industry and this study is thus a piece of industry-sponsored research. Andrea Millwood Hargrave's team used focus groups to find out more about which words people found offensive and the impact of the context of viewing on the degree of offence. Such complex questions as 'why?' and 'in what context?' are too vague to be used in a survey and take time and empathy to elicit. By organizing focus groups of subjects from similar backgrounds one is able to elicit more nuanced, complex ideas. In order to find out why people don't like to hear certain words on television programmes, the researchers conducted a series of focus groups.

This method is more suited to eliciting the degree of embarrassment felt by multi-generational families in the face of offensive language on posters or on television. The focus group element looked at the reactions of 14 different groups, in a discussion lasting two hours. The different groups comprised single white men, black parents, single women, same sex couples, and families with a learning-disabled person. The focus group organizers used video and poster extracts containing offensive language as 'prompts' for the discussions. The focus group study found that people associated swearing with aggression, vulgarity, and inability to express oneself appropriately. Participants reported that they didn't like to hear swearing around children. For example, one British Asian male said: 'If our child sees or hears that [on television], then it's going to think that's the norm' (Millwood Hargrave, 2000: 6). In general, concern over obscenity was expressed by parents of teenagers more frequently than by any other group. This research constitutes a part of the television industry's self-monitoring. It serves an administrative function, much as Lazarsfeld's Radio Research Unit of the 1940s; in other words it is of benefit to the industry to know the limits of acceptability. The advertising industry in particular does the kind of research, which falls under the rubric of 'administrative research' – often for proprietary reasons; the research is undertaken to better understand markets and to target campaigns more effectively.

Focus groups are usually interviewed about one specific topic for a limited time – usually one to two hours in an informal setting. Subjects are made to feel relaxed and comfortable and the focus group is facilitated by a person who is able to establish rapport. If, for example, the focus group comprises disabled people, then a person with a disability would be best to facilitate it. When Tim Healey and Karen Ross used focus groups to find out what older people thought about television they used 'older' people to facilitate those groups. This work, too, was sponsored by the television industry – in this case OnDigital and Carlton Television. The article discussed as the case study below was published in *Media, Culture and Society*, one of the leading academic journals in the field.

## Case Study

**Tim Healey and Karen Ross, 2002. Growing old invisibly: older viewers talk television. *Media, Culture and Society*, 24(1): 105–20.**

Focus groups provide the research method for Tim Healey and Karen Ross's study of the attitudes of older people towards their representation on television. In 2000 the British broadcaster Carlton Television and the digital service provider at the time, OnDigital, commissioned Coventry University to undertake this research on their behalf. Carlton were interested to find out what their loyal constituency of older viewers thought about their services, while OnDigital was concerned to know how to increase take-up of digital services among older people.

There were a total of 24 focus groups, comprising people describing themselves as 'older' and with an interest in talking about television. In addition, four groups of OnDigital subscribers were also organized – in total 228 people participated in the study. The researchers aimed to include subjects from a broad social and geographic spectrum, and recruited from friendship groups, lunch clubs and recreational facilities across Great Britain and Northern Ireland. The aim of the study was:

> To identify what viewers thought about the ways in which older age is portrayed, and how themes of age and aging are treated on television. (p. 107)

The first question was about general attitudes towards broadcasting, and here the single most important issue raised was the amount of swearing on television. Older people saw swearing and references to sex as something which broadcasters used to attract younger audiences for whom such language was ordinary and acceptable. The respondents in this study found such material embarrassing, especially when viewing with younger family members.

One of the key research questions was to find out whether older people thought broadcasters took any interest in them as audiences:

> In the group discussions, absolutely no one did believe that the broadcasters gave a moment's thought to their concerns or interests. (p. 109)

Elsie, in Watford, told the interviewer: 'They think if you're old, you just sit at home and watch the television'; while Sarah said: 'You're not important anymore, you're finished!' Older people found the kinds of programmes which were aired during the day to be of a very poor quality and they considered this offensive.

When asked about the representation of older people on television, they all reported that they found the images to be stereotyped. Healey and Ross report that older people were often shown as:

> dependent, frail, vulnerable, poor, worthless, asexual, isolated, grumpy, behind the times, stupid, miserable, ga-ga, pathetic and a drain on society. (p. 110)

*(Continued)*

*(Continued)*

In the focus group discussions, older people did note the stereotypes but they did not particularly find that a problem. They had contradictory opinions about programmes which specifically portrayed older people such as *Last of the Summer Wine* or *One Foot in the Grave*. The researchers report that: 'Such (unsurprising) contrary views are largely because one person's feisty grandpa is another's curmudgeonly old codger' (p. 111).

They found that the older people in their study had a sophisticated understanding of television and of the way they were portrayed.

The focus group is ideal for researching the responses, ideas and opinions of people in greater depth than a survey. A focus group is an organized discussion of a small group of people on a given topic.

## Advantages and disadvantages of focus groups

If you want to find out why people believe what they do, understand more of the nuanced reasons behind their answers, or question them about their opinions of particular media texts, focus groups are probably the best approach. The focus group is an ideal way to study how people feel about things or to delve into the complexities of their opinions and attitudes. It is a more textured method of analysis, but one plagued with problems of reliability and validity as a consequence.

Individual responses are often lost in the group – the extreme views may be encouraged if held by outspoken people. Sometimes a group mentality develops where some people feel more emboldened to speak than others. Usually ideas bounce off people and you find that you get more information through exchanging ideas in a group than if you just prompt people. You could not be expected to get such large numbers of respondents – both our case studies had external funding – but you could compare two different groups.

## Organizing your own focus group

Professional social researchers pay people to attend focus groups, but students reading this book are unlikely to have the money to do this. If you are thinking about focus group research, consider your access to potential subjects and try to design a study which allows you to use your friends and fellow students or members of your family, or place of worship, as subjects. So, once again, it is best to research an area in which you already have a lot of contacts if you want to use this method.

A focus group might be appropriate if you are interested in the responses of different people towards something. For example, you might want to study how different people respond to a television personality. Let's take Gok Wan, for example. He is a gay television presenter who fronts a number of television shows aimed at women, for example, *How to Look Good Naked.* One might use focus groups to see how men and women respond differently to his persona. Alternatively, you could have groups of 'gay' and 'straight' people and see how their responses differ. Dividing your subjects into different groups according to gender or sexuality would have the advantage of enabling both groups to talk more openly about their responses. If you had gay and straight people in the same groups to talk about sensitive issues to do with sexuality, you can see that they might feel too inhibited to talk openly. However, it has also been said that getting together groups of people of like minds tends to make the ideas they express more extreme, as people may feel the need to conform to what they perceive to be group norms.

If you were interested in how people of different generations use music, you might use focus groups as a part of your study. You could compare how 'young' and 'old' people use music in their lives by, first of all, asking likely candidates to attend focus groups. Getting together about four older people and four younger people in separate groups, you could ask them what they get out of music, what live music they go to, what radio stations they listen to and so on. You should lead the discussion so that you can be sure that both groups follow the same broad subject areas, and you should have a list of topics you want to cover in front of you at the time. You should record your focus groups, but you should also take brief notes as you go along. In this case, a survey, administered in advance, would help you to select candidates for your focus group. The focus group is an ideal way of getting people to discuss their attitudes and beliefs and has become a stalwart of audience research. Arthur Asa Berger gives some useful practical advice on focus groups in his book *Media Research Techniques* (1998a).

# ETHNOGRAPHY

The most direct way of finding out how audiences behave is by observing them in real life situations, using methods derived from ethnography (Abercrombie and Longhurst, 1998; Gray, 2003; Moores, 1993). Ethnographic methods are derived from anthropology, which usually involves the study of foreign people, but while anthropology addresses the exotic, ethnography more typically involves 'making strange' the ordinary and everyday. To conduct good ethnography, you must be detached and removed from the situation, and you observe others without allowing your presence to intervene. Ethnographers of the media have studied how people behave at work, as we saw in Chapter 4, but there are also many ethnographic studies of people's use of the media as audiences. James Lull has conducted several studies in which he looks at people watching television in various family situations and in different countries (Lull, 1990). Lull sent researchers to take notes on the dynamics of television viewing in a range of different households. He uses an army of researchers to do the observing for him and to report on their observations. Lull's work is exceptionally labour-intensive: he has a team of research assistants conducting the participant observation.

It is very expensive to conduct this kind of research and beyond the reach of most readers of this book in terms of scale and depth. However, it is perfectly possible for you to conduct small-scale ethnographic work observing people you know (and who won't feel too awkward about your being there). It is a good method to use in conjunction with interviews so that you can observe people and then ask them about their behaviour. This combination of methods was used by Tamar Liebes and Elihu Katz in their study of Israeli television audiences (Liebes and Katz, 1990). Liebes and Katz observed the responses of different ethnic and racial groups in Israel as they watched the American soap *Dallas*. Groups of friends were observed as they watched the broadcast programme and then interviewed about what they had just seen. Groups were recruited to reflect the ethnic composition of Israeli society and included Arabs, Moroccan Jews, recent arrivals from the Soviet Union and second-generation Israelis on a kibbutz. *The Export of Meaning: Cross-Cultural Readings of 'Dallas'* also includes a chapter (co-written with Sumiko Iwao) which reports on a study observing how Japanese viewers watched the programme. Liebes and Katz were concerned to appreciate how audiences with different relationships to the ideology of America interpreted the programme. The researchers asked the groups to retell the episode they had just seen and coded the subsequent conversations. They found that there were two main types of viewer involvement. The first is 'referential', whereby the viewer relates the programme to reality, especially to their own life situation. In the second, which they label 'critical', viewers discuss the programme in terms of its ideological construction. Most viewers slip between these different modes of involvement quite easily, but Liebes and Katz are able to conclude that the experience of viewing *Dallas* differs according to viewers' social attitudes and position.

The best subject for students conducting observational studies is an area of culture in which they are already participants. Victor Sampedro (1998) conducted an interesting participant observation study of overseas students' use of newspapers from their home countries while at university in the USA. Sampedro was inspired to conduct the study by his own experience of using the newspaper library to keep in touch with events back home. Sampedro observed the patterns of reading ethnographically (he was a participant observer, watching his subjects as he also read the foreign papers), and subsequently he interviewed the subjects about their use of the media. Sampedro's research prompted him to think about the role of the media in helping people to maintain their local identities despite being geographically displaced. The theoretical paradigm for the research (globalization and identity) was secondary in his thinking about this project. Clearly, the topic appealed to him because he shared a sense of identity and community with other foreign students who frequented the newspaper library. Stuart Cunningham and John Sinclair (2001) have assembled a broad collection of essays focusing on media use among Asian communities in Australia which explores some similar themes.

Ethnographic methods are often used in combination with other methods, commonly the interview. Ethnography requires a degree of critical distance that is sometimes difficult to attain when you are involved in the situation yourself. Take your time and give yourself plenty of 'time out' while conducting fieldwork – keep a journal of what happens at events you attend and try to update it frequently during the event. It might militate against your enjoyment of the occasion, but it will dramatically improve your research as a consequence! Remember that you are there to observe the impact of the event on others rather than participating yourself. You should be aiming to get a more critical distance and a deeper understanding of the social milieu which you inhabit.

The impact of new technology on the population in general has been the focus of ethnographic interest with early studies exploring the impact of television in both the US and the UK. Roger Silverstone and colleagues explore a range of audience responses to domestic media technology (Silverstone, 1999; Silverstone et al., 1991). Hillegonda Rietveld's research is about the dance culture she is a fan of and a DJ – a participant observation of dancing (Rietveld, 1998). With so many innovations and changes in technology there is lots of scope for research in this area (see, for example, Miller and Slater, 2000). Daniel Miller is an anthropologist whose work has focused on communities in India, the Caribbean and the UK (Miller, 2010). His work on fashion is fascinating; he explores how an object as simple as the *pallu*, the part of the *sari* that is worn over the shoulder, can be used to signify so many different things (Miller, 2010: 25ff). In a recent book he takes an anthropological approach to the use of *Facebook* by people in Trinidad, which provides our next case study (Miller, 2011).

## Case Study

**Daniel Miller, 2011. *Tales from Facebook*. Cambridge, UK/Malden, MA: Polity Press.**

The starting point for an anthropologist researching *Facebook* is that there is no such thing. The word *Facebook* stands for the social networking facility developed in the US. But what any given population actually

*(Continued)*

*(Continued)*

uses, based on that facility, quickly develops its own cultural genre and expectations, which will differ from others (p. 158).

Daniel Miller is an anthropologist looking at the consequences of the introduction of *Facebook* to the lives of people in Trinidad. He wants to know what impacts it has on the community and on social life.

The 'Trinis' (as the people of Trinidad refer to themselves) have invented new ways of using *Facebook* accommodating and adapting it to their social mores and values. *Facebook* is known by the terms *fasbook* and *macobook* in Trinidad. The word *fas* means being rather too familiar for comfort while *maco* is to be nosy and always prying into other people's business: both characteristics are held by Trinis to be part of their cultural identity; both characteristics have been attributed to *Facebook*. This congruence accounts partly for the way Trinis seem to have taken *Facebook* to heart. Moreover, in a country where so many people travel abroad to work, and/or have family in the UK or the US, social networking has become an important means of maintaining family links as well as forming new relationships.

Miller's fieldwork comprises in-depth interviews and observation of his subjects over about a year; the biggest section of the book is composed of 12 'portraits' of different *Facebook* users with titles like: 'Marriage Dun Mash Up. We watch a man's marriage break up. Why he blames *Facebook*'; 'Time Suck. What do teenagers who spend six hours a day on *Facebook* actually do?'; and 'It Was Just Sex. A sex video which features the lead singer of a band is leaked onto the internet – the consequences'. Each has a story to tell and each uses *Facebook* differently.

In the final section of the book, Miller discusses the implications of *Facebook* for anthropology and draws out the conclusions of his field-work for our understanding of the relationship of media technology to the social world.

Although the method of research involves observation and interview at the level of the *individual*, Miller is able to make generalizations about the broader Trini society, indeed the whole of society itself:

> The secret of *Facebook*'s success, along with that of similar social networks, lies not in change but in conservatism. Above all, *Facebook* really is quite literally a social network. Its importance lies in its perceived and actual ability to reconstruct relationships, especially within families and with absent friends, that had been gradually fading away due to the attrition of other aspects of modern life, such as increased mobility. (p. 217)

Miller uses ethnographic methods to help us understand this specific technology – *Facebook* – from the point of view of the culture. It is fascinating to see how illuminating it is on Trini life, culture and society to read these stories about individual uses of *Facebook*.

One group of audiences who are often the focus of research interest are children and young people, for example Sonia Livingstone's work on children (Livingstone, 2002; Livingstone and Helsper, 2007). The study of young people's media use is a recurring theme in the research. The ways youngsters incorporate the media into their everyday lives is explored by Linda Duits in her study of girls and young women's media use in the Netherlands (Duits, 2008). This study looks at two different groups of girls and how they develop their sense of identity in relation to fashion and media – based on in-depth interviews and observation of the girls.

An important use of ethnography is to listen to voices which were typically marginalized or unheard. Feminist scholars have particularly used ethnography because of the respect and empowerment it accords the subject. Radhika Parameswaran makes it clear:

> For feminist ethnographers especially, rigorous self-reflexivity has become an important channel to interrogate the research process and reveal power inequalities that arise in the field due to social constructions of gender, class, racial, sexual, and ethnic identification. (2001: 71).

John Sinclair, Audrey Yue, Gay Hawkins, Kee Pookong and Josephine Fox (2001) study how the Chinese community of the Asian diaspora living in Australia use the media. They conducted a survey of 50 households, ten from each of the five main Chinese communities, and recruited interviewers able to conduct surveys in both Mandarin and Cantonese as well as other relevant dialects. They wanted to follow up their research with more detailed, ethnographic study, but only four of the households would agree to submit themselves to this level of investigation. Here is a disadvantage of ethnography – that not everyone is willing to submit themselves to such a potentially invasive form of study. Ethnographies of audiences are aided by online studies which are able to investigate communities with very little awareness of the investigator being there.

Autoethnography is a mode of research in reference to oneself and theorizing from the particularity of one's own experience. This mode of research allows one to consider one's own experience (Reed-Danahay, 1997). Karen Boyle used her experience as a new mother to research the 'baby-screening' events at her local cinema (Boyle, 2010). This research involved several weeks of participant observation during which time Boyle attended the baby-screenings at the Grosvenor cinema in Glasgow with her baby and took notes on the activity. This was followed up with interviews with other mothers to discuss the particular pleasures they experienced and how they reconciled the roles of 'good mother' with cinema-going. Matt Briggs researches his own family dynamic in his article about the BBC children's series *Teletubbies* (2006). Ethnography can focus on the self, one's own community or a community of which you are not a part.

If you are thinking about ethnography, you should consider using groups you belong to and your own media use. Think about your friends and family and their media use. A good idea is to watch and then ask questions later. Observe how people behave in a particular social setting and try to reach conclusions about it. Develop a provisional hypothesis or research question and then test it in the field. Ethnography is best undertaken in a reflexive mode and requires a high level of researcher reflection and self-awareness. The method can be applied to real-world or virtual environments, but concentrates on behaviour.

Recent research on fans uses ethnography as a primary method. The work of Henry Jenkins looks at *Star Trek* fans ('trekkies') and observes their interactions when they gather at conferences as fans of the show (Jenkins, 1992). Gray et al. (2007) offer a good selection of essays in their book *Fandom*. Indeed, the literature on audiences constructed as 'fans' has grown into a separate genre of study which offers the beginner researcher plenty of food for thought (Hills, 2007).

## ORAL HISTORY

Interviewing is a very good way of finding out about people's behaviour and their attitudes to the past as well as the present, as we saw in Chapter 4. Oral history is an approach which, for its primary research, relies on interviews with people about their past experiences. It is a method developed in history and uses people's testimony about the past. One of the most powerful applications is the archive collected about the Holocaust – it is used to bear witness. In media studies it has been used to research media producers (see, for example, Mark Williams, 1999). The method can be used to good effect to investigate audiences in the past. Two studies which explore how British people responded to media technologies are Tim O'Sullivan's essay 'Television Memories and Cultures of Viewing, 1950–65' (1991), and Shaun Moores's essay 'The Box on the Dresser: Memories of Early Radio and Everyday Life' (1988) (see also Kuhn, 1999; Richards, 2003). O'Sullivan's study sets out to fill a gap in the existing literature on early television viewing. Most published research focuses on the institutions involved in television production, with the exception of some studies conducted by the BBC (Briggs, 1979; Silvey, 1974), O'Sullivan found that very little work had been done on how audiences experienced television viewing. He concludes that:

> Increased understanding of the domestic conditions and cultures which govern personal television viewing and use has a vital part to play in gaining greater critical insight into the shifting historical and contemporary significance of television and other communication technologies in the transformation of post-war British culture. (1991: 178)

However, very little work has been done in this area and there are lots of potential research topics for students to investigate using this method. One essay which does explore attitudes to radio in its early days is that by Shaun Moores which forms our next case study.

## Case Study

**Shaun Moores, 1988. The box on the dresser: memories of early radio and everyday life. *Media, Culture and Society*, 10: 23–40.**

In this oral history study about the early days of radio, Shaun Moores interviewed people at the Norris Street Old People's Day Centre and the Community Room at the Beaumont County Infant School in his home town of Warrington. Moores does not say how many people he interviewed for the study, but credits ten subjects by name and thanks several others. The study is based on the recollections of older people about their use of radio in the 1920s and 1930s.

Moores is investigating what happened to the status of leisure and entertainment during a crucial period in the social history of the British working class. Most of Moores's subjects were working-class people who lived in the Orford and Quay Bay areas of Warrington. Moores uses historical sources to set the scene of working-class life during this period. The key part of his study investigates the way radio contributed to a withdrawal of working-class social life into the interior. He shows how, with the introduction of the radio, a family audience was constructed, sometimes for the first time. Entertainment and leisure became centred around the household and the family during the 1920s and 1930s, as Moores demonstrates in this very engaging study.

The place to begin to look for subjects for oral history is at home. Asking the older generation about their media use at certain times can be very informative – for example, their recollections of the music scene when they were young. A good research question might be: 'How influential was punk music on people growing up in the 1970s?' If you have family or friends who grew up in a different country, an interesting research area is the way they used the media when they first came to this country. Here you might ask, 'How important is access to "news from home" to first-generation British citizens?' You could research what media were available from your subjects' background country (videos, newspapers, etc.) and ask them which of these they used. You could find out if they used any British media and whether these were useful in helping them to acclimatize to life in their new country. Individual interviews or focus groups would be useful approaches to take in gaining the information required from subjects, but oral history also requires a great deal of historical research.

# COMPARING METHODS FOR RESEARCHING AUDIENCES

In Figure 6.3 we list some of the advantages and disadvantages of the methods discussed in this chapter for conducting your own research into audiences.

**FIGURE 6.3** A comparison of the opportunities and challenges of selected methods for researching audiences

| Method | Opportunities | Challenges |
|---|---|---|
| **Surveys and Interviews** | Surveys provide a good means of getting data which can be readily analysed.<br><br>Interviews (closed or open-ended) allow you to collect first-hand data from subjects. | Survey questions have to be very carefully designed; care must be taken to operationalize the relevant variables.<br><br>Respondents may have more to say than you are asking them! |
| **Focus Groups** | An excellent method of getting nuanced responses to questions. The group dynamic can aid certain kinds of questions. Useful for getting debate going about media which you can present to the group. | People are not always willing to talk in groups; you may find people with stronger personalities swaying the feeling of the group. |
| **Ethnography** | Participant observation and the ethnographic interview are both methods which can produce rich data and complex insights. | It is not always appropriate to observe people in their own environments; there are serious 'ethical' considerations to overcome. |
| **Oral History** | A responsible means of researching which gives voice to the subject, allowing them to speak freely. | You have to rely on people's memories and be prepared to accept discrepancies between their accounts and published ones. |

We have seen how the use of more than one method can be quite illuminating in studying audiences. Andrea Millwood Hargrave's study (2000; discussed above) uses survey research and focus groups to study the mores and attitudes of today's television audiences. Often a survey is a good way to find out general information about a large population before focusing on a smaller sample for in-depth interviews or focus groups. This was also the method employed by the Global Disney Audiences Project, which investigated the meaning of Disney in audiences around the world (Wasko et al., 2001). If you are looking for factual information about audiences, the best approach is probably a closed-question survey. However, if you are interested in studying how people feel about something, then it is best to use a more nuanced method such as the in-depth interview or the focus group. The oral history interview is perhaps the most fluid of all these methods, allowing subjects to determine the course of the interview and to shape the discourse themselves. The selection of method, of course, depends on the way you are operationalizing your question – what exactly is it you wish to prove? How does your method enable you to address your research question?

## DISCUSSION

In this chapter, we have discussed some of the main ways in which audiences have been researched, and we have given you some guidelines for conducting your own audience research. In dealing with audiences, we come closest in media and cultural studies to the ethical considerations faced by many other researchers who use people in their research. We must always be wary of doing harm to people and remember that there are serious ethical considerations to be taken into account. You should never ask people to do anything that might cause them harm, physical or psychological. So you should not get into areas that people might find upsetting. Always get informed consent to anything and make sure that the subject knows what is going to happen. You don't necessarily have to give away what the survey is about if that might jeopardize your results, but always debrief the subjects and tell them as much as you can about your work.

The audience-research methods discussed in this chapter can also be combined with other methods discussed elsewhere in this book. For example, you could conduct a semiotic analysis of a film and then conduct focus groups to find whether your own interpretation is shared, or whether other people can provide different insights. Here you would be combining textual analysis with audience research. There is no right or wrong way to conduct audience research; you must just find the right method for your research question. The study of audiences is one of the most fruitful and productive areas of researching media and culture.

## FURTHER READING

Deacon, David, Michael Pickering, Peter Golding and Graham Murdock, 2007. *Researching Communications: A Practical Guide to Methods in Media and Cultural Analysis.* 2nd edition. London: Bloomsbury Academic.
This book provides some very useful descriptions of the methods discussed here; see especially Chapter 3, 'Selecting and Sampling', for a discussion on how many subjects you need for a focus group.

Gray, Ann, 2003. *Research Practice for Cultural Studies: Ethnographic Methods and Lived Cultures.* London: Sage.
For further discussion on organizing focus groups see Richard A. Kruger and Mary Anne Casey's *Focus Groups: A Practical Guide for Applied Research* (2009).

Priest, Susanna Hornig, 1996. *Doing Media Research: An Introduction.* Thousand Oaks, CA/London: Sage.

A very student-friendly guide to research methods one can apply to the study of the media. See Chapter 7, 'Interpreting', for an especially useful description of qualitative methods.

Tulloch, John, 2000. *Watching Television Audiences: Cultural Theories and Methods*. London: Arnold.

An engaging, wise and intelligent analysis of the place of audience research within cultural studies. Tulloch offers a thorough and thoroughly interesting survey of the diverse research methods which scholars have adopted in researching audiences, grounded in the relationship of theory to method.

Below are some links to journal articles which have been discussed in this chapter. Our case study on the ethnography of computer use among Latino families with children, by Lisa Tripp is available on the link below.

Tripp, Lisa M., 2010. 'The computer is not for you to be looking around, it is for schoolwork': Challenges for digital inclusion as Latino immigrant families negotiate children's access to the internet. *New Media and Society*. **13** (4): 552–567.

Victor Costello and Barbara Moore published an interesting study of television audiences using on-line survey methods published in *Television and New Media*. **8** (2): 124–143. http://tvn.sagepub.com/content/8/2/124.full.pdf+html.

## TAKING IT FURTHER ... ON YOUR OWN

*Thinking about yourself as part of an 'audience'*

Keep a diary of how you use the media and culture and with whom. How often are you part of a community of users? Consider how often you are co-present (in the same place) as other people using the same medium. How often are you sharing media with others at the same time? Conduct an 'autoethnography' of your own media use – reflect on the social situations in which you use the media. Do you ever feel yourself to be part of an 'audience'? How does being a member of an audience give you a sense of identity or belonging?

## TAKING IT FURTHER ... BEYOND THE CLASSROOM

*What is an audience?*

Select one media industry and identify how many different ways the users of this medium are treated as 'audiences' How is the audience 'constructed' through various discursive strategies? Look at industry statistics, academic journal articles, the newspapers, and blogs and websites of workers. How can you research audiences by bringing together these different approaches?

# PART 3
## PRESENTING YOUR WORK

# GETTING FINISHED

## Aims and Objectives

- This chapter offers some advice to help you finish your dissertation, giving you guidance on how to write up your work and present it.

- We discuss the parts of the dissertation and a typical layout of your final work. We consider each of the following parts in turn:

  - abstract

  - introducing your subject

  - writing a literature review

  - talking about theory

  - describing your methods

  - showing what you find

  - writing a conclusion

  - references and sources.

- We offer some suggestions for how to present your table of contents.

- We discuss the importance of understanding the rules and regulations including those relating to plagiarism and referencing.

- We consider the criteria for assessment and the importance of feedback.

- Where to go from here?

## INTRODUCTION

How you present your work will be an important determinant in how well your tutor is going to be able to evaluate your work. Your tutor will be looking to see how you have organized your work and to ensure you have met all the criteria for completion of the assessment. You need to think about presentation and style while you are working on your project, and think about how you are going to organize and submit your work while you are conducting the research. You have to give evidence for all the work that you have done: you don't get any marks for anything which is not actually presented. Your tutor is able to give you credit only for what you actually submit. This chapter will guide you through the main principles you should bear in mind when writing a project. It also includes some examples of tables of contents and how to present your dissertation in a professional and scholarly way. The success of your project depends on how well you can convey to the reader what you have done and why. Other works which can help you in writing up your project include books by Judith Bell (2010) and Derek and Ruth Swetnam (2009). For matters of style and presentation, refer to your university guidance in the first instance, as there may be specific criteria that will be applied at your institution; otherwise, see Richard Pears and Graham Shields's guide, *Cite Them Right* (Pears and Shields, 2010).

## CRITERIA FOR ASSESSMENT

In each institution, and on each degree course, there will be different criteria for assessment. Make sure you are familiar with the criteria your tutors will be using when they mark your work. These will usually be written in the module guide or course handbook. The kinds of things which your tutors will be looking for are:

1 *The originality of the idea*. How far is your research building on something new and original? As discussed in Chapter 3, this is not something which no one has ever thought of before, but something which comes from your own experience. You need to explain what is original about your work – why you chose to research this subject. Even if several other people are writing on the same 'topic', no one is telling it quite the way you do; make sure you get across how you have personally approached this subject and why.

2 *The 'so what?' question*. You are not necessarily going to solve all the world's problems, but the implications of the project for the broader field of study should be explained. Make sure you answer the 'so what?' question and spell out the generalizability of your work. Why is it important? Why should anyone care about your work?

3 *How well does your project build on your previous studies*? You need to demonstrate how your work relates to published research in the area. You should show that you have read widely and considered all relevant debates in the area.

4 *How well have you conceptualized the project*? The design and planning of the project will provide an important element of most assessments. Your tutor will want to know that you have thought carefully about the design and execution of your project. Whether your project is valid and reliable is also likely to be a criterion. You should ensure that your project investigates what you claim it does and does so in a manner which is appropriate. You will need to demonstrate that you have thought about the relationships among your *object of analysis*, the *theoretical paradigm* you are working within and your *methodology*.

5 *Structure, organization and presentation*. How well have you organized and presented your work? Is it easy to read and to find different parts of the dissertation? Make sure that your work is divided into meaningful chapters with headings which help the reader find their way round the project. Carefully proofread your work before submitting it. It is a good idea to give yourself a week or so to go through the final text carefully before you submit it to check your grammar and punctuation. You should also confirm the spelling of any unfamiliar words or names. Your work will benefit from being well written, so make sure that you check your style – often it helps to read it out loud to see if it makes sense. Although you don't get any extra marks for having brightly coloured binders and professionally bound dissertations, it is important to take care over presentation. Make sure that your work is neat and tidy and that you have structured and organized the chapter headings and subheadings appropriately. Your work should be typed, double-spaced, on one side of the paper and clearly labelled. Any illustrations or supplementary material (such as a DVD or data stick) should be carefully labelled and firmly attached, including your student name or number. Include a cover sheet with the title of your dissertation, the name and number of the unit or module, your course title and your name.

6 *Have you reflected on your work*? It is very valuable for you to think back over the project as you get ready to submit it and to think about how you think it has gone. Are there things you could have done better? Take advantage of the benefit of hindsight – would you have done it differently now? A good scholar always thinks back on their work and considers how they might have done better.

## PLANNING YOUR WORK

You need to think ahead to the presentation stage while you are conducting your study. You can begin to write elements which will go into the final version of the essay from the beginning. Make sure you keep a full record of every book, article, journal and television programme of relevance to your project as you come across them. Keep an annotated provisional bibliography – jot down everything you should, could or might refer to in your final dissertation. Go back to this list frequently and keep tabs on what you have managed to get hold of. If something turns out to be no good, make a note of why. If something is very useful, make a more detailed note of why, and think about how it relates to the other things you have on your list.

Keep a log or diary of what you do towards the project. Include things like making telephone calls (even if they weren't productive), going to the library and talking with your supervisor. This will help you to reflect on how you are progressing. The diary can provide a good basis for discussion with your supervisor in the early stages of the project.

It is very important to write an outline of your project as early as possible in the process, as we discussed in the first chapter of this book. Time spent at the beginning of the project will save you time in the long run. The more research you do on the planning stage, the less likely you are to encounter obstacles later in the process.

# THE PROJECT CONTENTS

You need to be aware of the elements that your project should contain. For example, do you need a table of contents? What should be in the main body of the text and what in the appendices? Your tutor will probably provide you with guidelines on what is required at your university, so you should check with the teaching staff if there are any particular requirements. In general, though, your final project should contain the following elements.

## The table of contents

The presentation of your material in clear sections is very important. It helps you to organize your material and helps readers find their way through the work. The table of contents should list the main chapter or section headings and, if necessary, the subheadings without going into too much detail. As a general rule, the table of contents should not exceed one page in length and need not comprise more than five lines. Remember that the most important function of the table of contents is to ensure that readers can find their way to specific sections if they wish, so do include page numbers. Table 7.1 gives an example of a generic table of contents which could be used for almost any kind of project! Use this as a template for organizing your own research project. Of course, the exact nature of the table of contents will vary from project to project and needs to reflect what you actually did in the project. A hypothetical table of contents for a project analysing the representation of femininity in magazines for black women is also provided, in Table 7.2.

**TABLE 7.1** A generic table of contents

| Title |
| --- |
| 1  Introduction |
| 2  Literature review |
| 3  Hypothesis |
| 4  Method |
| 5  The study |
| 6  Discussion |
| 7  Conclusion |
| 8  Bibliography |
| 9  Appendices |

## Introducing your work

It may sound obvious, but the introduction is the first thing the reader is going to read about your work, and it is important that it does several things clearly and concisely. First, it must specify what the project is about, indicating what the reader can expect from the rest of the essay. You need to state your research question here and say why you are interested in this topic. Don't be afraid to discuss your personal rationale: the reader will be more engaged if you have a personal reason for investigating the topic. For example, Karen Boyle explains at the beginning that she became interested in the 'Watch with baby' screenings at her local cinema when she herself began attending with her baby (Boyle, 2010). Boyle describes her own interest in the project at the beginning. As much of our work is based on personal experience it is necessary to state one's own involvement whenever that is appropriate; this not only makes the dissertation more interesting, it also adds to the *ethos* of you as writer. We saw in Chapter 1 how in classical rhetoric, an argument made by someone with experience can be much more credible. The introduction should also give a very concise précis of the research method and theoretical paradigm used – it should be an exposition of your research question telling us what you are going to do in the subsequent chapters and why. A brief résumé of the implications and significance of your work will also help here.

We have discussed the research question in Chapter 3 – you will need to think about how to design and present your research question and this should be stated clearly in the introduction. When you start you will need a draft of the introduction to make sure everything else follows, but be prepared to go back and change it in the light of changes you might make in the rest of the project. The introduction may not be finalized until you have completed the project. Sometimes it is best to write the introduction very quickly at first – just jot down on paper where you intend to go with the project. Later, when you have finished the entire project and written the conclusion, go back to the introduction and rewrite it completely, bearing in mind where you have actually gone with the project. Keep it brief and keep it interesting, and, although it is the first thing the reader sees, it should be the last thing you write. In our hypothetical example below, the introduction should state why the researcher wants to study the representation of femininity in magazines for black women. The introduction should indicate to the reader where the researcher is going to take them and what is at stake in the project.

**TABLE 7.2**  A hypothetical table of contents

The Representation of Femininity in Magazines for Black Women

1  Introduction

2  Previous literature on women's magazines and representations of femininity

3  Research question: Is the discourse of femininity in magazines for black women empowering?

4  Content analysis and discourse analysis: discussion of the method

5  Analysis of six issues of *Pride*

6  Discussion

7  Conclusion

8  Bibliography

9  Appendix: coding sheet

## Reviewing the literature

In any project, you will need to show that you have read widely by reviewing the literature on the topic. This could include books, journal articles, trade literature, videos or lectures. Whatever has informed your thinking needs to be discussed and reviewed here. Although it is called a 'literature review', it is really more of a survey of what has been written on your topic. Your literature review should include 'classic' texts as well as more recent articles and books about your topic. In other words, you are not supposed to evaluate whether the literature is good or bad, as you would in a book review for example, but you should say what the literature says that is of relevance to what you are going to say. In our hypothetical project (see the 'Hypothetical table of contents' above) we would: a) include the literature on women's magazines and on feminist debates about the representation of women generally; b) include discussion of literature about the representation of black women, whether related specifically to magazine representations or not; c) comment on the strengths and weaknesses of the literature overall; and d) draw out of the literature some key themes, and comment on the extent to which we agree with the authors discussed.

You should give credit to the source of your ideas – show you have read widely. Think about what others have said on the subject. It is a good idea to write the literature review early on in the project – you may come across something in your reading which makes you change your mind about the project. So read widely and give a draft of your literature review to your tutor as soon as possible.

The literature discussed should be organized thematically. Think about the main subject areas that the literature falls into: how can you categorize all the literature that you have read? You may want to put all the researchers of one persuasion together, or to discuss all the trade literature separately from the academic. For example, 'literature about women's magazines' might be one section, while 'black feminist perspectives' could be another. The literature review should present all the arguments which you are going to discuss.

It is a good idea to show the literature review to your supervisor at an early stage to ensure that you are covering enough ground and that your work is going in the right direction. Don't expect to change the literature review much once you get into the research, unless you come across some new literature during which alters the focus of your project. The point of the literature review is for you to find out what has been said before and to set out how you are going to push forward the sum of our knowledge in this area.

The literature review section should explain how your reading and knowledge of the field, allied with your personal interest discussed in the introduction, have informed the design of your project. Here you are locating your work among the existing scholarship in the field. One of the ways you prove that you have the right to speak, or *ethos* to speak, is by demonstrating that you, too, are something of an expert by virtue of the fact that you have read so widely. You have to give the reader reason to believe what you say – one of those reasons is that you understand the field and know where your own work fits in (for more discussion of ethos see Chapter 1, especially page 12). The literature review section of your project should lead logically into your research question or hypothesis.

## Stating your research question or hypothesis

Whatever the nature of your study, you need to be able to state in a clear, single sentence what you wish to demonstrate or test. It may or may not be in the form of a hypothesis, but should be emphasized in the text in boldface or underlining to indicate its importance. The research question should follow on from the literature review, and the relationship between the two needs to be spelled out clearly. In our example the research question is: 'Is the discourse of femininity in magazines for black women empowering?' The researcher would need to demonstrate how the question follows on from the literature discussed.

## Explaining your method

Having stated your research question, the next step is to say how you are going to conduct your research. Here you are specifying how you have operationalized the question or hypothesis. You need to be very clear about the relationship between the hypothesis and the method(s) employed. You must show that the method chosen is a valid and appropriate test of the question.

## Describe your study

Explain exactly what you did, when and why. Do not worry that you do not always see this in published research – for the purposes of the project, you will usually be expected to show how you conducted your study. Include discussion of any false paths you have followed – the reader will want to see that you have learned from your mistakes and that your ideas have developed in the process of designing and conducting your study.

Clarify your object of analysis. If it is a film study, state what films you looked at and why you chose those, and not others. If it is an interview-based method, explain how you found your interview subjects and what kind of interview you used (for example, open-ended or closed-end questions). Justify each design decision you made in academic terms, not expediency – 'I only interviewed five people because that was all I could be bothered to get' or 'that was how many people came over on Friday' is not an academic justification. However, 'small groups of close friends feel more comfortable talking about sensitive issues' may be a perfectly acceptable academic rationale for a focus group of five. In our example, content analysis of the kinds of women represented in conjunction with a discourse analysis of the context of representation are perfectly justifiable methods. Content analysis is a tried and tested method of analysing the content of media, while discourse analysis answers nuanced questions around issues of empowerment.

## Arguing your case/presenting your findings

The next stage in the project is to say what you found when you conducted your study. If you have done a more empirically based study, you will have to come up with facts and figures that you need to present in an uncluttered manner. Here you should expand on the findings to relate them to your original hypothesis or research question. Think carefully about what you have learned in researching the project and be clear and logical about presenting what you have found. This is the most important part of the write-up and the one that the reader will focus on the most, so make sure you bring out all the main points in this section. Content analysis is a quantitative method which will generate tables of data which you should present. In our example, you would produce one coding sheet for each issue of *Pride* you analyse, and one summary sheet of the overall findings.

## The conclusion

The final part of the text should conclude your work, showing how you have done what you set out to do in the introduction. The conclusion should briefly summarize the whole project, so make sure that you do refer to what you did in the previous sections. The conclusion should link in neatly with the introduction. Show in the conclusion how, having reached the end of your research, you have addressed the questions raised in the introduction. If necessary, go back and rewrite the introduction. It may seem like a cheat, but in fact it is just good writing style to 'telegraph' to the reader what is going to happen and why. Only when you know the whole plot from beginning to end can you sit down and write the first scene. The conclusion needs to relate directly to the introduction and to tie up any loose ends.

## The bibliography

Your bibliography should include everything that has informed your dissertation. It is a statement of the books and other material you have referred to. By including something in the bibliography, you are saying that you have read it; although it is not expected that you have read every word of the works it lists, the bibliography should include everything that you mention in the body of the text. It is correct academic procedure to include only those items that you have referred to in the text. But it is also essential that you include in your bibliography everything that you have mentioned in the project. See Richard Pears and Graham Shields' book *Cite Them Right*, (Pears and Shields, 2010).

It is very important that you give full and proper references at the end of your project. You need to give credit to every source, primary and secondary, that you have used in your work. Whenever you reference something, you are saying that you have used that work – never reference something that someone else has referenced. If you come across a quotation within an article, for example, you may not quote it in your work. If you think it is indispensable to your research to use that quotation, you should go to the original source. Find out if the person who actually used those words intended that they should be used in that way. Read the context in which they were first written. Maybe this is a better resource than the one you first found it in – great! When you have read the quotation in the original form and then you can use it in your own work; you have not actually accessed the work until you have read and understood it for yourself. Your first source may well have misunderstood the quotation or taken it out of context.

All statements of fact usually need to have a source: you should give a bibliographic reference for any statistic you use in your essay so that readers can verify your source. You do not have to include in your bibliography sources of information which may be considered 'general knowledge'. Therefore, if you need to use a reference book to find out when the Queen ascended to the throne or who directed *Sixth Sense*, you don't need to give a reference for your source or list it in your bibliography. See 'Style Matters' below for details of how to list your bibliographic and other material.

## Appendices

Footnotes are the notes at the bottom of the page: in general, it is best to avoid these. As a matter of style, if you have something to say, say it in the body of the text. Appendices are not usually included in your final word count (but check with your supervisor). Here you should include transcripts of interviews or samples of your questionnaire or 'instrument'. The appendix should include full details of data collected in the project.

# STYLE MATTERS

Let's consider some of the ways in which your presentation and style can be enhanced and improved. In this section, we look first of all at what not to do, and consider the problems of plagiarism and poor grammar and punctuation which so often let students down. Then we present a guide to writing your bibliographic and other reference information.

## A note on plagiarism

When you submit your essay, you are effectively saying that the work is yours. You put your name to it and you submit it for assessment along with all the other people in your class. If you present someone else's work as if it were your own, this is plagiarism. Plagiarism means copying and it is a form of cheating by stealing. When you copy work without giving the author credit for it, you are breaking the codes by which academics work – you are defying a professional norm which protects people's work from being appropriated by someone else. Never copy. Plagiarism can result in expulsion from the university. There are systems for testing how much of your work is similar to others, for example the website *Turnitin*.

## Quotations

You should use quotations in your essay, but take care not to use too many or to quote too much. It is fine to quote up to about five lines; anything longer should be paraphrased. You need to demonstrate that you have read and understood the relevant literature and often you can do this best by putting ideas in your own words. As a general principle, direct quotations should be used when an author's words cannot be easily summarized.

## Notes on references

There are two different general ways in which bibliographical information is presented in published work. One uses numerical notes in the text to refer the reader to a reference at the end of the page or document. This is sometimes called a 'note system' and includes the Chicago style and the Modern Language Association (MLA) style. The note system method is most fully explained in *The Chicago Manual of Style* (1993) and in Kate Turabian's *Manual for Writers* (Turabian, 1997). This system has the advantage that all the references are presented in the order in which they are mentioned in the essay – this can give a more fluid feel to the references. Its disadvantages are that it can be quite repetitive – a reference is separately listed each time it is mentioned, and it can be difficult to find specific references. The more commonly used style in the social sciences (a variation of which I have used in this book) is the author/date reference, or APA (American Psychological Association) style. In this system, the author and year of publication are mentioned in the body of the text, and the reader can find the specific reference by looking up the author's name in the alphabetical list of references at the end of the work. This system has the disadvantage that the greater level of information in the body of the text can be distracting to some readers. It has the advantage that the precise citations are easier to find in the bibliographic list of references. It is strongly recommended that you keep careful track of your sources in order to be sure that the referencing does not go astray.

## Citations in the text

In the author reference style, the name of the author is the one that should be given in the text. If you are referring to a book by one author you should always give that name in the text:

(Rose, 2007)

If you are giving a quotation you should also give the page number:

(Rose, 2007: 72)

Where you are citing an essay in an edited volume, you do not refer to the editors in the body of the text, but to the author of the particular essay you have read:

(Tripp, 2010)

The above could refer to an essay in a collected volume, a journal article or a book. The author reference system makes no distinction in the body of the text – you have to go to the bibliography to find out about the actual publication. Remember that it is only necessary in your essay to give the name of the author and the year of publication – the reader should then be able to consult the bibliography to get further information. Where there are two pieces by the same author published in the same year in your bibliography you should refer to one as

(Storey, 2009a)

and the other as

(Storey, 2009b)

In the bibliography, they should also be listed as 'a' and 'b'.

In some cases, as in some magazines and several websites, the author of the piece is not always given. In these instances, you should cite the institution publishing the piece as the author – for example, *The Economist* or the Periodical Publishers' Association. These institutional authors should be treated like any other and listed alphabetically alongside other authors in the bibliography.

## Writing your bibliography

Note carefully the use of punctuation and italics below. It is very important to follow the exact order. List the author's surname first in the bibliography, followed by a comma and then the first name.

### Single-author books

Where there is one author of a book, you should use the following format:

Jenkins, Henry, 2007. *Convergence Culture: Where Old and New Media Collide.* New York: New York University Press.

### Edited volumes

Where you are citing the whole volume, the format should be as follows:

Cunningham, Stuart and John Sinclair (eds), 2000. *Floating Lives: The Media and the Asian Diasporas.* St. Lucia, Queensland: University of Queensland Press.

Note that, although the first author is listed surname first and given name second, subsequent editors should be listed with their names in the usual order. It is necessary to invert the normal order of names only when you are making an alphabetical list by authors' last names. More frequently, you are likely to be referring to an individual essay in a collection, in which case you should use the following form:

Bell, Philip, 2001. Content analysis of visual images. In Theo van Leeuwen and Carey Jewitt (eds), *Handbook of Visual Analysis*. London: Sage, pp. 10–34.

Note that you should always give the page numbers for an essay in a collected volume, although this is not necessary for a whole book. The abbreviation used for pages is pp.

## Journal articles

For journal articles, you also need to list the page numbers of the relevant volume. This is the format to follow:

Napoli, Philip M., 2010. Revisiting 'mass communication' and the 'work' of the audience in the new media environment. *Media, Culture and Society* **32** (3): 505–516.

Note that the titles of articles in journals and of essays in collected volumes are given without capitalization; however, the titles of books and journals are capitalized. The volume number is printed in bold **32** and the issue number is in parentheses(3). There is a colon after the issue number followed by the page number.

## Newspaper articles

The entry for a newspaper article is as follows:

Meikle, James and Alison Flood, 2012. Sales of ebooks soar – but paperbacks are selling too. *Guardian*. 19 September. p. 11.

Most newspaper articles have bylines showing the author of the piece and you should always give the author's name whenever possible. In cases where no author is given, you should refer to the publication as the institutional author. Thus an article in the *Guardian* with no given author (for example, the editorial) would be listed with the *Guardian* as its author in the bibliography.

## Broadcast material

When citing broadcast material, you should always give the name of the series or producer. Give sufficient information about the production: company, title of the programme, title of the series, and the date and channel of first transmission. In long-running series, such as soaps or the news, always give the date of transmission. For a videotape or DVD, give the publication date.

## Websites

When doing research on the internet, always write down the URL, or web address, of every site you visit (for example, www.ppa.co.uk). URL stands for Uniform resource locator and appears in the address bar of your browser. You should also write down the name of the author, whether it is an institutional one (for example, the Periodical Publishers' Association) or a person. If you want to reference a page on the site with a named author, such as the director's message, you should use the person's name as the first part of your reference. For example, if referring to Derek Carter's message in the Annual Report of the Periodical Publishers' Association, you should do so as follows:

Carter, Derek, 2002. A message from the PPA Chairman. Periodical Publishers' Association. http://www.ppa.co.uk/annualreview/index.htm. Accessed: 7 February 2002.

If, however, you want to refer to information on the same website which does not have any named author, you should use the name of the organization publishing the information as the author. In the following example, the Periodical Publishers' Association is the institutional author:

Periodical Publishers' Association, 2002.

Note that you should always give the URL as it appears in the address bar. The easiest way to do this is to copy that data directly into your document, making sure that the punctuation remains unchanged. Any line breaks should be made after a dash or full stop, and no other punctuation (such as hyphens) should be added.

Wherever possible, you should cite the author of any web page and list the author's name as the first field in your references. This should be followed by the year of access, with the rest of the date following later; for example:

Paik, Nam, June 2002. Context. http://www.geocities.com/namjunepaik/ context.html. Accessed: 7 February 2002.

In the body of your text, there is no need to treat your electronic references differently from any other. If you are using a footnote style, you just list the reference as a number; if you are using an author reference, you use the author/date index. Thus, the references above would be cited in your text as follows: (Carter, 2002), (Periodical Publishers' Association, 2002) and (Paik, 2002).

The APA gives details of how to reference electronic sources on its website: http://www.apastyle.org/elecmedia.html#link.

As a general principle, remember that you are giving reference to the authors of the work you have read. As far as possible, you should always list the author in your bibliography and in your reference in the text. In the case of books, book chapters, journal articles and so on, it is usually pretty clear who the author is. But sometimes it is not possible to identify a person as an author. In magazines, journals and newspapers where no author is given, you should cite the title of the publication as the author: the author is almost certainly an employee of the publication and is speaking with the voice of the publication. In the case of a website or an official publication such as a company report, the author will be the company providing the website (e.g. nua) or report (e.g. Granada). Again, these are official mouthpieces of organizations that need to be referenced. It is never appropriate to use 'anon' or 'anonymous' as an author except in very rare examples such as quoting from traditional rhymes and poems. Almost everything you are likely to quote comes from a specific source that must be credited and acknowledged.

Several American universities have excellent writing centres which provide students with help on all aspects of essay writing. Dartmouth College has an excellent guide for students to use when writing their term papers. It is also very useful in giving information on how to reference different kinds of material. It is very easy to use and find your way around; see www.dartmouth.edu/~sources/. Another useful site is that of the University of Purdue's Online Writing Lab (OWL), which has readily printable data on a wide range of presentation topics, including using the APA and MLA styles: www.http://owl.english.purdue.edu/handouts/research/index.html. Your own study skills department should be able to provide you with further guidance and support.

## WHERE TO GO FROM HERE?

What happens when you have finished your dissertation, given it in and had a well-deserved break? For many students it is the last thing you do at university and it may be that it will take some time before you get it back. By the time you do look at it again you may find that you are in a new phase of life – perhaps you have left university and gone on to the world of work or further study. It is tempting with new things to do, to forget about the dissertation and, having worked so hard, to put it behind you as you go on with your life. I would advise you not to forget all that work you have done! Make sure you collect your dissertation and meet your tutor, and read the feedback and reflect carefully on what she or he says. This may well be the culmination of your university career, but it might be the beginning of a new phase in your life. Think carefully about what lessons you can learn about working on your own, about designing and setting your own targets, and about how you can present your work in future. I am sure there will be much good work to reflect on. Cherish the memory of the good work you have done and value it. Focus on the good things you have achieved and congratulate yourself on a job well done!

One of the main pedagogic goals of the dissertation or project is to enable students to research independently. When you work hard on your dissertation you find that you acquire resources that will serve you well in the future. Being able to conduct independent research means that you can take responsibility for your own ideas. You can design and execute a research project. You will have utilized the skills you learned on your degree and perhaps even developed some new ones. I hope that you will look back on the experience and realize how much you have learned about your subject, but also how much you have learned about yourself. You should gain a great deal of satisfaction looking back on the way you have designed, conducted and written your own research. Who knows, perhaps the experience will spur you on to research more and to continue with further study or publish your own book. When I started to write this, the second edition of *How to do Media and Cultural Studies*, it was the anticipation of reading your work in the future which inspired me. What will be the inspiration for your next piece of research?

# GLOSSARY

**'Administrative' research** – a term to refer to research undertaken with a commercial orientation, in order to advance the successful running and administering of an organization or institution. The term is most associated with Paul Lazarsfeld and his Bureau of Applied Social Research at the University of Columbia in New York. See discussion on pages 36–37

**Antecedent variable** – a variable which is not being measured in a study but which may be causing change in both the independent and the dependent variable; a variable with explanatory power which has not been considered in the study (see also **variable**).

**'App'** – short for 'application', a computer word for program. Rose to prominence with the introduction of the iPhone which first developed their use.

**A *priori*** – something which is already known or is self-evident.

**Archive research** – research undertaken based on archives (collections of material) which may be physical or virtual. See pages 81–89 for a discussion of archive research.

**Article** – in academic discourse an article (or paper) is the name given to a piece of work published in an academic journal.

**Audience** – the people who use the media and culture; audience could be used to refer to a group of people gathered in one place or at one time, for example, to see a play in a theatre. Equally, audience has come to refer to those people who have accessed any media or cultural artifact – the end-users of a product.

**Auteur study** – to research a text as the product of a specific author; to identify a single articulating intelligence, be it the director of a film, producer of a television programme or designer of a game. A form of study identified with the French film critics associated with the magazine, *Cahiers du Cinéma*. See discussion on pages 156–161.

**Autoethnography** – a research paradigm in which one's own experience is the object of analysis. See discussion on pages 195–196.

**Average** – see **mean/median/mode**.

**Causality** – the extent to which changes in one variable may be said to be caused by changes in another; how much one thing may effect change in another.

**Connotation/connotative** – used in semiotic analysis to refer to the implications of signs such as words or images, often as distinct from 'denotation' (what is said or shown); see discussion on semiotics on pages 124–131.

**Content analysis** – a method of researching texts which relies on counting occurrences of particular phenomona. See pages 131–143.

**Convergence** – (technologically) the phenomenon by which media forms are becoming more alike physically, typically through digitization; (economically) – the tendency for large corporations to have economic interests in a wide range of media and cultural outputs.

**Correlation** – a relationship between two variables; the degree to which two variables may change together without one necessarily causing the other (see also **causality**).

**Cyberculture** (see also **cybernetics**) – media and cultural artifacts created on the internet; a movement in literature.

**Cybernetics** – derived from the Greek use, meaning 'to steer or lead', later to mean 'govern'; more recently has come to refer to an automatic or computer system which replicates biologic ones, such as a robot which can imitate human behaviour.

**Data** – pieces of information such as facts or numbers; usually used to refer to the information gleaned from research. A plural of the word **datum**.

**Datum** – a single piece of information. The plural form of the word is **data**.

**Deductive** – If you use the classic social science method of taking a hypothesis (developed in theory) and applying that hypothesis to a situation, then you are using deductive thinking. This approach to the study of culture and media derives from a scientific approach associated with positivism.

**Denote/denotation** – used in semiotic analysis to refer to what is said or shown in a sign such as a particular word or an image. Used in opposition to **connotation**; see discussion on semiotics on pages 124–131.

**Dependent variable** (see **variable**) – the variable being measured whose variation comes as a consequence of the **independent variable**.

**Diachronic** – through time; a kind of analysis discussed by Saussure in contradistinction to *synchronic* (at the same time).

**Digital divide** – the gap between those who have access to computer technology and know-how and those who don't.

**Discourse analysis** – a kind of research involving the analysis of images or language as constituent of specific discursive positions; a mode of analysis derived in large part from Michel Foucault's work. See discussion on pages 143–149.

**Empirical/empiricism** – to do with numbers or measurement; relying on scientific method, as opposed to *interpretive* methods.

**Epistemology** – the science or study of knowledge; attempts by philosophers to identify and understand truth claims and laws of evidence. See discussion in Chapter 1.

**Ethnography** – the study of social practice (including media and cultural use and/or production) through an anthropological perspective.

**Feminism/feminist** – the movement which recognizes that women are treated unequally in society; people who recognize social inequalities of gender and who have a commitment to bring about change to those inequities.

**Focus group** – a method of research in which small groups of people focus on a single issue or theme. Typically it is used as a method of gathering the opinions and attitudes of groups of people. See discussion on pages 187–191.

**Fordist** – Henry Ford was the first manufacturer to fully exploit the principles of the 'production line' to his automobile factories. His name has subsequently been given to the factory system of producing objects and to the economies of scale which this system engendered.

**The Frankfurt school** – usually this is the name given to a loose affiliation of scholars who were associated with the University of Frankfurt and who moved to the USA to escape persecution during the Hitler era. Among them were Theodor Adorno, Max Horkheimer and Walter Benjamin. See discussion on pages 35–37.

**Globalization** – the tendency of the social world to become increasingly international in scale; the recognition of social and economic phenomena to be 'global' in reach.

**Heteronormativity** – the expectation that heterosexuality is not only 'normal' but the ideal and desired state for everyone. More specifically, heteronormativity assumes a romantic ideal of a male and female couple, married or with the expectation to be married (see Chrys Ingraham, 2008).

**Hypothesis** – a statement which can be proved or disproved; the argument or research question you are investigating in deductive research – the hypothesis is the statement of something that can be proved. See also **research question**.

**Iconoclasm** – the destruction of religious icons or images and, by extension, any argument or activity which radically challenges orthodoxy. See discussion on page 28–29.

**Iconoclast** – literally a person who destroys religious icons; by extension it can also refer to a person who goes against conventional ideas and thereby assaults established mores and values.

**Ideology** – a system of belief or ideas; often considered within the context of 'dominant ideology' (the ideology of the ruling class or elite).

**Independent variable** (see **variable**) – the variable which is hypothesized to be the cause or the determinant of any change in the **dependent variable**. If we say $CO_2$ emissions are responsible for global warming, then the $CO_2$ emissions are the independent variable and global warming the dependent; the researcher must prove the relationship.

**Inductive** – if you design your study from examining a real-world situation and then plan to develop an explanation from your observation, you are using inductive reasoning, for this goes from the specific case to the general; sometimes called 'exploratory' research and typical of cultural studies methods and ethnographic methods particularly.

**Industrial Revolution** – the period which marks the transition in Britain from a largely agricultural society to an industrial one; the age of the ascent of the machine, the heyday of which is usually considered to be 1750–1880.

**Inter-coder reliability** – this is a term most likely to come up during **content analysis**. When you have two different researchers coding different material using the same coding categories, it is necessary to measure the extent to which they are both coming up with the same results. By giving each coder the same sample to code and measuring the extent to which they are the same, one can find out what the inter-coder reliability is. This is a text not only of how well you have briefed and trained your researchers, but also how robust your coding categories are.

**Interpretive** – a research method which relies on the interpretive judgement of the researcher as compared to *empirical* studies.

**Machinima** – a form of user-originated film production in which the technology and content of games are used as the basis for the new product. See the Academy of Machinima Arts and Sciences website at http://www. machinima.com.

**Materialist** – based on the economic value of something; usually derived from Marxist approaches, the study of the material or economic base of how something is produced.

**Mean/median/mode** – different measures of 'average'. For example, if we take as our variable the number of hours a group of people watch television, we can express the average in different ways. The usual way of calculating an average is the *mean* which would be calculated by summing all the hours spent by each individual and dividing it by the number of people; the *median* would be arrived at by writing the numbers of hours in ascending or descending order and choosing the middle one; the *mode* would be the number of hours most people watch. Each way of calculating has different strengths and weaknesses depending on the particular variable; and each may produce a different number.

**Object of analysis** – that particular thing which you are going to examine.

**Pathos** – the appeal both to the emotions and to sympathy when making an argument.

**Peer review** – the process by which one's peers evaluate one's work; used with reference to academic journals which send out articles submitted to them to be 'reviewed' (evaluated) by other academics, usually anonymously.

**Population** – within statistics this refers to the entire group of people you want to make conclusions about (as opposed to the sample – the group of people you are investigating).

**Pro-sumer** – a portmanteau word composed of 'consumer' and 'producer' – used to refer to those people who are users or fans, but who also produce media or cultural content.

**Reliability** – in the case of quantitative research, the reliability is a measure of how well you have designed your study; could another researcher, using the same research instrument, come to the same conclusion? See also **inter-coder reliability**. Sometimes this is calculated as a number value, with 1 being perfectly reliable.

**Research question** – the question you wish to answer or address in your research; a statement of the goals of your research question (see pages 60–66).

**Sample** – in statistics this is the sub-set of people or artifacts you are examining.

**Semiotics** – the analysis of cultural phenomena for their ideological meaning; considering media or culture as composed of 'signs'. Within media and cultural studies, semiotics is the study of signs for their hidden (ideological) meanings. See pages 122–131.

**Sign** – the smallest unit of meaning; the sum of the 'signifier' and the 'signified' in semiotics.

**Social media** – forms of computer communication such as *Facebook* and *MySpace* which allow for individuals to communicate in a one-to-many way and also to participate in many-to-many communications.

**Sophistry** – a form of argument which may be highly sophisticated and engaging but which does not contribute to the sum of our knowledge.

**The sophists** – a group of Greek philosophers and educators who held that, since there was no credible way to prove anything actually existed, one might as well learn to speak well and not worry about its relationship to the real. See pages 15–16.

**Source credibility** – the extent to which you can trust your source to be impartial.

**Star study** – the examination of texts where the star is the primary object of analysis. We may now see 'celebrity' replace 'stardom' in much media studies research; see discussion on pages 161–165.

**Survey instrument** – in the social science tradition, an instrument is the particular kind of tool that you use to conduct your research. For example, if you were conducting interviews, you might use a questionnaire as your survey instrument.

**Thesis** – a systematic idea or an argument.

**User entrepreneur** – consumers or users who act in an entrepreneurial manner, designing and marketing products independent of any corporate affiliation; a person who designs and develops new products from the position of a fan or an audience member but who is not paid for their work or employed by any particular company.

**User-generated content (UGC)** – material which is submitted by non-professionals to media organizations and used as content by them, such as mobile phone footage of a witness used in a news report.

**Variable** – something which changes (varies) and which can also be measured; a feature of the real world which the researcher wishes to study and/or explain. See also **independent variable**, **dependent variable, intervening variable** and **antecedent variable**.

**Volume** – when referring to an article in a journal such as *Media, Culture and Society*, one will identify it by reference to the author, the title of the article, the title of the journal and the particular volume and probably issue of that journal.

# REFERENCES

Abercrombie, N. and B. Longhurst, 1998. *Audiences: A Sociological Theory of Performance and Imagination*. London: Sage.

Adorno, Theodor W., 1991. *The Culture Industry: Selected Essays on Mass Culture*. Edited by J.M. Bernstein. London: Routledge.

Adorno, Theodor W., 1994. *Adorno: The Stars Down to Earth and Other Essays on the Irrational in Culture*. Edited by Stephen Crook. London: Routledge.

Adorno, Theodor and Max Horkheimer, 1993. The culture industry: enlightenment as mass deception. In Simon During (ed.), *The Cultural Studies Reader*. London: Routledge.

Alexander, Bryant Keith, Claudio Moreira and hari stephen kumar, 2012. Resisting (resistance) stories: a tri-autoethnographic exploration of father narratives across shades of difference. *Qualitative Inquiry*. 18(2): 121–133.

Alim, H. Samy, 2006. *Roc the Mic Right: The Language of Hip Hop Culture*. London: Routledge.

Alim, H. Samy, Jooyoung Lee and Lauren Mason Carris, 2011. Moving the crowd, 'crowding' the emcee: The coproduction and contestation of black normativity in freestyle rap battles. *Discourse and Society*, 22(4): 422–39.

Althusser, Louis, 1979. *For Marx*. London: Verso.

Althusser, Louis, 1984. *Essays on Ideology*. London: Verso.

Altman, Rick, 1999. *Film/Genre*. London: British Film Institute.

Andén-Papadopoulos, Kari, 2009. Body horror on the internet: US soldiers recording the war in Iraq and Afghanistan. *Media, Culture and Society*, 31(6): 921–38.

Anderson, Benedict, 2006. *Imagined Communities: Reflections on the Origin and Spread of Nationalism*. 2nd edition. London: Verso Books.

Ang, Ien, 1985. *Watching 'Dallas': Soap Opera and the Melodramatic Imagination*. London: Methuen.

Ang, Ien, 1991. *Desperately Seeking the Audience*. London: Routledge.

Arceneaux, Noah and Amy Schmitz Weiss, 2010. Seems stupid until you try it: press coverage of Twitter, 2006–9. *New Media and Society*, 12(8): 1262–79.

Arnold, Matthew, 2009 [1869]. *Culture and Anarchy*. Oxford's World Classics. Oxford: Oxford University Press.

Arthur, Sue, 2009. Blackpool goes all-talkie: cinema and society at the seaside in thirties Britain. *Historical Journal of Film, Radio and Television*, 29(1): 27–39.

Askew, Kelly, 2002. Introduction. In Kelly Askew and Richard R. Wilk (eds), *The Anthropology of Media*. Cambridge: Blackwell. pp. 1–14.

Avraham, Eli and Anat First, 2010. Combining the representation approach with the framing concept: television news coverage of the Arab population in Israel during conflict. *Journalism*, 11(4): 481–99.

Babbie, Earl, 1989. *The Practice of Social Research*. 5th edition. Belmont, CA: Wadsworth.

Balio, Tino (ed.), 1976. *The American Film Industry*. Madison, Wisconsin: University of Wisconsin Press.

Balvanes, Mark, Stephanie Hemelruk Donald and Brian Shoesmith, 2009. *Media Theories and Approaches: A Global Perspective*. Basingstoke: Palgrave Macmillan.

Barker, Martin and Julian Petley (eds), 2001. *Ill Effects: The Media/Violence Debate*. 2nd edition. London: Routledge.

Barthes, Roland, 1967. *Elements of Semiology*. Translated by Annette Lavers and Colin Smith. New York: Hill and Wang.

Barthes, Roland, 1973. *Mythologies*. Translated by Annette Lavers. London: Paladin Books.

Barthes, Roland, 1981. *Camera Lucida*. New York: Hill and Wang.

Barthes, Roland, 1984. Rhetoric of the image. In *Image, Music, Text*. Translated by Stephen Heath. London: Fontana, pp. 32–51.

Barthes, Roland, 1987. *S/Z*. Translated by Richard Miller. New York: Hill and Wang.

Barthes, Roland, 1990. *The Fashion System*. Translated by Matthew Ward and Richard Howard. Berkeley and Los Angeles, CA: University of California Press.

Baudrillard, Jean, 1981. *For a Critique of the Political Economy of the Sign*. St Louis: Telos.

Baudrillard, Jean, 1983. *Simulations*. New York: Semiotext(e).

Bazin, André, 2004. *What Is Cinema?* Volumes I and II. Los Angeles: University of California Press.

Beharrell, Peter, 1993. AIDS and the British press. In John Eldridge (ed.), *Getting the Message: News, Truth and Power*. Glasgow University Media Group. London: Routledge, pp. 210–49.

Bell, Allan, 1991. *The Language of News Media*. Oxford: Blackwell.

Bell, Allan and Peter Garrett, 1998. *Approaches to Media Discourse*. Oxford: Blackwell.

Bell, Judith, 2010. *Doing your Research Project: A Guide for First-time Researchers in Education and Social Science*. 5th edition. Buckingham: Open University Press.

Bell, Philip, 2001. Content analysis of visual images. In Theo van Leeuwen and Carey Jewitt (eds), *Handbook of Visual Analysis*. London: Sage, pp. 10–34.

Benjamin, Walter, 1968. *Illuminations*. Edited and translated by Hannah Arendt. London: Fontana/Collins.

Berger, Arthur Asa, 1998a. *Media Research Techniques*. Thousand Oaks, CA/London: Sage.

Berger, Arthur Asa, 1998b. *Media Analysis Techniques*. Thousand Oaks, CA/ London: Sage.

Berkowitz, D., 1990. Refining the gatekeeping metaphor for local television news. *Journal of Broadcasting & Electronic Media*, 34(1): 55–68.

Berners-Lee, Tim, 1999. *Weaving the Web*. San Francisco: Harper.

Bertrand, Ina and Peter Hughes, 2005. *Media Research Methods: Audiences, Institutions, Texts*. London: Palgrave Macmillan.

Bickerton, Emilie, 2011. *A Short History of* Cahiers du Cinéma. London: Verso.

Bignell, Jonathan, 2002. *Media Semiotics: An Introduction*. 2nd edition. Manchester/New York: Manchester University Press.

Birks, Jen, 2010. Press protest and publics: the agency of publics in newspaper campaigns. *Discourse and Communication*, 4(1): 51–67.

Bordwell, David, Kristin Thompson and Janet Staiger, 1985. *The Classical Hollywood Cinema: Film Style and Mode of Production to 1960*. London: Routledge.

Bourdieu, Pierre, 1984. *Distinction: A Social Critique of the Judgement of Taste*. London: Routledge and Kegan Paul.

Boyle, Karen, 2010. Watch with baby: cinema, parenting and community. *European Journal of Cultural Studies*, 13(3): 275–90.

Braudel, F., 1975. *Capitalism and Material Life 1400–1800*. London: Fontana.

Briggs, Asa, 1961. *The History of Broadcasting in the United Kingdom. Volume 1: The Birth of Broadcasting*. London: Oxford University Press.

227

Briggs, Asa, 1965. *The History of Broadcasting in the United Kingdom. Volume 2: The Golden Age of Wireless*. London: Oxford University Press.

Briggs, Asa, 1970. *The History of Broadcasting in the United Kingdom. Volume 3: The War of Words*. London: Oxford University Press.

Briggs, Asa, 1979. *The History of Broadcasting in the United Kingdom. Volume 4: Sound and Vision*. London: Oxford University Press.

Briggs, Asa, 1995. *The History of Broadcasting in the United Kingdom. Volume 5: Competition*. London: Oxford University Press.

Briggs, Matt, 2006. Beyond the audience: Teletubbies, play and parenthood. *European Journal of Cultural Studies*, 9(4): 441–60.

Brooks, David, 2010. The messiah complex. *New York Times*. 7 January.

Browne, Ray B., 2006. *Against Academia: The History of the Popular Culture Association/American Culture Association and Popular Culture Movement 1967–1988*. Bowling Green University Popular Press.

Burchfield, Rebekah Lynn, 2010. *Pressed Between the Pages of My Mind: Tangibility, Performance, and Technology in Archival Popular Music Research*. PhD Dissertation. Bowling Green State University.

Burns, Robert B., 2000. *Introduction to Research Methods*. 4th edition. Sage: London.

Butler, Judith, 1990. *Gender Trouble: Feminism and the Subversion of Identity*. London/New York: Routledge.

Caldwell, John T., 2008. *Production Culture: Industrial Reflexivity and Critical Practice in Film and Television*. Durham, NC/London: Duke University Press.

Caldwell, John T., 2009. Cultures of production. Studying industry's deep texts, reflexive rituals, and managed self-disclosures. In Jennifer Holt and Alisa Perren (eds), *Media Industries: History, Theory and Method*. Malden, MA/Oxford: Wiley-Blackwell, pp. 199–212.

Carrington, Ben, 2008. 'What's the footballer doing here?' Racialized performativity, reflexivity and identity in Cultural Studies. *Cultural Studies <=> Critical Methodologie*, 8(4) 423–52.

Castells, Manuel, 1996. *The Information Age: Economy, Society and Culture. Volume 1: The Rise of the Network Society*. London: Blackwell.

Castells, Manuel, 1997. *The Information Age: Economy, Society and Culture. Volume 2: The Power of Identity*. London: Blackwell.

Castells, Manuel, 1998. *The Information Age: Economy, Society and Culture. Volume 3: End of Millennium*. London: Blackwell.

Caughie, John, 1981. *Dossier on John Ford in Theories of Authorship*. London: Routledge and Kegan Paul.

Cawley, Anthony, 2008. News production in an Irish online newsroom: practice, process and culture. In Chris Paterson and David Domingo (eds), *Making Online News: The Ethnography of New Media Production*. New York: Peter Lang, pp. 45–60.

Chang, Heewon V., 2008. *Autoethnography as Method (Developing Qualitative Inquiry)*. San Francisco, CA: Left Coast Press.

Chapman, James, 2006. *The BBC and the Censorship of The War Game (1965)*.

Charters, W.W., 1970 [1933]. *Motion Pictures and Youth: A Summary*. New York: Arno Press (original publication – New York: Macmillan).

Chibnall, Steve and Robert Murphy (eds), 1999. *British Crime Cinema*. London: Routledge.

Cole, C.L. and David L. Andrews, 2001. America's new son: Tiger Woods and America's multi-culturalism. In Donald L. Andrews and D.L. Jackson (eds), *Sport Stars: The Cultural Politics of Sporting Celebrity*. London: Routledge.

Coleman, James S., Elihu Katz and Herbert Menzel, 1966. *Medical Innovation: A Diffusion Study.* New York: The Bobbs-Merrill Co., Inc.

Collier, Malcolm, 2001. Approaches to analysis in visual anthropology. In Theo van Leeuwen and Carey Jewitt (eds), *Handbook of Visual Analysis*. London: Sage, pp. 35–60.

Collins, Richard, 1999. European Union media and communication policies. In Jane Stokes and Anna Reading (eds), *The Media in Britain: Current Debates and Developments.* London: Macmillan, pp. 158–69.

Cottingham, John, 1999. 'Descartes'. In Robert Audi (ed.), *Cambridge Dictionary of Philosophy.* Cambridge: Cambridge University Press.

Cottle, Simon, 2006. *Mediatized Conflict: Developments in Media and Conflict Studies*. Maidenhead, Berkshire: Open University Press.

Cottle, Simon, 2007. Ethnography and news production: new(s) developments in the field. *Sociology Compass*, I(1): 1–16.

Cottrell, Stella, 2011. *Critical Thinking Skills: Developing Effective Analysis and Argument.* 2nd edition. London: Palgrave Macmillan.

Crang, Mike and Ian Cook, 2007. *Doing Ethnographies*. London: Sage.

Cresser, Frances, Lesley Gunn and Helen Balme, 2001. Women's experiences of on-line e-zine publication. *Media, Culture and Society,* 23: 457–73.

Cumberbatch, Guy, 2000. *Television: The Public's View. An ITC Research Publication.* London: ITC.

Cunningham, Stuart and John Sinclair (eds), 2001. *Floating Lives: The Media and Asian Diasporas.* Lanham/Boulder/New York/Oxford: Rowman and Littlefield Publishers Inc.

Curran, James, 1979. The media and politics. *Media, Culture and Society*, 1(1): 1–3.

Curran, James, 2000a. Introduction. *Media Organizations in Society*. London: Arnold, pp. 9–16.

Curran, James, 2000b. Literary editors, social networks and cultural tradition. In James Curran (ed.), *Media Organizations in Society*. London: Arnold, pp. 215–39.

Curran, James and Jean Seaton, 2010. *Power Without Responsibility: The Press and Broadcasting in Britain*. 7th edition. London: Routledge.

Czitrom, Daniel J., 1997. *The Media and the American Mind: From Morse to McLuhan*. Chapel Hill, NC: University of North Carolina Press.

Danesi, Marcel, 2002. *Understanding Media Semiotics.* London: Arnold.

Deacon, David, 2007. Yesterday's papers and today's technology: digital newspaper archives and 'push button' content analysis. *European Journal of Communication*, 22(5): 5–25.

Deacon, David, Michael Pickering, Peter Golding and Graham Murdock, 2007a. *Researching Communications: A Practical Guide to Methods in Media and Cultural Analysis.* 2nd edition. London: Bloomsbury Academic.

Deacon, David, Michael Pickering, Peter Golding and Graham Murdock, 2007b. Counting Contents. Chapter 6 of *Researching Communications: A Practical Guide to Methods in Media and Cultural Analysis.* 2nd edition. London: Bloomsbury Academic, pp. 117–37.

de Beauvoir, Simone, 1961. *The Second Sex.* New York: Bantam Books.

De Lauretis, Teresa, 1991. Queer theory, lesbian and gay sexualities. *Differences: A Journal of Feminist Cultural Studies.*

Deleuze, Gilles, and Félix Guattari, 1994. *What is Philosophy?* Translated by G. Burchell and H. Tomlinson. London: Verso.

Deleuze, Gilles, and Félix Guattari, 2004. *A Thousand Plateaus: Capitalism and Schizophrenia.* Translated by B. Massumi. London: Continuum.

Dennis, Jeffry P., 2009. Gazing at the black teen: con artists, cyborgs and sycophants. *Media, Culture and Society*, 31(2): 179–95.

Department for Culture, Media and Sport, 2010. *Creative Industries: Economic Estimates.* London.

Deuze, Mark, 2009. Convergence culture and media work. In Jennifer Holt and Alisa Perren (eds) *Media Industries: History, Theory and Method.* Chichester, West Sussex: Wiley-Blackwell, pp.144–156.

Duffy, Brendan, 1999. The analysis of documentary evidence. In Judith Bell, *Doing Your Research Project: A Guide for First-time Researchers in Education and Social Science.* Buckingham: Open University Press, pp. 106–17.

Du Gay, Paul, Stuart Hall, Linda Janes, Hugh Mackay and Keith Negus, 1996. *Doing Cultural Studies: The Story of the Sony Walkman.* London: Sage.

Duits, Linda, 2008. *Multi-Girl-Culture: An Ethnography of Doing Identity.* Amsterdam: University of Amsterdam Press.

Duke, George, 2012. The Sophists (Ancient Greek). *The Internet Encyclopedia of Philosophy.* Martin, Tennessee: University of Tennessee Press. ISSN 2161-0002. www.iep.utm. edu/sophists. Accessed 4 July 2012.

Dyer, Richard, 1982. *Stars.* London: British Film Institute.

Dyer, Richard, 1987. *Heavenly Bodies.* London: British Film Institute.

Dysinger, W.S. and C.A. Ruckmick, 1970 [1933]. *The Emotional Responses of Children to the Motion Picture Situation.* New York: Arno Press (original publication – New York: Macmillan).

Eco, Umberto, 1978. *A Theory of Semiotics (Advances in Semiotics).* London: John Wiley and Sons.

Eco, Umberto, 1984. *The Role of the Reader: Explorations in the Semiotics of Texts (Advances in Semiotics).* London: John Wiley and Sons.

Eco, Umberto, 1986. *Semiotics and the Philosophy of Language (Advances in Semiotics).* London: John Wiley and Sons.

Eisenstein, Elizabeth L., 1979. *The Printing Press as an Agent of Change: Communications and Cultural Transformations in Early Modern Europe* (2 volumes). Cambridge, UK: Cambridge University Press.

Eldridge, John (ed.), 1993. *Getting the Message: News, Truth and Power.* Glasgow University Media Group. London: Routledge.

Eliot, T.S., 1948. *Notes Towards the Definition of Culture.* London: Faber and Faber.

Elsaesser, Thomas, 2011. James Cameron's *Avatar*: access for all. *New Review of Film and Television Studies*, 9(3): 247–64.

Elsaesser, Thomas, 2012. *The Persistence of Hollywood.* London: Routledge.

Engels, Friedrich, 1887. *1886 Appendix to the American Edition: The Condition of the Working Class in England.* New York. http://www.marxists.org/archive/marx/works/1886/02/25.htm. Accessed 25 September 2011.

Engels, Friedrich, 2011 [1845]. *The Condition of the Working Class in England* (first published 1845 in Leipzig). http://www.marxists.org/archive/marx/works/1886/02/25.htm. Accessed 25 September 2011.

Evans, Jessica and David Hesmondhalgh (eds), 2005. *Understanding Media: Inside Celebrity.* Milton Keynes: The Open University.

Everett, Daniel, 2008. *Don't Sleep, There Are Snakes: Life and Language in the Amazonian Jungle.* London: Profile Books.

Facer, K.J. Furlong, R. Furlong and R. Sutherland, 2003. *Screenplay: Children and Computing in the Home.* London: Routledge.

Feuer, Jane, 1982. *The Hollywood Musical.* London: Macmillan/British Film Institute.

Figenschou, Tine Ustad, 2010. Young, female, Western researcher vs. senior, male, Al Jazeera officials: critical reflections on accessing and interviewing media elites in authoritarian societies. *Media, Culture and Society*, 32(6): 961–78.

Foucault, Michel, 1991 [1975]. *Discipline and Punish: The Birth of the Prison*. 2nd edition. Translated by Alan Sheridan. London: Vintage Books.

Foucault, Michel, 1998 [1976]. *The History of Sexuality. Volume 1: The Will to Knowledge*. London: Penguin.

Foucault, Michel, 2002 [1972]. *The Archaeology of Knowledge*. 2nd edition. London: Routledge.

Friedan, Betty, 1963. *The Feminine Mystique*. New York: Dell Publishing.

Friedman, Lawrence S., 1999. *The Cinema of Martin Scorsese*. Oxford: Roundhouse Publishing.

Gans, Herbert J., 1974. *Popular Culture and High Culture: An Analysis and Evaluation of Taste*. New York: Basic Books.

Garber, Marjorie, 1992. *Vested Interests: Cross-Dressing and Cultural Anxiety*. London: Routledge.

Garrett, Peter and Allan Bell, 1998. Media and discourse: a critical overview. In Allan Bell and Peter Garrett (eds), *Approaches to Media Discourse*. Oxford: Blackwell, pp. 1–20.

Gauntlett, David, 1995. *Moving Experiences: Understanding Television's Influences and Effects*. London: John Libbey.

Gauntlett, David and Annette Hill, 2000. *TV Living: Television, Culture and Everyday Life*. London: Routledge.

Geertz, Clifford, 1973. *The Interpretation of Cultures*. New York: Basic Books.

Gerbner, George, 1996. Foreword. In Jowett et al., *Children and the Movies: Media Influence and the Payne Fund Controversy*. Cambridge, MA: Cambridge University Press, pp. x–xi.

Gerbner, George and Larry Gross, 1976. Living with television: the violence profile. *Journal of Communication*, Spring: 173–199.

Gerbner, George, Larry Gross, Marilyn Jackson-Beeck, Suzanne Jeffries-Fox and Nancy Signorielli, 1978. Cultural indicators: violence profile no. 9. *Journal of Communication*, 28: 176–207.

Giddens, Anthony, 1991. *Modernity and Self-Identity: Self and Society in the Late Modern Age*. Oxford: Polity Press.

Giddens, Anthony, 1998. *The Third Way: The Renewal of Social Democracy*. Oxford: Polity Press.

Gioia, F. (ed.), 2005. *The Popes – Twenty Centuries of History*. The Vatican: Libreria Editrice Vaticana.

Glasgow University Media Group, 1976. *Bad News*. London: Routledge and Kegan Paul.

Glasgow University Media Group, 1980. *More Bad News*. London: Routledge and Kegan Paul.

Glasgow University Media Group, 1982. *Really Bad News*. London: Routledge and Kegan Paul. http://www.glasgowmediagroup.org/content/view/5/18.

Goodwin, Peter, 1999. The role of the state. In Jane Stokes and Anna Reading (eds), *The Media in Britain: Current Debates and Developments*. London: Macmillan, pp. 130–42.

Goody, Jack [John Rankin] and Ian Watt, 1968. The consequences of literacy. In Jack Goody (ed.), *Literacy in Traditional Societies*. Cambridge, UK: Cambridge University Press.

Goosman, Stuart L., 2005. *Group Harmony: The Black Urban Roots of Rhythm and Blues*. Philadelphia: University of Pennsylvania Press.

Gopsill, Tim and Greg Neale, 2007. *Journalists: 100 Years of the NUJ*. London: NUJ/Profile Books.

Gorin, Valérie and Annik Dubied, 2011. Desirable people: identifying social values through celebrity news. *Media, Culture and Society*, 33(4): 599–618.

Gramsci, Antonio, 2011. *The Prison Notebooks*. Three volumes. New York: Columbia University Press.

Gray, Ann, 2003. *Research Practice for Cultural Studies: Ethnographic Methods and Lived Cultures*. London: Sage.

Gray, Jonathan, Cornel Sandvoss and C. Lee Harrington (eds), 2007. *Fandom: Identities and Communities in a Mediated World*. New York/London: New York University Press.

Greer, Germaine, 1976. *The Female Eunuch*. London: Paladin.

Griffiths, Anthony, 1980. *Prints and Printmaking: An Introduction to the History of Techniques*. London: The British Library.

Griswold, Charles, 2009. Plato on Rhetoric and Poetry, in Edward N. Zalta (ed.), *The Stanford Encyclopedia of Philosophy*. Fall 2009 edition. Stanford, CA: Stanford University. http://plato.stanford.edu/archives/fall2009/entries/plato-rhetoric/. Accessed 24 July 2011.

Habermas, Jürgen, 1989. *The Structural Transformation of the Public Sphere: Inquiry into a Category of Bourgeois Society*. Cambridge: Polity Press.

Haefliger, Stefan, Peter Jäger and Georg von Krogh, 2010. Under the radar: industry entry by user entrepreneurs. *Research Policy*, 39: 1198–213.

Hall, Stuart, 1981. Encoding/decoding. In S. Hall, D. Hobson, A. Lowe and P. Willis (eds), *Culture, Media, Language*. London: Hutchinson.

Hall, Stuart, 1997. *Representation: Cultural Representations and Signifying Practices*. London: Sage/The Open University.

Hall, Stuart, Chas Critcher, Tony Jefferson, John Clarke and Brian Roberts, 1978. *Policing the Crisis: Mugging, the State and Law and Order*. London: Macmillan.

Halliday, Jon, 1997. *Sirk on Sirk: Conversations with Jon Halliday*. London: Faber and Faber.

Hammersley, Martyn and Paul Atkinson, 2007. *Ethnography: Principles in Practice*. 3rd edition. London: Routledge.

Hamminga, Bert (ed.), 2005a. *Knowledge Cultures: Comparative Western and African Epistemology (Poznan Studies in the Philosophy of the Sciences and the Humanities 88)*. New York/Amsterdam: Rodopi.

Hamminga, Bert, 2005b. Epistemology from the African point of view. In Bert Hamminga (ed.), *Knowledge Cultures: Comparative Western and African Epistemology (Poznan Studies in the Philosophy of the Sciences and the Humanities 88)*. New York/Amsterdam: Rodopi, pp. 57–84.

Hammond, Philip, 2007. *Media, War and Postmodernity*. London: Routledge.

Hansen, Anders, Simon Cottle, Ralph Negrine and Chris Newbold, 1998. *Mass Communication Methods*. London: Macmillan.

Healey, Tim and Karen Ross, 2002. Growing old invisibly: older viewers talk television. *Media, Culture and Society*, 24(1): 105–20.

Hebdige, Dick, 1979. *Subcultures: The Meaning of Style*. London: Methuen.

Hebdige, Dick, 1988. *Hiding in the Light: On Images and Things*. London: Comedia/Routledge. Especially 'Object as image: the Italian scooter cycle' and 'The bottom line on planet one: squaring up to The Face'.

Henderson, Lesley, 1999. Producing serious soaps. In Greg Philo (ed.), *Message Received. Glasgow Media Group Research 1993–1998*. Harlow, Essex: Addison Wesley Longman, pp. 62–81.

Henry, John, 2012. *A Short History of Scientific Thought*. Basingstoke, Hampshire: Palgrave Macmillan.

Hesmondhalgh, David, 2007. *The Cultural Industries*. 2nd edition. London: Sage.

Higgins, C. Francis, 2006. Gorgias (483–375BCE). *The Internet Encyclopedia of Philosophy*. Martin, Tennessee: University of Tennessee Press. ISSN 2161-0002. www.iep.utm.edu/gorgias. Accessed 4 July 2012.

Hillier, Jim, 1985. Cahiers du Cinéma: *1950s: Neo-Realism, Hollywood, New Wave*. Boston, MA: Harvard University Press.

Hillier, Jim, 1992. Cahiers du Cinéma: *1960–68: New Wave, New Cinema, Re-evaluating Hollywood*. Boston, MA: Harvard University Press.

Hills, Matt, 2002. *Fan Cultures*. London/New York: Routledge.

Hills, Matt, 2007. Media academics as media audiences: aesthetic judgements in media and cultural studies. In Jonathan Gray, Cornel Sandvoss and C. Lee Harrington (eds), *Fandom: Identities and Communities in a Mediated World*. New York: New York University Press, pp. 33–47.

Hilmes, Michele, 2009. Nailing Mercury: the problem of media industry historiography. In Jennifer Holt and Alisa Perren (eds), *Media Industries: History, Theory and Method*. Chichester, West Sussex: Wiley-Blackwell, pp. 21–33.

Hobson, Dorothy, 1982. *Crossroads: The Drama of a Soap Opera*. London: Methuen.

Hoggart, Richard, 1957. *The Uses of Literacy: Aspects of Working-Class Life with Special Reference to Publications and Entertainments*. London: Chatto and Windus.

Holmes, Susan, 2001. 'As they really are, and in close-up': film stars on 1950s British television, *Screen*. 42: 167–87.

Holt, Jennifer and Alisa Perren (eds), 2009. *Media Industries. History, Theory and Method*. Chichester, West Sussex: Wiley-Blackwell.

hooks, bell, 1987. *Aint I a Woman?: Black Women and Feminism*. London: Pluto Press.

Horst, H., Herr-Stephenson, R. and Robinson, L., 2009. Media ecologies. In Mitzuko Ito, S. Baumer, M. Bittanti, D. Boyd, R. Cody, R. Herr-Stephenson et al., 2009. *Hanging Out, Messing Around and Geeking Out: Kids Living and Learning with New Media*. Cambridge, MA: MIT Press.

Iedema, Rick, 2001. Analysing film and television: a social semiotic account of *Hospital: An Unhealthy Business*. In Theo van Leeuwen and Carey Jewitt (eds), 2001. *Handbook of Visual Analysis*. London: Sage, pp. 183–206.

Independent Television Commission, 2001. *1999 Attitudes to Television Questionnaire*. London: ITC.

Inglis, Fred, 1993. *Cultural Studies*. Oxford: Blackwell.

Ingraham, Chrys, 2008. *White Weddings: Romancing Heterosexuality in Popular Culture*. New York/London: Routledge.

Innis, Harold Adam, 1945. The English press in the nineteenth century: an economic approach. *University of Toronto Quarterly*, 15(1): 37–53.

Innis, Harold Adam, 1986 [1950]. *Empire and Communications*. Edited by David Godfrey. Victoria, BC: Press Porcépic.

Innis, Harold Adam, 2008 [1951]. *The Bias of Communication*. 2nd edition with new introduction by Alexander John Watson. Toronto: University of Toronto Press.

Ito, Mitzuko, S. Baumer, M. Bittanti, D. Boyd, R. Cody, R. Herr-Stephenson et al., 2009. *Hanging Out, Messing Around and Geeking Out: Kids Living and Learning with New Media*. Cambridge, MA: MIT Press.

Jacobs, Norman (ed.), 1961. *Culture for the Millions*. Princeton, NJ: Van Nostrand.

Jenkins, Henry, 1992. *Textual Poachers: Television Fans and Participatory Culture*. London: Routledge.

Jensen, Klaus Bruhn (ed.), 2002. *A Handbook of Media and Communication Research: Qualitative and Quantitative Methodologies*. London: Routledge.

Jowett, G., I.C. Jarvie and K.H. Fuller, 1996. *Children and the Movies: Media Influence and the Payne Fund Controversy.* Cambridge, MA: Cambridge University Press.

Katz, Elihu and Daniel Dayan, 2003. The audience is a crowd, the crowd is a public: latter day thoughts on Lang and Lang's 'MacArthur Day in Chicago'. In Elihu Katz, John Durham Peters, Tamar Liebes and Avril Orloff (eds), *Canonic Texts in Media Research: Are There Any? Should There Be? How About These?* Cambridge: Polity, pp. 121–36.

Katz, Elihu and Paul Lazarsfeld, 1955. *Personal Influence: the Part Played by People in the Flow of Mass Communication.* Glencoe, IL: The Free Press.

Katz, Elihu, John Durham Peters, Tamar Liebes and Avril Orloff (eds), 2003. *Canonic Texts in Media Research: Are There Any? Should There Be? How About These?* Cambridge: Polity.

Kitzinger, Jenny, 1999. A sociology of media power: key issues in audience reception research. In Greg Philo (ed.), *Message Received.* Glasgow Media Group Research 1993–1998. Harlow, Essex: Addison Wesley Longman, pp. 3–20.

Krippendorff, Klaus, 1980. *Content Analysis: An Introduction to Its Methodology.* Beverly Hills, CA/London: Sage.

Kristeva, Julia, 1982. *Power of Horror.* Translated by Leon Roudiez. New York: Columbia University Press.

Krueger, Richard A. and Mary Anne Casey, 2009. *Focus Groups: A Practical Guide for Applied Research.* 4th edition. London: Sage.

Kuhn, Annette, 1994 [1984]. *Women's Pictures: Cinema and Feminism.* 2nd edition. London: Verso Books.

Kuhn, Annette, 1999. Cinema-going in Britain in the 1930s: report of a questionnaire survey. *Historical Journal of Film, Radio and Television*, 19(4): 531–43.

Kuhn, Thomas, 1962. *The Structure of Scientific Revolutions.* Chicago: University of Chicago Press.

Kumar, Ranjit, 1999. *Research Methodology: A Step-by-Step Guide for Beginners.* London: Sage.

Lacan, Jacques, 1968. The mirror-phase as formative of the function of the I. *New Left Review,* 51: 71–7.

Lazarsfeld, Paul K., 1967. Preface to Lazarsfeld, Paul F., Bernard Berelson and Hazel Gaudet, 1968 [1944], *The People's Choice: How the Voter Makes up his Mind in a Presidential Campaign.* Columbia Paperback Edition. New York/London: Columbia University Press.

Lazarsfeld, Paul F. and Robert K. Merton, 1948. Mass communication, popular taste, and organized social action. In L. Bryson (ed.), *The Communication of Ideas.* New York: Harper, pp. 95–118.

Lazarsfeld, Paul F., Bernard Berelson and Hazel Gaudet, 1968 [1944]. *The People's Choice: How the Voter Makes up his Mind in a Presidential Campaign.* Columbia Paperback Edition. New York/London: Columbia University Press.

Liebes, Tamar and Elihu Katz, 1990. *The Export of Meaning: Cross-Cultural Readings of 'Dallas'.* New York/Oxford: Oxford University Press.

Lindlof, Thomas R. and B.C. Taylor, 2002. *Qualitative Communication Research Methods.* 2nd edition. London: Sage.

Lister, Martin and Liz Wells, 2001. Seeing beyond belief: cultural studies as an approach to analysing the visual. In Theo van Leeuwen and Carey Jewitt (eds), *Handbook of Visual Analysis.* London: Sage, pp. 61–91.

Livingstone, Sonia, 1990. *Making Sense of Television: The Psychology of Audience Interpretation.* Oxford: Pergamon.

Livingstone, Sonia, 1998. Relationships between media and audiences: prospects for audience research studies. In Tamar Liebes and James Curran (eds), *Media, Ritual and Identity.* London/New York: Routledge, pp. 237–55.

Livingstone, Sonia, 2002. *Young People and New Media: Childhood in the Changing Media Environment*. London: Sage.

Livingstone, Sonia and E.J. Helsper, 2007. Gradations in digital inclusion: children, young people and the digital divide. *New Media and Society*, 9(4): 671–96.

Lowenthal, Leo, 1961. *Literature, Popular Culture and Society*. Palo Alto, CA: Pacific Books.

Lowood, Henry and Michael Nitsche, 2011. *The Machinima Reader*. Cambridge, MA: MIT Press.

Lukács, György, 2000 [1923]. *History and Class Consciousness: Studies in Marxist Dialectics*. Cambridge, MA: MIT Press.

Lull, James, 1990. *Inside Family Viewing: Ethnographic Research on Television's Audiences*. London: Routledge.

Lutz, Catherine A. and Jane L. Collins, 1993. *Reading* National Geographic. Chicago: University of Chicago Press.

Lutz, Catherine A. and Jane L. Collins, 2002. The color of sex: postwar photographic histories of race and gender. In Kelly Askew and Richard R. Wilk (eds), *The Anthropology of Media: A Reader*. Oxford: Blackwell, pp. 92–116.

Lynch, Jane, 2012. *Happy Accidents*. London: Fourth Estate.

Lyotard, Jean-François, 1984. *The Postmodern Condition: A Report on Knowledge*. Translated by Geoff Bennington and Brian Massumi. London/Minnesota: University of Minnesota Press.

Lyotard, Jean-François, 1992. *The Postmodern Explained: Correspondence 1982–85*. London/Minnesota: University of Minnesota Press.

MacCabe, Colin, 1999. *The Eloquence of the Vulgar: Language, Cinema and the Politics of Culture*. London: British Film Institute.

MacDonald, Dwight, 1957. A theory of mass culture. In Bernard Rosenberg and David M. White (eds), *Mass Culture: The Popular Arts in America*. Glencoe, IL: The Free Press.

Machinima.com. 2011. Date accessed: 6 July 2011.

Mackay, Hugh and Tim O'Sullivan, 1999. *The Media Reader: Continuity and Transformation*. London: Sage/Open University Press.

MacKenzie, Donald and Jude Wajcman, 1999. *The Social Shaping of Technology*. 2nd edition. Buckingham: Open University Press.

Malinowski, Bronislaw, 1997 [1932]. *Argonauts of the Western Pacific*. Read Books.

Marc, David and Robert J. Thompson, 1995. *Prime Time, Prime Movers: From 'I Love Lucy' to 'L.A. Law' – America's Greatest TV Shows and the People who Created Them*. Syracuse, NY: Syracuse University Press.

Maréchal, Garance, 2010. Autoethnography. In Albert J. Mills, Gabrielle Durepos and Elden Weibe (eds.), *Encyclopedia of Case Study Research,* Volume 2. Thousand Oaks, CA: Sage, pp.43–45.

Marshall, Bill and Robynn Stilwell, 2000. *Musicals: Hollywood and Beyond*. Exeter, England/Portland, OR: Intellect Books.

Marshall, P. David (ed.), 2006. *The Celebrity Culture Reader*. London: Routledge.

Martin-Barbero, Jesus, 1993. *Communication, Culture and Hegemony: From the Media to Mediations*. Translated by Elizabeth Fox and Robert A. White. London: Sage.

Marx, Karl, 1990 [1867]. *Capital: Critique of Political Economy*. Volume 1. London: Penguin Classics.

Marx, Karl, 1992 [1885]. *Capital: Critique of Political Economy*. Volume 2. London: Penguin Classics.

Marx, Karl, 1992 [1894]. *Capital: Critique of Political Economy*. Volume 3. London: Penguin Classics.

Marx, Karl and Friedrich Engels, 1964 [1848]. *The Communist Manifesto*. New York: Simon and Schuster.

Marx, Karl and Friedrich Engels, 1974 [1845]. *The German Ideology*. Edited by C.J. Arthur. London: Lawrence and Wishart.

McKee, Alan, 2011. *YouTube* versus the National Film and Sound Archive: which is the more useful resource for historians of Australian television? *Television and New Media*, 12(2): 154–73.

McLeod, Kembrew, 1999. Authenticity within hip-hop and other cultures threatened with assimilation. *Journal of Communication*, 49(Autumn): 134– 50.

McLuhan, Marshall, 1962. *The Gutenberg Galaxy: The Making of Typographic Man*. Toronto: University of Toronto Press.

McLuhan, Marshall, 1995 [1964]. *Understanding Media: The Extensions of Man*. London: Routledge.

McMahon, Jennifer L. and B. Steve Csaki (eds), 2010. *The Philosophy of the Western*. University Press of Kentucky, Lexington.

McMillan, Kathleen and Jonathan Weyers, 2011. *How to Write Dissertations and Project Reports*. Harlow, Essex: Pearson Education Ltd.

McQuail, Denis, 2010. *Mass Communication Theory: An Introduction*. 6th edition. London: Sage.

McRobbie, Angela, 2008. *The Aftermath of Feminism: Gender, Culture and Social Change*. London: Sage.

Metcalf, Andy and Martin Humphries, 1985. *The Sexuality of Men*. London: Pluto Press.

Miller, Daniel, 1998. *A Theory of Shopping*. Cambridge: Polity Press.

Miller, Daniel, 2010. *Stuff*. Cambridge: Polity Press.

Miller, Daniel, 2011. *Tales from Facebook*. Cambridge, UK/Malden, MA: Polity Press.

Miller, Daniel and Don Slater, 2000. *The Internet: An Ethnographic Approach*. Oxford: Berg.

Mills, C. Wright (ed.), 1956. *The Power Elite*. London: Oxford University Press.

Millwood Hargrave, Andrea, 2000. *Delete Expletives?* London: The Advertising Standards Authority, British Broadcasting Corporation, Broadcasting Standards Commission and the Independent Television Commission (jointly funded research).

Modleski, Tania, 1982. *Loving with a Vengeance: Mass-Produced Fantasies for Women*. New York/London: Methuen.

Monk, Claire, 1999a. From underworld to underclass: crime and British cinema in the 1990s. In Steve Chibnall and Robert Murphy (eds), *British Crime Cinema*. London: Routledge, pp. 172–88.

Moores, Shaun, 1988. The box on the dresser: memories of early radio and everyday life. *Media, Culture and Society*, 10: 23–40.

Moores, Shaun, 1993. *Interpreting Audiences: The Ethnography of Media Consumption*. London: Sage.

Morgado, Marcia A., 2007. The semiotics of extraordinary dress: a structural analysis and interpretation of hip-hop style. *Clothing and Textiles Research Journal*, 25(2): 131–55.

Morgan, David L. and Richard A. Krueger, 1998. *The Focus Group Tool Kit*. London: Sage.

Morley, David, 1980. *The 'Nationwide' Audience*. London: British Film Institute.

Morley, David, 1986. *Family Television: Cultural Power and Domestic Leisure*. London: Comedia.

Morley, David, 1992. *Television, Audiences and Cultural Studies*. London: Routledge.

Morley, David and Roger Silverstone, 1991. Communication and context: ethnographic perspectives on the media audience. In Klaus Bruhn Jensen and Nicholas W. Jankowski (eds), *A Handbook of Qualitative Methodologies for Mass Communication Research*. London: Routledge, pp. 149–62.

Morrison, D. 1998. *The Search for Method: Focus Groups and the Development of Mass Communication*. Luton: University of Luton Press.

Mottram, James, 2000. *The Coen Brothers: The Life of the Mind*. London: BT Batsford.

Mulhern, Francis, 1979. *The Moment of 'Scrutiny'*. London: New Left Books.

Museveni, Yoweri K., 2005. The power of knowledge. In Bert Hamminga (ed.), *Knowledge Cultures: Comparative Western and African Epistemology (Poznan Studies in the Philosophy of the Sciences and the Humanities 88)*. New York/Amsterdam: Rodopi, pp. 11–22.

Napoli, Philip M., 2010. Revisiting 'mass communication' and the 'work' of the audience in the new media environment. *Media, Culture and Society,* 32(3): 505–16.

National Institute of Mental Health, 2011. 'Dr. Jay Giedd of the National Institute of Mental Health on development of the young brain'. Posted: 2 May 2011. Accessed: 13 June 2011. http://www.nimh.nih.gov/media/video/giedd.shtml.

Neale, Steve, 1980. *Genre*. London: British Film Institute.

Neale, Steve, 1999. *Genre and Hollywood*. London: Routledge.

Neale, Steve (ed.), 2002. *Genre and Contemporary Hollywood*. London: BFI.

Neale, Steve and Frank Krutnik, 1990. *Popular Film and Television Comedy.* London/New York: Routledge.

Neale, Steve and Murray Smith (eds), 1998. *Contemporary Hollywood Cinema*. London/New York: Routledge.

Negroponte, Nicholas, 2000 [1995]. *Being Digital.* London. Vintage Books.

Nichols, Bill, 1991. *Representing Reality: Issues and Concepts in Documentary*. Bloomington, Indiana: Indiana University Press.

Ong, Walter J., 1982. *Orality and Literacy: The Technologizing of the Word*. London: Methuen.

Ortner, Sherry B., 2010. Access: reflections on studying up in Hollywood. *Ethnography*, 11(2): 211–33.

O'Sullivan, Tim, 1991. Television memories and cultures of viewing, 1950–65. In John Corner (ed.), *Popular Television in Britain: Studies in Cultural History*. London: British Film Institute, pp. 159–81.

The Paley Center for Media, 2008. *She Made It.* Various contributors. http://www.shemadeit.org/watch/default.aspx?page=2. (Accessed: 6 June 2011).

The Paley Center for Media, 2011. *Next Big Thing.* http://www.paleycenter.org/nbt-next bigthing (Accessed: 6 June 2011).

Parameswaran, Radhika, 2001. Feminist media ethnography in India: exploring power, gender, and culture in the field. *Qualitative Inquiry*, 7: 69–102.

Paterson, Chris, 2008. Why ethnography? In Chris Paterson and David Domingo (eds), *Making Online News: The Ethnography of New Media Production*. New York: Peter Lang, pp. 1–11.

Paterson, Chris and David Domingo (eds), 2008. *Making Online News: The Ethnography of New Media Production*. New York: Peter Lang.

Pears, Richard and Graham Shields, 2010. *Cite Them Right: The Essential Referencing Guide*. 8th edition. Basingstoke: Palgrave, Macmillan.

Peirce, Charles S., 1958. *Selected Writings (Values in a Universe of Chance)*. Edited by P. Wiener. New York: Dover Press.

Peters, John Durham, 2004. *Mass Communication and American Social Thought 1919–1968*. Lanham, MD: Rowan and Littlefield.

Peterson, Ruth C. and Louis Leon Thurstone, 1976 [1933]. *Motion Pictures and the Social Attitudes of Children.* New York: Arno.

Petrie, Duncan and John Willis (eds), 1995. *Television and the Household: Reports from the BFI's Audience Tracking Study*. London: British Film Institute.

Philo, Greg (ed.), 1996. *Media and Mental Distress*. Glasgow Media Group. Harlow, Essex: Addison Wesley Longman Ltd.

Philo, Greg (ed.), 1999. *Message Received*. Glasgow Media Group Research 1993–1998. Harlow, Essex: Addison Wesley Longman Ltd.

Pickering, Michael and Gabriele Griffin (eds), 2008. *Research Methods for Cultural Studies*. Edinburgh: Edinburgh University Press.

Plato, 2007. *The Republic*. Melissa Lane (Introduction). 3rd edition. Translated by H.D.P. Lee and Desmond Lee. London: Penguin Classics.

Plesner, Ursula, 2011. Studying sideways: displacing the problem of power in research interviews with sociologists and journalists. *Qualitative Inquiry*, 17(July): 471–82.

Popp, Richard K. and Andrew L. Mendelson, 2010. 'X'-ing out enemies: *Time* magazine, visual discourse, and the war in Iraq. *Journalism*, 11(2): 203–21.

Powdermaker, Hortense, 1951. *Hollywood, the Dream Factory: An Anthropologist Looks at the Movie-Makers*. Boston: Little Brown and Company.

Priest, Susanna Hornig, 1996. *Doing Media Research: An Introduction*. Thousand Oaks, CA/London: Sage.

Propp, Vladimir, 1968. *Morphology of the Folktale*. Austin, Texas: University of Texas Press.

Punch, Keith F., 1998. *Introduction to Social Research: Quantitative and Qualitative Approaches*. London: Sage.

Radway, Janice, 1984. *Reading the Romance: Women, Patriarchy and Popular Literature*. Chapel Hill, North Carolina: University of North Carolina Press.

Ramamurthy, Anandi, 1997. Constructions of illusion: photography and commodity culture. In Liz Wells (ed.), *Photography: A Critical Introduction*. London/New York: Routledge.

Raphael, Amy, 2011. *Danny Boyle: In His Own Words*. London: Faber and Faber.

Redmond, Sean and Su Holmes, 2007. *Stardom and Celebrity: A Reader*. London: Sage.

Reed-Danahay, D.E. (ed.), 1997. *Auto/ethnography: Rewriting the Self and the Social*. Oxford: Berg.

Richards, Helen, 2003. Memory reclamation of cinema going in Bridgend, South Wales, 1930–1960. *Historical Journal of Film, Radio and Television*, 23(4).

Rietveld, Hillegonda, 1998. *This is Our House*. Hampshire: Ashgate Publishing.

Ringrose, Jessica and Valerie Walkerdine, 2008. Regulating the abject: the TV make-over as site of neo-liberal reinvention toward bourgeois femininity. *Feminist Media Studies*, 8(3): 227–46.

Roberts, James Paul, 2010. Revisiting the creative/commercial clash: an analysis of decision-making during product development in the television industry. *Media, Culture and Society,* 32(5): 761–80.

Rogers, Everett M., 2003 [1962]. *The Diffusion of Innovations*. 5th edition. New York: Free Press.

Rojek, Chris, 2001. *Celebrity*. London: Reaktion Books.

Rojek, Chris, 2004. *Frank Sinatra*. London: Polity Books.

Root, Jane, 1986. *Open the Box: About Television*. London: Comedia.

Rose, Gillian, 2001. *Visual Methodologies: An Introduction to the Interpretation of Visual Materials*. London: Sage.

Rose, Gillian, 2007. *Visual Methodologies: An Introduction to the Interpretation of Visual Materials*. 2nd edition. London: Sage.

Rosenberg, Bernard and David M. White (eds), 1957. *Mass Culture: The Popular Arts in America*. Glencoe, IL: The Free Press.

Rosengren, Karl Erik (ed.), 1981. *Advances in Content Analysis*. London: Sage.

Routledge, 2011. *White Weddings*. Retrieved 30 April 2011, from Routledge, Taylor and Francis Group: http://cw.routledge.com/textbooks/9780415951333/.

Rubin, Martin, 1999. *Thrillers*. Cambridge: Cambridge University Press.

Sampedro, Victor, 1998. Grounding the displaced: local media reception in a transnational context. *Journal of Communication*, 48: 125–43.

Sandvoss, Cornell, 2005. *Fans: The Mirror of Consumption*. Malden, MA: Polity.

Sapsford, Roger, 1999. *Survey Research*. London: Sage.

Saussure, Ferdinand de, 1983. *Course in General Linguistics*. Translated by Roy Harris. London: Gerald Duckworth.

Scannell, Paddy, 2003. Benjamin contextualized: on 'The Work of Art in the Age of Mechanical Reproduction'. In Elihu Katz, John Durham Peters, Tamar Liebes and A. Orloff (eds), *Canonic Texts in Media Research: Are There Any? Should There Be? How About These?* Cambridge: Polity, pp. 74–89.

Scannell, Paddy, 2007. *Media and Communication*. London: Sage.

Scannell, Paddy and David Cardiff, 1991. *A Social History of Broadcasting. Volume 1: 1922–1939. Serving the Nation*. Oxford: Basil Blackwell.

Schatz, Thomas, 1981. *Hollywood Genres: Formulas, Film-making and the Studio System*. Philadelphia: Temple University Press.

Schlesinger, Philip, 1987 [1978]. *Putting Reality Together: BBC News*. 2nd edition. London: Methuen.

Schudson, Michael, 2003. *The Sociology of News*. New York: W.W. Norton and Company.

The Science Museum, 2011. *The King George III Collection*. The Science Museum website. http://www.sciencemuseum.org.uk/onlinestuff/stories/the_king_george_iii_collection. aspx. Accessed 15 August 2011.

Seban, Jean-Loup, 1999. Encyclopedia. In Robert Audi (ed.), *Cambridge Dictionary of Philosophy*. Cambridge: Cambridge University Press, p. 264.

Seiter, Ellen, 2005. *The Internet Playground: Children's Access, Entertainment, and Mis-Education*. New York: Peter Lang.

Seiter, Ellen, 2008. Practicing at home: computers, pianos and cultural capital. In T. McPherson (ed.), *Digital Youth, Innovation, and the Unexpected*. Cambridge, MA: MIT Press, pp. 27–52.

Seymour-Ure, Colin, 1996. *The British Press and Broadcasting Since 1945*. 2nd edition. Oxford: Blackwell.

Shannon, Claude, 1949. *The Mathematical Theory of Communication*. Urbana, IL: University of Illinois Press.

Shoemaker, P.J., 1991. *Gatekeeping*. Newbury Park, CA: Sage.

Shoemaker, P., and T. Voss, 2009. *Gatekeeping Theory*. New York: Routledge.

Silverstone, Roger, 1994. *Television and Everyday Life*. London: Routledge.

Silverstone, Roger, 1999. *Why Study the Media?* London: Sage.

Silverstone, Roger, et al., 1991. Listening to a long conversation: an ethnographic approach to the study of information and communication technologies in the home. *Cultural Studies*, 5(2): 204–27.

Silvey, Robert, 1974. *Who's Listening? The Story of BBC Audience Research*. London: Allen and Unwin.

Simonson, Peter, 2010. *Reconfiguring Mass Communication: A History*. Chicago, IL: University of Illinois Press.

Simonson, Peter and Gabriel Weimann, 2003. Critical research at Columbia: Lazarsfeld and Merton's 'Mass Communication, Popular Taste, and Organized Social Action'. In Elihu Katz, John Durham Peters, Tamar Liebes and Avril Orloff (eds), *Canonic Texts in Media Research: Are There Any? Should There Be? How About These?* Cambridge: Polity, pp. 12–13.

Sinclair, John, Audrey Yue, Gay Hawkins, Kee Pookong and Josephine Fox, 2001. Chinese cosmopolitanism and media use. In Stuart Cunningham and John Sinclair (eds),

*Floating Lives: The Media and Asian Diasporas*. Lanham/Boulder/New York/Oxford: Rowman and Littlefield Publishers Inc., pp. 35–90.

Smith, Debra C., 2008. Critiquing reality-based televisual black fatherhood: a critical analysis of *Run's House* and *Snoop Dogg's Fatherhood: Critical Studies in Mass Communication*, 25(4): 393–412.

Stacey, Jackie, 1994. *Star Gazing: Hollywood Cinema and Female Spectatorship*. London: Routledge.

Stonewall, 2010. *Unseen on Screen: Gay People on Youth TV.* London: Stonewall. Electronic version available via www.stonewall.org.uk.

Storey, John, 2009a. *Cultural Theory and Popular Culture: An Introduction*. 5th edition. Harlow: Pearson Education Limited.

Storey, John, 2009b. *Cultural Theory and Popular Culture: A Reader*. 4th edition. Harlow: Pearson Education Limited.

Surgeon General's Scientific Advisory Committee on Television and Social Behavior, 1972. *Television and Growing Up: The Impact of Televised Violence*. Report to the Surgeon General, United States Public Health Service. National Institute of Mental Health, Bethesda, MD.

Swetnam, Derek and Ruth Swetnam, 2009. *Writing Your Dissertation: The Best-Selling Guide to Planning, Preparing and Presenting First-Class Work*. 3rd edition. Oxford: How-To-Books Ltd.

Thompson, E.P., 2002 [1963]. *The Making of the English Working Class*. London: Penguin History.

Thompson, John B., 1995. *The Media and Modernity: A Social Theory of the Media*. London: Polity.

Thompson, Kristin and David Bordwell, 1994. *Film History: An Introduction*. New York: McGraw-Hill.

*The Times of India*, 2010. Hindu temple attacked, idols destroyed in B'desh: Official. http://articles.timesofindia.indiatimes.com/2010-02-06/south-asia/28137103_1_idols-hindu-temple-miscreants. Last accessed 13 September 2011.

Tonkiss, Fran, 1998. Analysing discourse. In Clive Seale (ed.), *Researching Society and Culture*. London: Sage, pp. 245–60.

Tripp, Lisa M., 2010. 'The computer is not for you to be looking around, it is for school-work': challenges for digital inclusion as Latino immigrant families negotiate children's access to the internet. *New Media and Society*, 13(4): 552–67.

Tripp, Lisa M. and R. Herr-Stephenson, 2009. Making access meaningful: Latino young people using digital media at home and school. *Journal of Computer-mediated Communication*, 14(4): 1190–207.

Tuchman, Gaye, 1972. Objectivity as strategic ritual: an examination of newsmen's notions of objectivity. *American Journal of Sociology*, 77(January): 66–70.

Tuchman, Gaye, 1980. *Making News: A Study in the Construction of Reality*. New York: Highlighting.

Tulloch, John, 2000. *Watching Television Audiences: Cultural Theories and Methods*. London: Arnold.

Tunstall, Jeremy, 1977. *The Media are American: Anglo-American Media in the World*. London: Constable.

Tunstall, Jeremy, 1983. *The Media in Britain*. London: Constable.

Tunstall, Jeremy, 1993. *Television Producers*. London: Routledge.

Tunstall, Jeremy, 1996. *Newspaper Power: The New National Press in Britain*. Oxford: Clarendon Press.

Tunstall, Jeremy, 2007. *The Media were American: U.S. Mass Media in Decline*. Oxford: Oxford University Press.

Turner, Graeme, 1996. *British Cultural Studies: An Introduction*. 2nd edition. London: Routledge.

Turner, Graeme, 2004. *Understanding Celebrity*. London: Sage.

Turnock, Robert, 2000. *Interpreting Audiences and the Death of a Princess*. London: British Film Institute.

UNESCO, http://www.unesco.org/new/en/media-services/single-view/news/ten_years_on_remembering_the_tragic_destruction_of_the_giant_buddha_statues_of_bamiyan_afghanistan. Accessed: 13 September 2011.

van Dijk, Teun, 1988. *News as Discourse*. Hillsdale, New Jersey: Erlbaum.

van Leeuwen, Theo and Carey Jewitt (eds), 2001. *Handbook of Visual Analysis*. London: Sage.

van Sterkenburg, Jaco, Annelies Knoppers and Sonja De Leeuw, 2010. Race, ethnicity, and content analysis of the sports media: a critical reflection. *Media, Culture and Society*, 32(5): 819–39.

van Zoonen, Liesbet, 1994. *Feminist Media Studies*. London: Sage.

Walker, Peter, 2011. Dale Farm evictions: protesters remain locked to vehicles and concrete as bailiffs prepare to begin clearance of illegal Traveller site in Essex. 20 October. *Guardian* Newsblog: http://www.guardian.co.uk/uk/2011/oct/20/dale-farm-evictions-live?INTCMP=SRCHNews Blog. Accessed: 3 December 2011.

Wardle, Claire and Andrew Williams, 2010. Beyond user-generated content: a production study examining the ways in which UGC is used at the BBC. *Media, Culture and Society*, 32(5): 781–99.

Wasko, Janet, Mark Phillips and Eileen R. Meehan (eds.), 2001. *Dazzled by Disney? The Global Disney Audiences Project*. London/New York: Leicester University Press.

Wayne, Mike, 2003. *Marxism and Media Studies: Key Concepts and Contemporary Trends*. London: Polity Press.

Weber, R.P., 1985. *Basic Content Analysis*. Beverly Hills, CA: Sage.

Wheeler, Mark, 1997. *Politics and the Mass Media*. Oxford: Blackwell.

White, David Manning, 1950. The gate-keeper: a case study in the selection of news. *Journalism Quarterly*, 27: 383–96.

Williams, Dmitri, Nicole Martins, Mia Consalvo and James D. Ivory, 2009. The virtual census: representations of gender, race and age in video games. *New Media Society*, 11(5): 815–34.

Williams, Kevin, 1998. *Get Me a Murder a Day! A History of Mass Communication in Britain*. London: Arnold.

Williams, Kevin, 2010. *Read All About It! A History of the British Newspaper*. London: Routledge.

Williams, Mark, 1999. Considering Monty Margetts's Cook's Corner: Oral history and television history. In Mary Beth Harolovich and Lauren Rabinovitz (eds), *Television, History and American Culture: Feminist Critical Essays*. Durham, North Carolina/London: Duke University Press, pp. 36–55.

Williams, Raymond, 1961. *The Long Revolution*. Harmondsworth: Penguin Books.

Williams, Raymond, 1963 [1958]. *Culture and Society 1780–1950*. Harmondsworth: Penguin Books.

Williams, Raymond, 1975. *The Country and the City*. St. Albans, Herts: Granada Publishing.

Williams, Raymond, 1983. *Keywords*. London: Fontana.

Williams, Raymond, 1989a. *Raymond Williams on Television*. Edited by Alan O'Connor. London: Routledge.

Williams, Raymond, 1989b. *Resources of Hope: Culture, Democracy, Socialism.* Edited by Robin Gable. London: Verso.

Williamson, Judith, 1978. *Decoding Advertisements: Ideology and Meaning in Advertising.* London/New York: Marion Boyars.

Willis, Paul (ed.), 2005. *Stardom: Hollywood and Beyond.* Manchester: Manchester University Press.

Wolf, Naomi, 1990. *The Beauty Myth: How Images of Beauty are used Against Women.* London: Chatto and Windus.

Wood, Robin, 1981. *Howard Hawks.* London: British Film Institute.

Wright, Will, 1979. *Six-Guns and Society: A Structural Study of the Western.* Berkeley, CA: University of California Press.

Žižek, Slavoj, 1989. *The Sublime Object of Ideology.* London/New York: Verso.

Žižek, Slavoj, 2010. Return of the natives. *New Statesman,* 4 March.

Zuckerman, Harriet, 1972. Interviewing an ultra-elite. *The Public Opinion Quarterly,* 36(2) Summer: 159–75.

# INDEX